DRE

MW01121906

WHICH CHURCH IS ~~RIGHT?~~ WRONG

An In-depth Study for the End-time Church

Based upon the story of the church
of the Laodiceans (Revelation 3:14-22)
as compared to the Bride of Christ.

PRESS

ACW Press
Eugene, Oregon 97405

Table of Contents

Revelation 3:14-22

The following is the scriptural text from which the story of this book is taken:

14 "And to the angel of the church of the Laodiceans write, 'These things says the Amen, the Faithful and True Witness, the Beginning of the creation of God:

15 "I know your works, that you are neither cold nor hot. I could wish you were cold or hot.

16 So then, because you are lukewarm, and neither cold nor hot, I will vomit you out of My mouth.

17 "Because you say, 'I am rich, have become wealthy, and have need of nothing'—and do not know that you are wretched, miserable, poor, blind, and naked—

18 "I counsel you to buy from Me gold refined in the fire, that you may be rich; and white garments, that you may be clothed, that the shame of your nakedness may not be revealed; and anoint your eyes with eye salve, that you may see.

19 "As many as I love, I rebuke and chasten. Therefore be zealous and repent.

20 "Behold, I stand at the door and knock. If anyone hears My voice and opens the door, I will come in to him and dine with him, and he with Me.

21 "To him who overcomes I will grant to sit with Me on My throne, as I also overcame and sat down with My Father on His throne.

22 "He who has an ear, let him hear what the Spirit says to the churches."

(New King James Version)

Expectations for the Readers of the Book

1. A need for a greater awareness of each church organization's accountability to Christ's great love for His church organism, the Body of Christ.
2. A better understanding of the oneness of the Godhead and how each functioning member relates to each other in the divine building program of the church.
3. The prophetic fulfillment of the *Father's* ultimate purpose for the church by the *Holy Spirit* preparing a mature, blameless Bride for His deserving *Son*.
4. A tool to help the end-time church be more watchful and ready at His Coming.
5. The importance of church unity and why it requires Christian growth and development toward spiritual maturity in the leadership of each church to achieve it.
6. Changing from a self-centered church focus as a particular church organization to having a daily Christ-centered focus toward the one church organism, the Body of Christ. Spiritual maturity (being more like Jesus) wants to please the Head of the Body and that is one answer to the problem of a divided end-time church.
7. A passionate love for a compassionate Bridegroom provides the basis for becoming an eligible Bride.
8. The greatness of Christ to His church cannot be overemphasized compared to insignificant doctrines that do not change lives, promote church unity or glorify God.
9. Though each end-time church organization may have a desire to please Him, each needs to be made aware that she may well be her own worst enemy. (A high opinion of the Laodicean Church of herself caused Him to have a very low opinion of her.)

Why a Need for this Book?

The title of "Which Church Is Wrong?" is based on a story about the worth and importance of one church in the eyes of her Judge. Because of her attitude of self-sufficiency, the Laodicean Church had become a "wrong church." The pivotal scripture on the commentary concerning that church is based on what she said, "I am rich, have become wealthy, *and have need of nothing*." There is a need for a book to be written about a church that boldly declared, "I have need of nothing."

The difficult task of knowing that a church is right can be better understood through knowing the attitude and characteristics of a church that the Lord had declared wrong. The church of the Laodiceans had a good beginning but her Judge, who "loved the church and gave Himself for her," was also interested in her having a good ending.

Coming to an understanding of what was wrong with a church like the one at Laodicea might be compared to what is right and important that the Lord is looking for in a church. If Christ loved the church so much that He died *for her sake*, the church needs to reciprocate that love through fervent worship and Christian service *for His sake*.

There is an old adage, "A picture is worth a thousand words," but sometimes it takes a thousand words to paint the picture. When it comes to understanding Bible truth, the Holy Spirit is able to paint a needful picture that can be seen through the eyes of faith. That picture surpasses the worth of ten thousand words with no eternal value.

Gross immorality was not the issue concerning the Laodicean Church. This story is about a self-pleasing church that became so self-centered that she forgot the main purpose for her existence, which was doing things to please Him. She could not please the Lover of her soul by loving the riches of this world more than she loved Him.

Finally, the most important need for writing the book is to give insight into a scene that takes place in heaven. The end of this story is the beginning of a greater story where there is great excitement in heaven and it escalates "as the sound of many waters and as the sound of mighty thunderings." Why all the excitement? "For the marriage of the Lamb has come, and His wife has made herself ready." Within the scriptural text of the story of the Laodicean Church is contained the reward that awaits the overcoming church.

Introduction

From Being Lukewarm
to Becoming an Overcomer

The Laodicean Church had a perfect birth at her beginning, but the negative commentary about her is that she compromised her love for the Lord of the church. As a rich, self-sufficient church, she became contented with the riches and wealth of this world rather than pursuing a fervent love for God's eternal riches in Christ Jesus. Riches and wealth gave to her the best that the world had to offer. What more could she want? The best that God has to offer! But her attitude of complacency and contentment caused her to become lukewarm toward Him who loved her and gave Himself for her.

The positive side of the story is that everyone in that church organism had the opportunity to repent and accept the Lord's invitation to open the door and dine with Him. Anyone who came back into a wholehearted, loving fellowship with the Lord had an opportunity to share in the exalted reward of an overcomer.

This book is a scriptural analysis of the seventh church (the church of Laodicea) in the book of Revelation. As a Judge of righteous living, the Lord gave encouragement, motivation, counsel and admonition to all seven churches of Asia Minor. He is an awesome Judge as well as a loving, merciful Savior. What is so amazing about the story of the Laodicean Church, who had become a big disappointment to Him, was the humble invitation that He was offering to anyone who would repent.

Is it possible for a church to be orthodox in her Christian faith, and yet, not have a passionate, heartfelt love for Jesus? In order to know the

Christ of the Scriptures in His fullness, there is a need to be continually led by the Holy Spirit in diligent worship, study and practice of all teachings in the Scriptures concerning Him.

The Laodicean Church was deceived in thinking that she could obtain the Lord's approval and favor through self-glory. Self-reliance is the crux of the fallen sin nature that caused that church to fall short of the glory of God (Rom. 3:23). By having a "need of nothing" attitude, she was declaring her independence from other members in the Body of Christ. An independent know-it-all salvation based upon self-fulfillment had replaced a dependent know-so salvation based upon the grace of God. She had many things to learn about the Christ of the Scriptures and His great work of redemption. She needed to rely and submit to the work of the Holy Spirit in that church in order to come into a mutual heart-to-heart relationship with her Lord over the church. The Holy Spirit has come to glorify Christ.

An English poet, Alexander Pope, once said, "Some people never learn anything because they understand everything too soon." The Laodicean Church was guilty of jumping to a wrong conclusion about herself, without acknowledging a need for knowing more of the fullness of God's great salvation through His liberating truth.

Jumping to quick conclusions in understanding truth hinders the Holy Spirit in leading God's people into receiving the full benefits of additional truth. He has come to lead and guide the church into all truth. Members of a church may conform to an ecclesiastical or theological system of truth without ever being challenged in having an exciting and a loving enthusiastic dependence upon feeding from the Bread of Life.

In hearing teachings from the Scriptures, the Laodicean Church needed to develop three columns in her thinking. One column should have been given to "yes," that is what the Bible says. Another column should have been given to "no," that is not what the Bible says. A third column should have been given to, "I don't understand" or a "pending file." Because the fullness of spiritual things takes time to learn and to apply to our lives, a mindset against a truth ends spiritual progress in that area. A third column, therefore, was needed, and that self-satisfied church had no need for a pending file in her thinking.

The Need to Depend upon Him

The world might want to stir up controversy by asking, "Which church is right?" But this book is basically about a church that the Lord declared wrong. Jesus told the Laodicean Church, in so many words, that she did not know her own true spiritual status toward Him. The objective is to be in such an ongoing fellowship with the Head of the church that a church member can have the same testimony as the apostle Paul. Paul proclaimed, "For I know whom [not what] I have believed and am persuaded that He [not my church] is able to keep what I have committed to Him until that day" (2 Tim. 1:12). Paul rejoiced in his know-so salvation by the grace of God through faith in Him.

There are many important truths in the Scriptures, but the church of the Laodiceans did not wait humbly before the Lord for Him to make them known unto her. She had a need to be led by the Holy Spirit in order that she would not make a careless decision concerning the ever-expanding revelation of the gospel message. The Holy Spirit has come to lead the church into all truth, but He resists the proud. Without help from the Holy Spirit, the leadership of that church would continue to sit in the seat of those in self-conceit that would lead to defeat.

The gospel story is a message of comparisons. Jesus had walked with the Laodicean Church in the greatness of her past, but now He was standing on the outside of a church door that had been closed to Him. Her past greatness was based upon the fact that she was a functioning member in harmony with the rest of the Body of Christ.

Because her assumption of self-worth before God was based upon her material abundance, the Laodicean Church was lifted up in pride and self-righteousness. Her sense of self-sufficiency and self-centered love was robbing her of an inheritance that belonged to her through Christ's self-giving love. She was guilty of an attitude of self-centeredness, as being the greatest, but the Head of the church, as her Judge, didn't agree. She had put herself at the top, but the Lord told her that she belonged at the bottom. Because the Laodicean Church had her focus totally on her own self-worth, she lost her focus on the impotance of His great worth to her.

It is important, therefore, how a church is related to Jesus as both the Beginning and the End in the Christian journey. The King of the Jews, who was rejected by His own people, belongs to the Father who sent Him, and the church belongs to Jesus who sends her. The heart of church life is all about being in harmony with her functional Head. That called for the Laodicean Church to learn to lean on the Holy Spirit as He directs each one to hear the personal invitation to open the door to a personal Savior and dine with Him. Complete salvation is walking with Him from beginning to the end.

The actions of the church at Laodicea had caused her to lose her passionate zeal for the Savior of her soul. That was not taken lightly by the

Lord, and her lukewarm attitude toward Him was met with strong words of disapproval and rebuke. He said, "I will vomit you out of my mouth." She could not have a wrong attitude toward other members in the Body and live a life of dependence upon the functional Head of the Body.

What caused that church to become so self-sufficient and self-centered? Could it have been that the good news had become old news, not realizing the walk of faith in the newness of life is a continual challenge? When a church has a need to go forward to the next level, she should not say, "I have arrived." Christ Jesus, who is "the way" to the Father, gives true meaning to Christian living.

That church needed to repent from her lukewarm disposition toward Jesus. The message of repentance was for her to change her thinking from within, which would cause a change in her speech and outward behavior. That is also where the message of being a disciple of Christ leads. Being His disciple means following Him and dining with Him on a daily basis. The God of new creation living is in the changing business, where all things are becoming new in Christ Jesus.

That church organizational leadership should have put more emphasis on the church organism to follow on to know the Christ of the Scriptures through the discipleship message. Emphasis upon the greatness of that church organization to its membership was food for a church-centered focus. She needed to be emphasizing a Christ-centered focus as being members of the church organism, the Body of Christ.

She said, "I have need of nothing." Having a need for God is the very foundation of the gospel message. If a sinner doesn't believe that he or she is a sinner, there will be no need to repent and come into the saving knowledge of the Lord Jesus Christ. If Christians see no need for the working of the Holy Spirit in their daily walk, they will not humble themselves before the Holy Spirit in order to be led by Him. If a church group feels like they stand alone, as being the only right church, they will see no need to seek the guidance of the Holy Spirit to walk into additional truth by dining with Him.

Her claim of having a need of nothing deceived her in thinking that she was in right relationship with the Judge of the church. But her attitude of having exclusive access and control under the Head of the church as a church organization had to mean that no other church could have a good relationship with Him. The Head cannot be separated from the rest of the members of the Body. That "no-need" church couldn't be the greatest!

Building invisible church walls by self-important and self-sufficient thinking kept that church from being led by the Spirit of God, but the Holy

Spirit was still willing to speak and direct anyone that had a willing heart to hear. The Laodiceans probably didn't fully realize that building invisible walls separated her from other churches, but at the same time, she was also building an invisible roof that had separated her from the Lord over that church. She could make no further progress in walking in the light.

A lesson might be learned from the church at Laodicea. She was not declared wrong because of preaching false doctrine, nor was it for being in gross sinful immorality. It was her self-centered thinking. She was rich and wealthy and had no need in the realm of temporal, material things. But her self-centered thinking had blinded her to her great need in the realm of eternal, spiritual things in a loving fellowship with the Lord.

It is easier to see the wrong in other churches and be blinded to the wrong in our own church. But when a challenge is given to deny self, a spirit of compromise may cause a church to try to find a middle ground, but there is no middle ground between right and wrong, hot and cold, or being for Him or against Him in walking in the truth.

In daily living, there is a mixture of saying or doing that is either right or wrong. A person may be right one moment, and say or do the wrong thing the next moment. But for a church organization that is taking her congregation on a spiritual journey, it is very important that she is headed in the right direction.

A good Bible example of the contrast of being right one time and wrong the next is what Peter spoke on two different occasions concerning Jesus of Nazareth. When Jesus asked His disciples the question, "Who do you say that I am?" Peter answered with the words, "You are the Christ, the Son of the living God" (Matt. 16:15-16). Jesus commended Peter that He spoke the words that the Father had given him.

A short time later, however, Jesus began to tell His disciples "that He must go to Jerusalem, and suffer many things from the elders and chief priests and scribes, and be killed, and be raised the third day." At that moment, Peter began to rebuke Jesus saying, "Far be it from You, Lord; this shall not happen to You!" But He turned and said to Peter, "Get behind Me, Satan! You are an offense to Me, for you are not mindful of the things of God, but the things of men" (vv. 21-23).

I believe Jesus addressed Peter as Satan (figuratively). Proud, impetuous, outspoken Peter was motivated by his soulish reasoning and emotions and not by satanic influence. As an unenlightened soul in decision making, Peter was demonstrating the self-life as "the things of men," where a builder builds his foundation upon the sand and not upon the rock of the "things of God." Christ was being directed by the Father toward laying the rock foundation for building the church. He would die a criminal's death on the cross as atonement for sin.

Peter was acting like Satan by using his intimidating and dominating tactics, in opposing Jesus from doing His Father's will. But when it comes to saying or doing the wrong thing in the sight of God, a right attitude of the heart is more important than spiritual ignorance. The Holy Spirit can teach and lead a repentant heart toward the right objective. Developing a fervent heart toward Jesus would lead anyone in that church out of a luke-warm condition into a fellowship of feasting with Jesus.

If a church organism doesn't continue to follow and fellowship with the Lord Jesus Christ, she will not grow and mature spiritually in Him. As the Head, He is the focal point for the unity of the organic Body of believers. Members of the church organism that belonged to that church organization should have had a wholehearted love toward Him and one another. Jesus said, "By this [new commandment] all will know that you are My disciples, if you have love for one another." When God's people are taught to love the church organism, they love the Head and all other members in the Body of Christ.

As each member of the Body of Christ submits to the Head of the Body, each member of the Body functions in harmony with one another. The functioning Body is one with many members and one member cannot say to another member, "I have no need of you" (1 Cor. 12:21). From the Head to the feet, each member of the Body of Christ depends on one another to function for the glory of God in the end-time church.

Church Humanism

What is the difference between church humanism and secular humanism? Secular humanism rejects the claims of Christ's Headship over their lives, but church humanism neglects the claims of Christ by not submitting to His Headship over the church. In Christianity, if a church or anyone thinks they have no need, then that wrong attitude becomes the greatest need. In church humanism, all the emphasis is placed upon being accountable to a church organization, and none is placed upon being accountable to Christ as the Head of the church organism. Trusting in an organizational church system might be at the expense of the glory that Christ should receive as the functioning Head over His church organism.

Humanism, as a Christian cult, glorifies self-enlightened thinking, undermining the need for a personal Savior. It builds upon the sands of self-reliance and not upon Jesus Christ and Him crucified. It glorifies in the self-life rather than the Christ-life.

Secular humanism, as a philosophy, believes that all the good things that riches and wealth may bring come only by the intellect and ability of man to achieve them, and not as a blessing from God. Secular humanists believe, therefore, that civilization can arrive at its ultimate fulfillment and self-satisfaction without God's help.

The church of the Laodiceans thought that she had already arrived at divine fulfillment as a church. Her saying, "I have need of nothing," can be interpreted that she no longer had any need for daily, divine direction by the Holy Spirit, and she didn't need to seek for a closer daily personal relationship to Christ as the Head over the church. Instead of acknowledging Him in all her ways, His authority and guidance was being replaced with making decisions by leaning to her own understanding, and doing what she thought was the reasonable thing to do.

Secular humanism can be described by a story I once heard about a man who believed that he was a self-made man, and he worshipped his creator. There is also an old saying about a strong-willed person who would cut off his nose to spite his face. Because of his fallen nature, man is his own worst enemy.

When some areas of humanistic teachings declare themselves as a specific religious institution, it becomes a religion of works and self-centered thinkers that are accountable to no one but their religion of self-assurance and self-reliance. But the freethinkers of secular humanism, as a whole, have no need to be authorized or recognized as a religious institution. Modern humanistic teachings deny the God of the Bible and His relationship to humanity. It promotes its own independent secular ideology against the Christ of the church in modern secular educational institutions supported by taxpayer's money.

As a result, humanistic thinking is having a penetrating impact upon the end-time church. The last two verses in the Book of books says, "He who testifies to these things says, 'Surely I am coming quickly.'" Amen. Even so, come, Lord Jesus! The grace of our Lord Jesus Christ be with you all. Amen." As we see the day approaching, His people, who are eagerly waiting for Him, are seeing more clearly the importance of being ready at His Appearing.

The church members of Laodicea were not waiting on God for divine fulfillment as followers of Christ. She had already arrived at her own self-prescribed or self-appointed fulfillment. That church was not waiting on God to go forward in spiritual progress, but because of her self-reliant attitude, the

Son of God was doing the waiting on those in that church to open their heart's door to Him. Those who answered the invitation would have the spiritual fellowship that is needed for spiritual advancement in Christ.

Which Church Is Right?

Based upon the study of the Scriptures, it is easier to find out which church is wrong, like the Laodicean Church, than which is the right church. A church needs to receive the Scriptures humbly concerning the high standards that God has concerning His overcoming, glorious church. We must rely upon the mercies of God through faith, for with God all things are possible.

After the Jews rejected their King, the emphasis of the early apostles was upon the resurrected, ascended Christ and the building plan for His church, but the church would eventually grow to become a Gentile church. Only twice does Christ refer to the church, and that is recorded in the book of Matthew. Beginning with Acts 2:47, however, the church is mentioned seventy-four times in the rest of the New Testament.

The first disciples of Jesus believed Him to be the Messiah, and they were looking for Him to set up a visible kingdom. The hope of an immediate visible kingdom disappeared when the King of the Jews was crucified on a Roman cross. But when He was resurrected from the dead on the third day, the hope of an immediate visible kingdom was revived. Though it has been almost two thousand years since He ascended to the Father, He is coming back again to set up a visible kingdom on earth.

The "right church" label has been put upon a countless number of church organizations by expressions and attitudes. No church denomination or organization wants to be operating as a wrong church to the Lord. After all, the evaluation of the Judge is the only one that counts, and the Laodicean Church was found lacking.

To the unchurched, which church is right is a variable. A church may be right for one generation and wrong for the next generation. That's the way it was with the Laodicean Church. A generation before the writing the book of Revelation, the Laodicean Church was right based upon Apostle Paul's epistle to the Colossians. In Colossians Paul refers to the Laodiceans as a sister church with similar support as being right.

The temperature of water, which can be compared to human emotions, can be characterized in three main categories: lukewarm, cold and hot. In the natural realm, lukewarm water nauseates a thirsty soul. Most people like to drink cold drinks and hot coffee or tea, but nothing lukewarm. That can be compared to the spiritual realm of an emotional relationship with Jesus. The

Holy Spirit is the One who directs and guides a thirsty soul to the Fountain of Living Waters. Thirsty souls never receive a lukewarm reception from Him. In the light of what Christ has done for the church, a lukewarm or halfhearted attitude toward Him is as bad as not having a heart toward Him at all.

At the time of His Appearing, the visible church needs to be right at that given moment, and Jesus said that He is coming at a time when the church is not expecting Him. So a Christian life needs to be lived one moment at a time. If the Holy Spirit is unable to work within a church organization in preparing its members to qualify for the Rapture, that church could be labeled, in a post-Rapture context, as a wrong church.

It could be said that church members who are taken in the Rapture would be "the right church." Jesus said, "I tell you, in that night there will be two men in one bed: the one will be taken and the other will be left. Two women will be grinding together: the one will be taken and the other left." "Two men will be in the field: the one will be taken and the other left."

At the time of the Rapture of the church, there will be a separation of people who have been very close with one another in the realm of time. Will there be two seated together in a church; one will be taken and the other left? If some church members qualify and others do not and they attend the same church, can the leadership of that church organization be blamed? One may have had a heart toward the things of the world while the other one had a faithful heart toward the words of Jesus.

In the parable of the ten virgins, there was only one difference between the wise and the foolish. The five foolish virgins did not have an extra supply of oil in their flask for their lamps. While they went out to buy that needed oil the Bridegroom came, and those who were ready went in with Him to the wedding and the door was shut and could not be opened.

How can the church prepare for His coming? Self-analysis of any church related to the coming of the Lord is unreliable. Critics of the apostle Paul in the Corinthian Church claimed that he was wrong and that he was not qualified to be an apostle. Though Paul knew in his heart that he was right, and he had the experience and the testimony of his apostleship with the Lord, he would not rely on self-analysis in reference to his position with the Judge. Paul said, "He who judges me is the Lord" (1 Cor. 4:4).

Whether it is greatness with a church or with an individual, the Lord's analysis is what will hold true and not self-analysis. His judgment is the final analysis. Much time is wasted through self-analysis in Christianity outside of the context of Scripture, for everything will be judged in the light of what has been written in the Scriptures.

Being Identified with His Greatness

What makes any church great? Being identified in daily fellowship with the Christ of the Scriptures, the functional Head of His church, is being identified with His greatness. The lowly bride elect will be identified with Him in His exaltation. A church label is not necessary to achieve greatness with Him. A church label may be needed for identification in a world of business enterprises that includes God's business, but it is not of primary importance to those who are being led by the Spirit.

There is no greatness in a label. The Christian faith, which works by love, is what bonds many church organizations together as one church organism. True Christianity understands that Christ paid the price. He is the One that puts a church on the right pathway toward true greatness in losing her self-identity in Him as the Body of Christ.

The church organism within a church organization is what makes the evangelistic efforts of the organization successful. As a church organization grows in numbers through evangelistic efforts, the increased life in the church organism should also grow and develop toward the image of the Father's firstborn Son. The quality of the church organism should grow strong along with the quantity of the church organization.

Since He is the church organism called the Body of Christ, His "life-giving spirit" of the divine church organism grows and develops across the lines of a countless number of human church organizations of one church to hundreds of other churches. A church organization has no spiritual life without the life of the church organism that comes through planting the seeds of evangelism and feeding upon the Bread of Life for spiritual growth and development.

Because it takes the Spirit of Truth to administer it, no new revelation truth comes to the proud in heart. When more truth comes, a church becomes excited about the glory of His truth. But persevering day after day into more new truths transforms the church into the same image of Christ "from glory to glory" (2 Cor. 3:18). It is not the place of worship but the heart of the worshipper that counts with God, for the time has come when those who worship the Father must worship Him by His Spirit through His Truth.

The signs of the time point to the soon coming of the Lord. It is, therefore, most important that we find ourselves in right fellowship with Him at His Appearing. The magnitude of that event will be the greatest that has ever occurred in human history. "The dead in Christ will rise first;" then, those in the end-time church who qualify "shall be caught up together...to meet the Lord in the air" at that great event. It is important to know how to qualify, and that event should not be taken lightly but soberly.

Chapter 1 begins with the Laodicean Church having a right beginning. That can be contrasted with the past history of many revival movements of evangelical churches in modern America. Chapter 10 ends the Lord's appeal where anyone in that church that heard His voice and opened the door could receive the reward of the overcomer. Will only a remnant in the Laodicean Church receive that reward? Will the end-time church, for the most part, take advantage of the lessons that need to be learned to be ready at His Appearing as presented in each chapter of this book?

Jesus gave many sober warnings for His disciples to be ready at His Coming. "Take heed, watch and pray; for you do not know when the time is" (Mark 13:33). The word *watch* is used four times in the last five verses of Mark 13. That is not an overemphasis on Jesus' part. It is a warning of the gravity of the event and the importance for the church to be ready when He comes again. Watch means how the church is waiting and preparing for His Return. Jesus is telling the end-time church to be ready with a whole-hearted vigilance toward His great love at the time of His Appearing.

The Lord gave that warning because He didn't want anyone in the church to be found asleep at the time of His Appearing (Eph. 5:14). Jesus is coming for the church at an unexpected moment in time. He wants her to be ready and alert, walking with Him while looking for Him. But luke-warm end-time churches, like the Laodicean Church, are unaware and unconcerned that they have a need to be watching and ready.

Chapter 1

True Greatness

See the Need to Press Forward to the Next Level

"Therefore *let us go on* and get past the elementary stage in the
teachings and doctrine of Christ, the Messiah, *advancing
steadily toward* the completeness and perfection that belongs to
spiritual maturity" (Hebrews 6:1, AMP).

The church of the Laodiceans had a great beginning. She was part of
the early church movement in cities throughout the regions sur-
rounding the Mediterranean Sea and beyond. Now when the day of
Pentecost had fully come "there were dwelling in Jerusalem Jews, devout
men, from every nation under heaven" (Acts 2:1, 5).

That was all in the plan of God. After those Jews had experienced
the saving power of God in Jerusalem, they all went back to their specific
region and city and began assembling themselves together as a church.
Along with the establishing of new churches by the apostles, the church
began to grow and branch out to other cities.

Of the three thousand who entered into the saving knowledge of
Christ Jesus on the day of Pentecost, some were from the region of
Pamphylia (v. 10). Pamphylia was the region that included the city of
Laodicea in Asia Minor. The church in each city of that region probably
had their beginnings shortly after the day of Pentecost. So approxi-
mately sixty years of church history had taken place from the time of the

Feast of Pentecost in Jerusalem to the time of John's writing the book of Revelation.

The Father, as the divine Architect, has a plan for building the church and it is nothing like the plan of man. The Father was the One who initiated the plan and His plan is the greatest. The church needs to persevere in the Scriptures and submit to the leading of the Holy Spirit in order to become a finished product of His complete redemptive plan.

Christ is the only One who can give spiritual life to the church. He is the Head of the church organism that gives life and authority when He is honored in the midst of a church gathering, regardless of its size. As the Father has given the Son the authority to make the plan work, the Holy Spirit gives the ability or power to carry out the redemptive plan to its fullness over all opposing forces.

The greatness of the church of the Laodiceans could only be found in a wholehearted devotion and affection to the One that gave birth to that church. Without Him, she could do nothing! Without Him she was nothing! At the beginning, He dwelt in her midst in order that the purposes of God might be fulfilled. True greatness, therefore, is found in the Head that watches over the Body of Christ.

Near the end of his epistle to Colossians, Paul informed them about a fellow servant, *Epaphras,* who had a great zeal for both the Colossian Church and the Laodicean Church. After the epistle was read among the church at Colosse, Paul also wanted it read to the church at Laodicea (Col. 4:13, 16). Apparently the apostle Paul wanted the epistle to the Colossians to fulfill the spiritual needs of both churches.

The Laodicean Church represented one integral part of the whole Body of Christ during that period of time in church history. The greatness of her past was the excitement and enthusiasm in her relationship to her Lord and Savior. So the spiritual unity that existed in the early church was of great concern to Him who is Head over the church.

It is interesting that Paul speaks of Epaphras as having great zeal toward the nearby sister church, Laodicea, as well as the church in Colosse. Years later, the Laodiceans had lost their Christian zeal in Christian love and service to anyone outside their own sectarian walls.

To the church at Colosse Paul wrote: "For I want you to know what a great conflict I have for you and those in Laodicea, and for as many as have not seen my face in the flesh. For though I am absent in the flesh, yet I am with you in spirit, rejoicing to see your good order and the steadfastness of your faith in Christ" (Col. 2:1, 5).

Paul reported both churches as having good order and the steadfastness of their faith in Christ. But the Lord's message to the Laodicean Church in the book of Revelation showed that a disorderly walk had developed in her thinking toward the Head and the rest of the Body of Christ by declaring, "I have need of nothing." But at the time of writing his epistle to the Colossians, the apostle Paul had endorsed the Laodiceans as having the right attitude necessary to be an important member of the Body of Christ. In the book of Revelation, the Head of the Body was ready to vomit her out of His mouth.

Apparently the issue with the Laodicean Church was not a doctrinal issue. Early in the course of church history, she apparently had kept herself clean of those who would lead her astray with "another Jesus," which leads to receiving "a different spirit" that is not the Holy Spirit, and "a different gospel" that is not based upon God's grace. If she were engaged in false doctrine, the apostle Paul would not have commended her along with the church at Colosse. Also the Lord Jesus Christ would not have given "anyone" in that church an invitation to dine with Him in wholehearted fellowship.

Paul had a good endorsement of the Laodiceans along with the Colossians, "rejoicing to see your good order and steadfastness of your faith in Christ." People from both inside and outside the church could observe that church's good order.

Her steadfastness of faith toward the Lord, however, had changed over a short period of time. Approximately thirty years had elapsed between the writing of Colossians and the book of Revelation. It took approximately one generation, therefore, for this compromise of halfhearted love and devotion toward Christ to take place.

In answering the question, "Which church is right or wrong?" the Laodicean Church of the Apostolic Age is a good example of a church being right at the beginning, but at some point in time, becoming self-centered and lukewarm toward Jesus. She no longer had a personal Christ at the center of church activity; therefore, she had become a wrong church.

Laodicean Church / Hebrew Christians

The Laodicean Church and Hebrew Christians had a different disposition and attitude toward relating to other Christians in the Body of Christ, but both had the same need to press forward to greater things in Christ. The Hebrew Christians, like the Laodicean Church, were reluctant to press forward in the walk of faith in experiencing the fullness of the Christ of the Scriptures.

Though the Hebrew Christians, as part of the church organism throughout the churches, did not have the problem of self-sufficiency or an extreme egotistical attitude as did the church of the Laodiceans, they also were neglecting a "so great a salvation" (Heb. 2:3). Both had a need to draw closer to Him and go forward together up to the next spiritual level with others in the Body of Christ toward spiritual maturity.

Because of their spiritual heritage and victories of the past as the chosen people of God, the Jewish people were identified as the privileged people of God. But now the Hebrew Christians needed to know that privilege was located in having a proper, wholehearted personal relationship with the resurrected, ascended, soon-coming King of Glory. According to the Scriptures, both Christian groups continually had a spiritual challenge set before them to press forward in Christ.

After repeated warnings in the New Testament by the Lord, telling the church what is needed to be ready, will she be ready for His Second Coming? Or will only a small remnant actually be ready at His Coming? The end-time church should not underestimate the importance of His appeal for watchfulness in being ready.

Let Us Go Forward

Since God's people are by nature a people that wants to go their own way (Is. 53:6), the Holy Spirit's appeal to the church is a collective "Let us." No church should ever have a collective "I am," like the Laodicean Church, who had a need to change her "I have need of nothing" declaration to a "Let us go forward to spiritual maturity" declaration. "Let us" means an all-inclusive Church Body, with its many members working together for a common purpose and goal in Christ Jesus. That purpose is to glorify the Father through the Son.

The phrase, "Let us," is used thirteen times in the epistle to the Hebrews. It was used as a challenge to all Hebrew Christians, who were members of the church located in various cities throughout the regions, to go forward in togetherness as one in Christ. It is important that church members of a church organization have the freedom to receive the challenge to go forward in the fullness of the Christ of the Scriptures.

The Lord was offering the challenge to go forward in fellowship by dining with Him to "anyone" in the Laodicean Church who could hear His voice. Who are the ones who hear His voice? Because David was "a man after God's own heart," he heard the voice of the Lord. There is always a need to share the teaching message of the Christ of the Scriptures with other members in the maturing Body of Christ as well as the evangelistic message that is proclaimed to a perishing world.

The Hebrew Christians, like many dedicated church families in modern America, had the privilege of having a good background in the knowledge of the Old Testament Scriptures from their childhood (2 Tim. 3:15). Hebrew Christians had a better background of the Old Testament Scriptures than did Gentile converts. But because many had a need "of repentance from dead works" (6:1), their knowledge became more of a hindrance than a help to them. James wrote that faith without works is dead faith. The Hebrew Christians were reminded that works without faith is dead works.

The Hebrew Christians had a need for growing in faith toward the reality of a resurrected Christ; they had remained Christians without experiencing any spiritual growth and development toward Christian maturity. The writer of Hebrews told them at the end of chapter five, before he gave them the challenge to go forward in spiritual growth and development in chapter six, "You have come to need milk and not solid food. For everyone who partakes only of milk is unskilled in the word of righteousness, for he is a babe" (5:12-13).

Perhaps most church members in the Laodicean Church felt more comfortable with a milk diet, "What has Christ done and can do for me?" But moving forward from self-centered Christian thinking leads to the discipleship message of self-denial and cross-bearing. Jesus was appealing to them to accept His invitation to come and dine with Him on solid food, "What do you want me to do, Lord?" There is always a full spread when one dines at the King's table. God's children should develop a hunger for the Bread of Life in coming to a table with such a variety of wholesome, spiritual food that is always available for those who hunger and thirst after righteousness.

At the time of the writing of the book of Revelation, I doubt if anyone was still living that was a charter member of the church at Laodicea. Those were the church members who had received salvation at the Feast of Pentecost in Jerusalem about sixty years earlier. But within two generations, could that church possibly have developed an attitude of "I got it all when I received Jesus," or "I have experienced Acts 2:4 and don't need anything more?" The baptism of the Holy Spirit was given to the church as a spiritual gateway for use in ministerial and spiritual gifts in the work of the Lord and not merely as a spiritual goal to achieve.

The greatest ministry in using the Acts 2:4 experience is the ministry of prayer. Paul learned to lean on the Holy Spirit in helping Him in the prayer ministry, besides learning to fellowship with Him in Spirit and in truth.

Prayer is the most important ministry. When used effectively, it reveals from where all authority for success comes. It is where all Christians have been called to dine together with Him in worship and prayer fellowship.

The Laodicean Church, as a collective group, was not accepting the challenge where she could say, "Let us go forward," but she had a collective "I am rich, have become wealthy" problem as if she had finally arrived at the highest goal attainable in receiving God's blessings. The Spirit of Truth, up to the time the Lord appealed to her to repent and open the door to Him, was unable to lead the Laodiceans very far in understanding and acting upon very many Bible truths.

The Hebrew Christians needed to forget their long past heritage as a privileged ethnic group with God. They needed to press forward together toward a greater future. The Laodicean Church also needed to forget her short heritage as a privileged church with past spiritual achievements and present material gains and press forward to a greater future in experiencing "the unsearchable riches of Christ" (Eph. 3:8).

The Bride Desires to Come after Him

In order to do God's will, anyone who works with people in Christian service should develop a lowly attitude of servitude and practice cross-bearing in obedience to doing God's will. We are to lose our soul-life for His sake (Matt. 16:25). He bore our cross at Calvary as a sacrifice for sin; now He calls His disciples to become identified with Him and bear the cross of losing the self-life for His sake as His example in everyday living.

As there are different levels in knowing God's will for your life (the good, well pleasing and perfect), there are different areas of expression in self-denial and cross-bearing in being committed to God as "a living sacrifice." A Christian will not go very far in knowing God's will for his life if he thinks more "highly of himself than he ought to think" (Rom. 12:1-3).

There needs to be the renewing of the mind where "nothing (is to) be done through selfish ambition or conceit, but in lowliness of mind let each esteem others better than himself. Let each of you look out not only for his own interests, but also for the interests of others. Let this mind be in you which was also in Christ Jesus" (Phil. 2:3-5).

In conclusion, self-denial is how the self-life relates to God in obeying His will. Cross-bearing relates to how the body is laid down as a living sacrifice in Christian service in helping others. That is like the example of Christ laying His body down with outstretched arms to be nailed to the cross at Calvary in service to all humanity.

Committed Christians put their bodies on God's altar as living sacrifices unto God in how they relate to the world, which is an enemy of God. Laying one's body on God's altar, not as a dead sacrifice under the old covenant but as a living sacrifice under the new covenant, is true spiritual service to the one true church organism. The milk of God's Word is learning what Christ did for the church. The solid food of God's Word is receiving His strength that is needed to follow His example of laying down the self-life in everyday living.

The church of the Laodiceans is a prime example of a church that saw no need and had no desire to obey the message of Christ that exhorted its members to come after Him. But the Laodiceans, as a church, needed to deny her self, pick up her cross daily in order to fellowship with Him.

In dealing with the Laodiceans, the Christ of love was still bearing the cross of sorrow and sadness for a people who wanted to go their own way and do their own thing for their own sake. But Jesus said, "Whoever loses his (soul) life for My sake will find it" (Matt. 16:25). A good illustration of the soul-life is that it represents the will (I want), the intellect (I think) and the emotions (I feel). All three of these areas of soulish expression became evident in the self-centered church of the Laodiceans.

Before the marriage of the Bridegroom and His Bride can take place, His Bride has to make her own wedding garment. (Of course, she needs the help of the Holy Spirit to do it.) The wedding garment is described as "fine linen, clean and bright, for the fine linen is the righteous acts of the saints" (Rev. 19:8).

Doing things for Jesus' sake are outworked righteous acts of the saints that go into making the wedding garment. The wedding cannot take place until the bride is ready, and the bride cannot be ready until her wedding garment is complete. Righteous behavior is the acts of the Holy Spirit working through each believer as good things are done for others without personal gain. It is usually done at your personal expense.

A Need for Spiritual Nourishment

To lose her independent self-identity in the Body of Christ, the "have need of nothing" church should have exhorted her people with the words, "Let us go forward, advancing steadily toward spiritual maturity in a unified effort in fellowship with the rest of the Body of Christ." But she did not have the spiritual discernment, strength and insight that must be received from the solid food of the gospel message to do so.

As a result she was spiritually shortsighted and impotent, being all wrapped up in her self. Obeying Christ's discipleship message would have taken that church out of an attitude of self-centeredness. The church of the Laodiceans needed more spiritual nourishment than the pure milk of God's Word that provides for basic spiritual nutrition.

Her lukewarm attitude toward the Lord caused the church of the Laodiceans to lose her taste for Him. She needed to have her hunger for the spiritual Bread of Life restored. But before members of that church could accept an invitation to feed upon Him even as the milk of the word, they would need to be "laying aside all malice, all guile, hypocrisy, envy, and all evil speaking."

Then they would once again "desire the pure milk of the word, that you [they] may grow thereby, if indeed you [they] have tasted that the Lord is gracious" (1 Pet. 2:1-3). Before the spiritually proud can be fed and receive spiritual nourishment in a no-need church system, they first need to lay aside all the carnal characteristics that promote disunity in the Body of Christ.

An appetite for mundane things instead of heavenly things had caused that church to lose her taste for the pure milk of God's Word, which is personified in Jesus. At one time she had "tasted that the Lord is gracious," but now she had more of a hunger for the worldly, the riches of the temporal, and for the things that perish with the using. Self-satisfaction kept her from seeing a need to continue to seek Him in His fullness, for only in Him can true satisfaction be found.

Along with a hunger for Him, she also needed to have a thirst for Him. Because only He can satisfy the eternal thirst in the heart of humanity, He is life's great Thirst Quencher. "As the deer pants for the water brooks, so pants my soul for You, O God" (Ps. 42:1). If anyone hears His voice and opens the door, "the fountain of the water of life freely" will be given to that thirsty soul.

The beginning of the church at Laodicea was analogous to a rose bush full of beautiful, sweet-smelling roses unto the Lord. Because of self-centeredness that had crept into that church, the beautiful roses had withered and died, and now the rose bush appeared as a plant full of ugly thorns of selfishness in the sight of the Lord.

In order to go forward toward spiritual maturity, the Laodiceans needed to submit to the Holy Spirit for Him to give her a revelation of God's ultimate plan and purpose for the church. "Where there is no revelation, the people cast off restraint; but happy is he who keeps the law" (Prov. 29:18). As God's people, that lukewarm church needed to have a fervent love for Him, instead of just having a love for the church that they attend.

Forward to the Next Level

Whatever spiritual level a church becomes positioned in, spiritual things at that level may become too familiar. The longer she stays at that level the more commonplace they become. It usually becomes a spiritual plateau where there is no further spiritual progress in the upward spiritual journey toward experiencing fullness in Him. That church would like to have brought Christ down to her standard rather than going forward to the next level toward His standard. If she fails to submit to the Holy Spirit, who leads into all truth, to lead her to the next level, that church will never go to a higher spiritual level.

The Holy Spirit might move upon a remnant of people in that church, and through revival fires, a Christian movement may begin. That spiritual movement goes to the next level. With the blessings of God upon her as His privileged people, if she begins to develop the same self-centered characteristics as did the Laodicean Church, she too will be unable to move forward to the next spiritual level.

Church services begin to become more and more formal and ritualistic. The Laodicean Church could offer Him a form and a ritual in a church worship service but deny Him an affectionate heart in everyday Christian fellowship and service.

When a church is on one spiritual level, she is unfamiliar with anything that may be happening on the next level. How could she? She has never been there! She doesn't know what she is missing. She knows nothing about the upward journey or all the new-creation realities that are becoming new in Christ Jesus at the next level. She may misunderstand all of God's tests that are involved in getting to the next spiritual level.

Because she hasn't been there to experience the spiritual atmosphere at the next level, that church would be foolish to say that she had no need to know the many more spiritual blessings that God has to offer. Her spiritual pride would keep her from admitting that a higher level of spiritual experiences even existed. The walk of faith in the spiritual realm is an unfamiliar realm. As a church walks in time in the realm of sense-knowledge experiences, she may also learn to walk in the realm of the eternal Spirit by faith in new-creation spiritual experiences.

There are many things in the physical realm that we don't know anything about, and there are many more new things yet to be discovered. If that is true in the realm of the temporal, how much more do we need to experience new things in the realm of the eternal? The declaration of the temporal riches of the Laodiceans became like a dark cloud that came between her and the light of "the Sun of Righteousness" that gives warmth and healing energy to a church (Mal. 4:2).

The Lord was ready to reveal to anyone in that church, who would answer the knock at the door, the way out of such spiritual stagnation. Only the light of God's Truth can penetrate and absorb any specific realm of spiritual darkness. The sanctifying truth of God's Word separates from worldly influences and sets the hungry apart unto God.

The walk in the Spirit is a walk of faith, not sight. The walk of faith is exciting, challenging, rewarding, but it is never easy. In the school of spiritual growth and development, a church will make mistakes through growing pains, but she can learn from her mistakes. Many spiritual truths can be learned by the humbling process that is involved with on-the-job training in the walk of faith.

Moving forward to the next level may be illustrated by an experience that I received as a young man working with the U.S. Forest Service in blister-rust control in the state of Idaho during the summer of 1947.

In our work for the forest service, a group of young men just out of high school were camped at the base of a mountaintop named Moose Mountain. When we first saw it from a distance, it appeared much smaller than it actually was. But once we set up camp at its base, we realized how big it actually was. Yet, we in camp did not understand the immensity of energy required to reach the summit of that snow-capped mountain.

Fourth of July was a day off from work. A few of us in camp planned days in advance to get up at daybreak, climb the mountain, throw snow balls at one another, eat a snack lunch, and be back in camp by middle of the day. But we underestimated the project! The more we climbed upward toward the snow-capped top, the more accurately we understood the total height of the summit.

That's the way it is in the renewing of the mind through commitment in fellowshipping with Jesus. The more progress is made toward having the mind of Christ, the more accurately we understand the magnitude of the assignment. There is always a need for a challenge to pass another trial or test along the way in order to go to the next spiritual level.

Being inexperienced at mountain climbing, we did not understand that the closer that we got to the summit, the more difficult it would be to ascend because the thin air of the atmosphere made it more difficult to breathe. We could only ascend a short distance at a time before resting. We made frequent stops along the way to rest, but with a determination to reach our destination, we reached the top. At the summit we experienced new things like seeing a small glacier and playing in the snow in the middle of the summer.

Descending from the top of the mountain was much easier, but it was after dark when we arrived back at base camp exhausted. But we had been enlightened, on a small scale, about what was demanded of people who climb a mountain to its snow-capped summit. The opposite of not knowing is being enlightened.

That is an illustration of the unknown element in a new experience in the realm of the physical. In going to the next spiritual level, there is also the unknown element. In the walk of sanctifying truth, old things are passing away and all things are becoming new and exciting in new creation living in Him.

We cannot climb up to Him, but He is eager to meet us where we are so that He can lift us up to where He is. If it is necessary for Him to knock, we need to open the door. The message to the overcomers in the Laodicean Church was: "Humble yourselves in the sight of the Lord, and He will lift you up." Through faithful fellowship with Him, the overcoming church is being lifted a little higher today in Him than she was the day before. Overcomers in the end-time church are going forward to the next level by "beholding as in a mirror the glory of the Lord, are being transformed into the same image from glory to glory." The overcoming church is a triumphant church! She shall "be conformed to the image of His Son, that He might be the firstborn among many brethren."

Chapter 2

The Greatest Need

A Need to See That She Is a Very Needy Church

"Because you say, 'I am rich, have become wealthy, and *have need of nothing*'—and do not know that you are wretched, miserable, poor, blind, and naked" (verse 17).

The Lord had to deal with the "have need of nothing" attitude with blunt and harsh words. Because "the love of money is the root of all kinds of evil," here was a church with a multitude of spiritual needs declaring that she had no need, but she had an ego problem. That church's ego was enthroned upon her heart where the Lord should have been. A good theological acronym for ego is Edging God Out.

The ego of the church of the Laodiceans had replaced the sovereignty of the Lord over that church. In her zeal for self-glory, her ego needed to abdicate its throne of glory for Jesus' sake. To be conquered by the nature of the Christ-life for God's glory, that church's ego must be denied of her zeal for self-glory. Members of the family of God are to lose their various self-identities into the love and oneness of being identified with the Father's firstborn Son.

When people or organizations of the world make the same statement of having need of nothing, it indicates that they think they have all that the world has to offer them in this temporal life. But when it comes to the church, she is not dealing only with the physical but also with the spiritual.

Her pursuit is not only in the realm of temporal blessings but also in the realm of eternal rewards.

A church saying, "I have need of nothing," would cover both realms. It is quite possible for a church to be satisfied and self-sufficient in the material realm, but to proclaim self-sufficiency in the spiritual realm is a statement of spiritual ignorance and arrogance.

The worst state that an individual or church can be is a position where they think they have no spiritual needs. "Blessed are the poor in spirit, for theirs is the kingdom of heaven" (Matt. 5:3). The greatest need of the Laodicean Church was a need for a wholehearted love toward Him. Though she was out of control with a rebellious soul, the One who loved her and "poured out His soul unto death" for her was making an appeal for her wholehearted love.

The ultimate purpose of God's plan of salvation is the revelation of His great love for Adam's fallen race. A people, who were once dead in trespasses and sins, now have an opportunity to receive the gift of eternal life through the redeeming blood of Christ Jesus.

How can a finite mind understand such infinite love? (Eph. 3:19). There needs to be a wholehearted response on the part of the church toward God's amazing grace through Christ Jesus. The Lover of her soul requires that His great love for the church be taken seriously and reciprocated.

The evangelistic message to the world is that Christ is the Redeemer of mankind, "who gave Himself a ransom for all, to be testified in due time" (1 Tim. 2:6). The Father, through the Son, met the greatest need for lost humanity in giving eternal life to a lost race of people who are dead in trespasses and sins. The Father "so loved the world that He gave His only begotten Son" (John 3:16).

But when it comes to the message to the church, Christ, the Bridegroom, "loved the church and gave Himself for her…that He might present her to Himself a glorious church" (Eph. 5:25b-27a). That presents a challenge for the Father to create a masterpiece in Christ for the benefit of eternal fellowship with the Son by the Holy Spirit. The Father's creative workmanship that He prepared beforehand, as the Bride, will be taken out of the Body of Christ in the paradise of heaven. Christ has the honor of presenting the glorious Bride, for whom He died, unto Himself for eternity.

The Bridegroom Needs a Bride

The proud church of the Laodiceans would not be a submissive bride for the Father's Son. For a church to say "I have need of nothing" is a statement of sovereignty. Behind that statement was the pursuit for self-glory and self-sufficiency. Only God is sovereign. An all-sufficient God, the highest authority over all things, has need of nothing. But the paradox behind the story is the Father-God of the universe is a God of love, and love needs to be shared and fulfilled through His great plan of salvation for Adam's fallen race. The Son of God has a need to be loved by the church for which He died. Since Christ loved the Laodicean Church so much that He died for her, His great love therefore, became open and vulnerable toward her, and that church was walking on His loving heart with her hobnailed boots of spiritual indifference.

God created Adam, knowing that he would transgress His law, but that presented a need to be worked out by the Father through His Son. "Christ was the Lamb of God slain before the foundation of the world" (Rev. 13:8). For that reason, there was a need for the Son to suffer for a fallen race of people.

Christ suffered for the benefit of lost humanity that whoever believes in Him might have everlasting life. That serves the most important need for lost humanity, but the love of the Son of God for a maturing church that is able to reciprocate His love is a personal need that is being fulfilled by the end-time church. And as sure as there is a God in heaven, the need of God's ultimate purpose for the church shall be completed.

What about the need of a fervent love in question for the Son of God? God's Son is the Lord over a new creation, and He longs to have a loving fellowship with new-creation people. The highest position of fellowship with the Lord is unique. The Father's ultimate purpose for His church is for her to grow and develop into the fullness of spiritual maturity into the image and likeness of His firstborn Son.

Out of the church, as the Body of Christ in time, will come forth the Bride of Christ in eternity. As the Body of Christ has many members, yet being one spiritual body, the Bride and the Bridegroom, which are two, will become one with the same glorified body.

The oneness of all evangelical churches having fellowship one with another for time and eternity should be in the same manner that the Father and the Son have unity and fellowship with one another in the Godhead. Jesus prayed to the Father, "And the glory which You gave Me I have given them, that they may be one just as We are one: "I in them, and You in Me; that they may be made perfect in one, and that the world may know that You have sent Me, and have loved them as You have loved Me."

The Holy Spirit is working with all churches by God's grace to lead them into that oneness by losing their individuality with the Son, as the Son lost His individuality with the Father. The model for unity of the church, therefore, begins with having unity with the Son as He has fellowship with the Father.

Early in her Christian walk, the Holy Spirit makes a church conscious of the reality of her collective needs. Becoming need-oriented for spiritual progress and staying in focus to that need is very important for a church, and that primary need should be especially upon Him who loves her with an everlasting love.

God's love is eternal. The eternal unchanging Father has always loved the eternal unchanging Son and the eternal Spirit of Love reveals and imparts to the church the love that the Son has for her. By the Spirit of Love, the church has an invitation to become one with the Godhead through the Son of His dear love. The unity of the Godhead is the model for the unity of the end-time church with her Head.

The Son was sent into the world to show forth the Father's love and mercy to fallen humanity. The Son, who gave Himself for the church, requires the church to persevere in spiritual growth and development in order to reciprocate that love in a greater measure. The church in Laodicea was indebted to love Him fervently and passionately as He loved her, but her self-centeredness had blinded her from seeing that accountability to His great love.

With that divine overture of grace, a church should humble herself before the greatness of His majestic love for a fallen race. Why God loves Adam's race so much is one of "the secret things [that] belongs to the LORD our God." But one of those things emphasized and revealed in the Scriptures as belonging to His church (Deut. 29:29) is the need for God's people to love the LORD our God with all our heart. God should be first place in the hearts and lives of all church members.

Adam's Need for a Bride

Though the first man was made perfect as an object of God's love, he was incomplete in respect to God's total creative plan and purpose for him. Adam appreciated the fellowship with the animals that God had created. He probably was the first pet lover on planet earth. But there was a need; something was lacking in Adam's life. There was none of Adam's own kind to be the object of his love.

After Adam was put in charge of the garden to care for it and keep it, he classified and named all the cattle, the birds and every beast of the field. That required great intelligence on Adam's part. There was also an element of time involved to complete the task. "But for Adam there was not found a helper comparable to him" (Gen. 2:20).

God could have created Adam and the woman—also giving her a name—on the same day, but there was a time element between the creation of Adam and the creation of the woman. God had a purpose for doing that. Adam was alone long enough to see that He had a need for fellowship from one of his own kind. God waited until Adam saw that he had a need before He supplied that need. To make provision for Adam's loneliness and completeness, God created for him one of his own kind; He took a rib out of Adam and created one that was "bone of his bone and flesh of his flesh." Paul made a comparison to that story in reference to the church as "members of His body" (Eph. 5:32).

Christ, who gave Himself for the sins of the world as the Last Adam, was resurrected from the dead as the Second Man, being the Head over a new-creation people. Like the first man that had a need for one of His own kind, the Second Man also has a need. He longs for "a helper comparable to Him" (Gen. 2:18). Adam cleaving to his God-given bride is the creative mystery to which Paul refers concerning Christ and the church.

A self-centered church, like the Laodiceans, was incapable of loving anyone but herself, nor did she have the capacity to love Him the way that He deserves to be loved. Christ had proved His love for that lukewarm church, and the Lover of her soul has a need to be loved in the same manner that He loves.

Since the woman was made a "helper" along the side of Adam, she was equal to Him as one of a kind. She was made a helper to the keeper of the garden. She was to serve God on the same level of fellowship while ruling with Adam. As God's appointed helper, Adam's bride was to work together with Adam as one. As the woman was taken out of Adam to be a helper to Adam in ruling over the Garden of Eden with Adam, the Bride will be taken out of Christ to be His helper in ruling over the Kingdom of God with Christ.

Adam named his bride "Eve" for self-identity reasons after the fall (Gen. 3:20). At the beginning, she was created from Adam, became a part of Adam, and lost her self-identity in Adam. She had no name except the name of her bridegroom. "Male and female created he them; and blessed them, and called their name Adam, in the day when they were created" (Gen. 5:2, KJV). As Jesus spoke and acted in the name of the Father, the church is to speak and act in the name of Jesus. That means everything that is being done for the glory of God is also fulfilling the will of God.

The many end-time church organizations in America have a need for self-identity as any other business in a world of private enterprise and individualism, but that practice of self-identity is relative to being in the world but not being of the world. In God's business, He only has one unified, maturing church organism, functioning in obedience under one Head as the Body of Christ.

The church is the Father's business, with the Holy Spirit sent as the divine Helper to help the church fulfill His ultimate purpose through the Son for the Father's glory. A church organization at the beginning had no self-identity. The only identity of the early church organization was the city where the church was located.

The Exalted Destiny of the Church

The church of the Laodiceans had a need to be motivated and challenged to go forward toward spiritual maturity. God's destiny for His church is on a much higher level than human reasoning might "ask or think." The ultimate destiny that God has for His church can only be understood by divine revelation given by the Holy Spirit through the Scriptures.

The church of the Laodiceans thought she had arrived, but she had an experience with Him only as her "Beginning." There was also a need of having even a closer daily experience with Him until He became a greater reality as her "End." He is the Alpha and Omega to the church. Because she became sidetracked on the journey to the "End," she experienced self-deception through self-achievement that gave her false security.

The Bible pictures the church at the present, in time, as the Body of Christ with Him as the functional Head. The Bible pictures the future of the church, in eternity, as the Bride of Christ with Him as the waiting, grateful Bridegroom. We, therefore, need to see a local church as part of the whole church organism, a body of believers experiencing spiritual growth and development for the glory of the Father.

Too many church members may look to a church organization as nothing more than an inanimate commodity of natural assets and liabilities similar to any other secular enterprise. But a church organization, as a self-identity, may develop so much influence over the church organism that the organization itself replaces the Christ of the church over their lives. Christ will have no part in a loving courtship with a church organization that wants to dominate everything. Christ desires to fellowship with a church with a submissive attitude toward His great love.

The thought life of the masses of professing Christians of the end-time church is molded more around the church to which they belong than the Christ of the church who loves them and wants them to think that, above everything else, they belong to Him. He is to be the love and center of the Christian life.

But "anyone" in that church organism was given an opportunity to make a humble decision through repentance and reverse the order. By opening the door of their hearts through hearing His voice, they could have a restored loving fellowship with a personal Lord. The Christ of the church would be restored to His proper domain over their hearts and lives.

A quest for personal greatness is what motivated the church of the Laodiceans to pursue a self-centered course of personal attainment. In the world there is nothing wrong in having fame and fortune, but with a church, God must take the initiative. He is the One who gives the fame and provides the fortune. In realization of this, a church that has been blessed abundantly by God has a need to be thankful and praise Him for His grace and goodness toward her.

In her humility, a church knows that she has been blessed by His grace in the past, but she also knows not to rely on self-confidence but put her confidence in the Lord. The challenge for the church to work out her "own [complete] salvation with fear and trembling" (Phil. 2:12) by God's grace is to know Him in His redemptive fullness. In her humility, the Bride becomes the church that abides in Him as one like David who God said was "a man after My own heart, who will do My will" (Acts 13:22).

All progress in the growth and development of the church organism is by faith, in order that she may please God. The church as a family is called "the household of faith." There is no place for selfish ambition, whether it is in the many ministries of the church or as a church herself. Selfish ambition between churches that compete against one another does not glorify God. A Christian businessperson might pray and ask for divine guidance and wisdom in dealings in secular affairs. When those prayers are answered, God should get the recognition and the glory.

But in the work of the Lord, personal ambition should be denied in order that it will not become competitive. The many members of the Body of Christ do not compete against one another for the sake of the well-being of the Body. Each member of the Body works in harmony with the Head of the Body. Each member functions according to the directions of the Head and in cooperation with one another.

One member of the Body should not become dissatisfied, but see its importance as related to other members of the Body. "But now God has set the members, each one of them, in the body just as He pleased" (1 Cor. 12:18). God has an ultimate plan for the church and it was in the heart of God before the foundation of the earth (Rev. 13:8).

God never makes a mistake and He surrenders His sovereignty to no one. Sovereignty is not in a church system. Sovereignty is not in the many members of the Body. Sovereignty is in the Head of the Body. That means wherever a right church is found, the functional Head is teaching and testing for spiritual growth and development.

Humanity has a natural tendency to be self-assertive and self-reliant in the goal of becoming the greatest and the best in the affairs of the world in dealing with "the things of men." That approach can be carried over into the affairs of the church, which deals with "the things of God." But that tendency needs to be denied with the application of self-denial and cross-bearing.

Jesus said, "If anyone desires to come after Me, let him deny himself, and take up his cross daily, and follow Me" (Luke 9:23). The daily challenge is so great that there must be a desire with a whole heart to come after Him. Otherwise, that commandment will not be obeyed. That was the same challenge that the Lord was making to "anyone" in the church of the Laodiceans.

For anyone with a heart to do the work of the Lord, the Lord of the work will see to it that the tests will come. "My brethren, count it all joy when you fall into various trials, knowing that the testing of your faith produces patience. But let patience have its perfect work, that you may be perfect and complete, lacking nothing" (James 1:2-4). God will have a tested people.

The *lacking-nothing* church is at the end of the pilgrimage. That journey is one of self-denial and being a cross-bearer "for His sake." In the journey of a disciple, there is always a need for a closer walk with Him. The Bridegroom will declare His humble bride elect complete, lacking nothing at the end of journey. That is the time when there is a "need of nothing." The battle is over! The race has been won! The wedding is taking place! When a church declares, like the church of the Laodiceans did at the beginning of the race, in her self-importance that she has "need of nothing," she is only deceiving herself. When the Bride has won her Bridegroom, she has won it all. It is at the end, not the beginning, where a church might rightly say, "We got it all when we received the complete Christ of the Scriptures, and we have followed Him until the end."

Those who desire to follow Christ to the end, no matter what trials might come their way, will pass the test because they want God's best.

Working only for temporal rewards can be very superficial. The praises of men are soon silenced by death; then, only that which was pleasing to the Lord will truly count. That church organization saw no need to accept the Lord's challenge of coming after Him in discipleship (Luke 9:23). Now the appeal was to "anyone" in the church organism to come after Him by accepting the invitation to fellowship with Him by dining with Him.

That church had achieved a self-appointed purpose. Since she had arrived, she didn't need any help from anybody else in the Body of Christ. She had begun with Him as her Head, and the Lord wanted to bring her to the Father's appointed purpose for the church. The journey of discipleship was still ongoing, but she had deceived herself that she had arrived. She had achieved the ultimate in material prosperity, and she became blinded to the requirements that were needed for soul prosperity. She desired to receive heaven's rewards from His throne without keeping herself humble before His cross. She did not want to follow the example that the Lord Jesus Christ had set before her.

The Body of Christ is not sovereign in itself. The sovereignty is in the Head of the Body. The church of the Laodiceans needed to be reminded of the Head who is sovereign over the church. Who is the greatest in the church? Which one will sit on His right or His left when He comes into His kingdom? That was not left to the judgment of His disciples or His church. That is the Father's choice and He is the only one that has the authority and is qualified to make that kind of judgment.

What Is an Independent Church?

Because the church of the Laodiceans said, "I have need of nothing," she was an independent church, independent of God and independent of all other churches. Perhaps the church leadership depended on one another, and the church members depended on the church leadership. But the church itself was full of independent people. Mankind is independent by nature. "All we like sheep have gone astray; we have turned, every one, to his own way; and the LORD has laid on Him the iniquity of us all" (Is. 53:6).

Being an independent church has different meanings to different members in the Body of Christ. In some church circles the term "independent" is right. It means that a local church is "right" because it is operating independently of any one of the hundreds of denominational churches in the land.

The first time I visited a citywide pastors' prayer group, I was met with introductions from other members of the group by the host pastor. In one introduction, a pastor who was not affiliated with any denomination asked, "Do you pastor an independent church?"

"We are much more independent than we need to be," was my reply.

His question was based upon the church as an organization. My answer was based upon the function of the church as a body, a spiritual organism, of which Christ is the Head. As members of a body of believers, we find it difficult to put off the independent "old man" nature in order that we might put on the dependent "new man" nature. It is the new nature that will submit to the Chief Shepherd as the functional Head of a local assembly through His obedient undershepherds.

One of the consequences that came through the fall is the attitude of an independent soul-life toward God and the way He does things. The nature of an independent soul-life finds it most difficult to submit to the teachings of Jesus on how each church group should relate to God and to one another.

But in most denominational church circles, the thinking of being an independent church is "wrong." If a local church does not choose to line up under the leadership of some denominational church (more wisely their own), it is "wrong." If local church leadership is working independently and not operating under a given denominational leadership, she is working independently of God. Although the leadership in the hundreds of denominations in America is usually appointed by the vote of man, each leadership believes that it is acting on behalf of God.

In the church of the Laodiceans, modern-day denominations were not the issue; she just had an independent attitude toward God and all others. That attitude caused her to be lukewarm and halfhearted in her relationship with the Christ of Christianity. He was standing on the outside knocking on the closed door of that independent church.

Replacing a Wrong Focus with a Right Focus

When God blesses a church with success and prosperity, the focus of the heart is very important. Where is the focus going to be? Is the focus going to be upon herself? Is the focus only going to be upon the material blessings and success? Or is there going to be a steadfast focus upon the LORD who blesses His church with many good things?

(1) Look WHO God Has Blessed!

First, the focus is set upon the church that God has blessed. The Lord blessing her with material prosperity led that church to become self-centered in her thinking. Everything centered on self. She became self-satisfied in her self-sufficiency. Having a wrong concept about her self-worth, she developed a wrong attitude in being self-sufficient. With a focus only on temporal things, she said, "God has blessed me with riches and wealth." She concluded, now "I have need of nothing."

God prospers and blesses a local church in order that she might be used in loyalty to His cause. She might become a blessing to others, and not for her to become self-centered and selfish. She needed to receive the righteousness of God in Christ Jesus by faith, and let God's out-worked righteousness bring forth acts of righteousness on her part for the glory of God. "And to her [the Bride] it was granted to be arrayed in fine linen, clean and bright, for the fine linen is the righteous acts of the saints" (Rev. 19:8).

She might have seen her status before the Lord as being rich in Christian service. The Lord saw her as a self-centered church that cared only about her self-glory and nobody else. Love of self had kept that church from obeying the first and great commandment. She was rich in material goods, but she needed to know how to become rich in faith, "for whatever is not from faith is sin" (Rom. 14:26).

God had blessed her with riches, and perhaps church attendance, more than many others; therefore, God had put His approval on her above all others. A church may be right before the Lord in one generation, yet lose her focus and emphasis on His greatness in what He means to her, and become wrong the next generation. The thermometer of emotional temperatures toward Him changes over a period of time. At the beginning God received the glory, but now her statement indicates self-promotion. In seeking her own greatness, the Lord lost His greatness above everything else in her thinking.

In her erroneous non-scriptural reasoning and competitive attitude, she concluded that her riches made her as a privileged church with God, but she was neglecting the so great salvation of her Lord Provider. Being privileged through the prosperity that God had provided caused her to become a proud and rebellious people in heart.

Self-importance had taken center stage away from Jesus in that local church. She was rich with material things, but she needed to cast off the stronghold of haughty thinking and "bring every thought into captivity to the obedience of Christ" (2 Cor. 10:5).

She needed to buy what the Lord had to give. He paid a high price for her to become fervent in devotion to Him. He could not accept a halfhearted apathetic affection toward Him. She needed a broken and a contrite spirit before Him. God gives help to the church that knows she is needy and asks of Him to supply that need. He is a very present help in the time of need.

The Lord told her, "Do [you] not know that you are wretched, miserable, poor, blind, and naked." Though the rebuke was strong and stern, it was a rebuke of love. The authority of Christ over the church is clothed with His love toward His church. He desires to reward a church, not rebuke her, but true love tells it like it is.

Possibly that church didn't want to face the truth about herself. But there was a way out. Members of that church still had access to His great love, but they were the ones who had to open the closed door to enter into fellowship with Him. Entrance into the New Jerusalem through her twelve gates will be an open-door policy (Rev. 21:25).

That church was being judged for her self-centered works. That was not a judgment of condemnation with the world. That was a judgment of members of a church with the possibility of reaping eternal rewards. "Anyone" who heard His voice and entered into a mutual dining with Him in spiritual food of God's Word had the opportunity of winning the crown of the overcomer with Him.

(2) Look at God's BLESSINGS upon My Church

Next, the focus is set on the blessings that God had provided for His people. That story, as told, speaks many things between the lines, but one thing is quite clear. That church loved the riches that made her a wealthy church, at least according to her assessment and the standard for that time. If a person has been blessed in the realm of the physical, with great talent, great family status, impressive good looks, and exceptional intelligence, it is human nature for that person to have a tendency to have great pride.

That church had her focus on the natural and not on the spiritual, for none of these things is of any value in the spiritual realm. God wants His people to enjoy His blessings, for all good things come from above. If you do not know how to handle the blessings, God's right things can become wrong to the user of them.

There is nothing wrong in being prosperous in the Lord. But "no one [or collectively] can serve two masters; for either he [or they] will hate the one and love the other, or else he [or they] will be loyal to the one and despise the other, you can not serve God and Mammon" (Matt. 6:24). Notice that it does not say that you should not serve God and mammon. It says that you cannot.

Material blessings can serve a church well, but it is not well with a church that serves the material blessings. That church had a need to obey the first and great commandment of loving God above all others. Her halfhearted love toward Him and unfaithfulness led to faithlessness. "Without faith, it is impossible to please God."

The Laodicean Church was in bondage to mammon. Mammon is a spirit of this world that brings people into servitude to materialistic thinking. The media of television is a strong influence in promoting that kind of materialistic and sensual thinking in these last days.

His disciples, who followed Him during His journey toward the cross, were at various times taken up with temporal things. Here was their Messiah and they were following Him to help Him set up His kingdom on the earth. They could not understand Him. When He told them about His rejection and the prophetic message concerning the death that He was sent to die, they were afraid to ask Him. Their natural thinking was to receive a throne with Him without going through the cross-life of suffering with Him.

But they would find out that you have to go through the cross to get to the throne of the overcomer, and this was what Jesus was offering to "anyone" in that church through daily fellowship in eating spiritual food with Him. Walking with the Christ of the Scriptures in faithful commitment doesn't set well with the worldly-minded of the church. Knowing Him "in the fellowship of His suffering" would help qualify the "anyone" to receive the reward with the overcoming church.

(3) Look to GOD who provides the blessings

Finally, the focus should have been set on the goodness of God who provided her the riches and the wealth. She couldn't have been blessed with good things without help from the Blesser. She needed to recognize it was God's love toward her that helped her to prosper. An attitude of gratitude from a whole heart with a meek and lowly spirit would have been pleasing to the Lord. Then, the Holy Spirit could continue to lead her into spiritual growth and development as a prosperous church.

One of the most popular and renowned chapters in the Bible is the Twenty-third Psalm. That chapter is popular because of its emphasis on a close relationship with a personal Lord. The Lord Jesus Christ desires having a very close loving, personal relationship to a church before she gets too religious.

Verse 4 is a favorite verse that is usually quoted at a funeral service. At that time the focus is on walking "through the valley of the shadow of death." But the central thought is "I will fear no evil for you are with me." The Shepherd Lord is with His church at the time of death as well as in life.

That Psalm begins with, "The LORD is my shepherd; I shall not want." A king that once was a shepherd boy wrote those words. He became a man "after God's own heart" (Acts 13:22). God is an emotional God. When He becomes the center of the life of a church, she has His heart.

In other words, if the Lord becomes someone special to a church, she becomes someone special to Him. Christ gave Himself for the church "that He might purify for Himself His own special people, zealous for good works" (Tit. 2:14). His special people do good works by the leading of the Holy Spirit for the glory of the Father and the Son.

If Psalms 23:1 is contrasted with Revelation 3:17, you see that the crux of the Christian life is about looking unto God in order that you might learn to depend upon Him. David said that he had need of nothing because the Lord was his Shepherd. The church of the Laodiceans said that she had need of nothing because she was rich and wealthy.

King David's focus was upon the Lord who supplies every need. That develops wholehearted worship where true security is found. When the "poor in spirit" trust in the Lord, needs of the poor are supplied. True satisfaction is found in the Lord. When He is recognized as the Lord Provider, He should get the glory for providing every need.

If the love for temporal things of the world come between God and a church, there is a divided heart, a lukewarm devotion and a lack of affection toward the Lord. That displeases the Lord very much. The church of the Laodiceans was not a church "after God's own heart." That was the decisive factor and the problem with that church. Her prosperity had made her selfish, proud and self-centered. She sought for self-glory where there was no place for God's glory. This world's riches cannot give true satisfaction, for they provide a foundation of false security.

After the Israelites had been delivered from Egyptian bondage and had taken the riches and wealth of Egypt with them, God told His people, "And you shall remember the Lord your God, for it is He who gives you power to get wealth" (Deut. 8:18a). But it didn't take the children of Israel long to forget to whom they should give thanks for the wealth that they took from the Egyptians. Egypt was a type of the world. They were drawn away from God, their Deliverer, by making the idol of the golden calf from the gold that they had brought with them out of Egypt.

From the time God delivered His people from Egyptian bondage, she enjoyed prosperity as a nation "in the land of milk and honey." She did not give God the glory for that prosperity, which peaked in the building of the

Temple during the reign of Solomon. The attitude of Israel, as God's privileged people, hindered her from becoming God's humble people.

As with any church group, or with a nation like Israel, there is nothing wrong with collective prosperity. But the prosperity of the Laodicean Christians gave them a wrong attitude. That church's collective prosperity gave her an attitude of collective pride and superiority. Not only did she egotistically think it, but she also boastfully proclaimed it, "I have need of nothing." As a church, she became an island unto herself in God's vast ocean of family concern and care for His people.

All good things come from above and there is where the hearts and minds of the Laodicean Church should have been. She should have had a heart "for those things which are above, where Christ is, sitting at the right hand of God. Set your mind on things above, not on things on the earth" (Col. 3:1-2). [Note: that epistle was also read to the Laodiceans (4:16).] But when she became proud, there would be no purpose in reading it. She couldn't have received the message without a humble heart. Heaven is in the realm of the eternal, and it is where the true citizenship of the church is, and where her first allegiance ought to be. Anything of the earth is in the realm of time; it is temporal and secondary.

Christ was to become the Father's treasure to that church in everyday living, but the treasures of the world had taken His place. The church always has a need for more of God's heavenly treasure to be revealed in her earthen vessels. To do this, the visible earthen vessels need to declare His invisible excellence, "That all people may know that the glory and power may be of God and not of us" (2 Cor. 4:7). The Father's purpose is to reveal the Son through earthen vessels. Paul said, "When it pleased God, who separated me from my mother's womb…to reveal His Son in me" (Gal. 1:15-16).

The religious leaders of Israel represented a people who had waited hundreds of years for the coming of their Messiah, but when He showed up, they had no need for Him. They weren't ready to receive Him. The leadership in the Laodicean church was like the scribes and the Pharisees who were under the sound of Jesus' voice, but they did not have ears to hear what He had to say or eyes to see the miracles that He did in the Father's name for the Father's glory.

Like other local churches of the Apostolic Age, I'm sure that church felt she was truly ready and worthy for His Second Coming. But she was not! The love for gold, not the love for God, was the center of her life. When a church has been blessed with riches and wealth, she needs to have the right focus. A wrong focus is when emphasis is placed upon the church herself who is the recipient of God's blessings, or the emphasis is placed only on the blessings, forgetting the Lord who provides the blessings. The right focus is upon God, who is the giver of all good things.

A Need to Walk in Truth

If that church had a wholehearted love for the truth, she would have a wholehearted love for Him, for He is Personified Truth. She needed to love the truth in order that she might accept the challenge to walk in truth. No matter how much truth the Spirit of Truth has already revealed to local churches, as long as they continue to be submissive to His guidance, He will lead and guide them into all truth. Knowing the fullness of truth is beyond human limitations. The church needs the help of the Holy Spirit.

In her bid for greatness, the Laodicean Church was indirectly claiming she already had all truth, and she had more favor with God than did other churches. She saw no need to become more passionate for His loving presence and fellowship as the Truth.

Like the victories given by God to Israel in the Old Testament, at one time that church did have the favor of God. But based upon a great past and the blessings of increased riches and wealth, she had developed a self-centered focus that resulted in a sense of false security. Her security and salvation was not based upon a present close loving fellowship with Him.

As a lukewarm church, she no longer denied the self-life and neither would she pick up her cross daily in order that she might follow Him as the Christ of the Scriptures. The members of that church had an identity with the Christ of the cross, but they had become enemies of the cross of Christ. "For many walk, of whom I have told you often, *and now* tell you even weeping, that they are the enemies of the cross of Christ" (Phil. 3:18).

That scriptural reference is not about the enemies of Christ, which the world is full of in these last days; but it is about the enemies of the cross of Christ, which the church is full of in these last days. There must have been more church members in the time of Paul than there were those who denied themselves and followed on to know Him in Christian discipleship.

Here were Christians who had their minds set "on earthly things." The Laodiceans' riches and wealth of this world represented things of this earth (v. 19). First, that message which Paul taught the Philippians wasn't taught once or twice to that church. He said, "I have told you often." And now, the problem of the enemies of the cross of Christ had become so severe that Paul even wept while telling about it. That kind of preaching is not being heard from the majority of the pulpits of the end-time church. But throughout Paul's epistles, we see his concern for the well-being of the church organism.

If Paul were still alive in these last days, he would shed many tears over so many who oppose the challenge of the message of self-denial and being a cross-bearer for Jesus' sake. Multitudes of Christians are not willing to hear messages that call for a personal commitment or sacrifice on their part. Many church members love to hear the story about the Babe of Bethlehem, but they do not like to hear the message of what is required of them being identified with the cross of Christ. The central theme for Christian living should be to "come after Him" in order that a church may live and teach His ways.

John, the elder, wrote his third epistle to Gaius, whom he loved in the truth. Gaius was more committed than was the average church member. He was also a disciple of the Lord Jesus Christ. John told Gaius, "I have no greater joy than to hear that my children walk in truth" (3 John 4). That scripture illustrates what it took for John to experience a greater joy in Christian service as an elder in the church.

Paul wrote what caused him to weep in mourning while expressing why so many professing Christians failed to walk in the fullness of gospel truth. The church at Laodicea was not walking in the truth, and the Lord found no joy in admonishing her. He told her, "I could wish you were cold or hot" (v. 15).

When anyone sees that they have a spiritual need, the problem is half solved. If a sinner sees a need for a Savior, there is *joy over one sinner that repents* and enters into the saving knowledge of the Christ of the Scriptures. If anyone in that church saw a need to repent in order to walk in the knowledge of saving truth of the Christ of the Scriptures, Christians, like John the elder, would experience *"no greater joy."*

The church of the Laodiceans would like to have found a middle ground of compromise between right and wrong, good and evil, hot and cold. Because at times it is impossible to get all the facts, the human limitation of judges of this world's court system may try to find a middle ground in sentencing the guilty, but there is none.

But the Judge of heaven, who knows all the facts, says that there is no middle ground. That church was lukewarm and halfhearted toward the Lover of her soul and that attitude was inexcusable on her part. The exciting part about that story is the merciful Lord over that church. Look to Him! He forgives! He restores! Laodicean church members were given an opportunity to revive the courtship with the promised Bridegroom back on a loving, passionate foundation. He is wonderful!

After new converts come into the saving knowledge of the Lord Jesus Christ, they find it necessary to walk by faith in the truth of the saving knowledge of Christ Jesus. They find that saving, liberating truth has a price tag. "Buy truth and sell it not" (Prov. 23:23). The Lord of grace had truth that that church needed to come to Him and learn.

A church needs to do whatever it takes to have a fervency and love for the truth. If God's people ever expect to walk in the fullness of truth, they need to develop an uncompromising, enduring love for the truth. Walking in the truth leads to experiencing the fullness of salvation, which covers being qualified to "be caught up together in the clouds with them [dead in Christ] to meet the Lord in the air" (1 Thess. 4:17).

If we do not love the truth, the whole truth and nothing but the truth so help us God, we are in danger of being deceived in these last days. In reference to the coming of the lawless one, Paul warned the church at Thessalonica to be aware of his deceptive ways.

"Because they did not receive the love of the truth, that they might be saved. And for this reason God will send them strong delusion, that they should believe the lie" (2 Thess. 2:10-11). Loving the truth is what separates being a participant in one of the two Comings in these last days. There is the Coming of the lawless one and the Second Coming of the Righteous One.

A Church Is Nothing without Him

God's redeemed people have need of so many things, and there were people in that church who recognized they had needs. But as a church system, that church would not recognize any need. James in his epistle said, "If any have need of wisdom, let him ask of God." That church had need of wisdom and the book of Proverbs had the right scripture for her. "There is one who makes himself rich, yet has nothing" (Prov. 13:7a).

The church of the Laodiceans was an example of the first half of that verse. Paul, as an apostle of Christ Jesus, was an example of the last half of the verse. "One who makes himself poor, yet has great riches" (13:7b). In 2 Corinthians 6:10, Paul speaks "as having nothing, and yet possessing all things." That church needed to dine with Him, for in God's Word is where "the unsearchable riches of Christ" are found (Eph. 3:8).

Paul told the Corinthian Church in his first epistle that if he had been gifted with many spiritual gifts, but he didn't have love, he would be "nothing." He could also give away everything that he had, even to the sacrifice of his own body, and if he didn't have love, it would profit him "nothing" (13:1-3). Paul had the right attitude toward the Lord and His people.

That church needed to learn to serve one another in the Body of Christ in love. The God of love cannot be imparted to others without first becoming a receiver of Him. That church needed to be reminded of His deep affection toward her. "We love Him because He first loved us" (1 John 4:19).

In the Sermon on the Mount, Jesus says Christians are like the "salt of the earth," but if the salt loses its flavor, "It is then good for nothing but to be thrown out and trampled underfoot by men" (Matt. 5:13). Because the Laodiceans had developed a lofty attitude about herself that was not scriptural, that "need of nothing" church had become a "good for nothing" church in the eyes of the Lord.

Misplaced emphasis on what is truly important in rightly dividing the word of truth caused that church organization, over a short period of time, to compromise and become unworthy in the sight of the Lord. She should have been ever mindful of the greatness of Christ's self-giving love that paid for her redemption through His blood. "Knowing that you were not redeemed with corruptible things, like silver or gold…but with the precious blood of Christ, as of a lamb without blemish and without spot" (1 Pet. 1:18-19).

In teaching the parable of the Vine and its branches, Jesus was kind in saying to His disciples, "Without Me you can do nothing" (John 15:5b). In reality, branches that do not abide in the vine are nothing. The church is like branches of the Vine, Christ Jesus, and she has one ultimate purpose for living and that is to abide in the Vine to bring forth "much fruit" in order that the Father might be glorified (v. 8). Any church living in these last days should have a desire to glorify the Father by bringing forth "much fruit." The seed of the mature fruit that abides in the Vine will reproduce after its own kind.

Jesus, the Great Physician, was speaking to the scribes and Pharisees, who had the same problem as the church of the Laodiceans. As religious leaders of the nation of Israel, they did not acknowledge having a need for anything from Jesus. They were self-righteous, having no need for the gospel message that reveals the righteousness of God. They were seekers for self-glory so they had no need to learn how they might be better advocates of God's glory.

The self-righteous Pharisees criticized Jesus for eating with the tax collectors and the sinners. When Jesus heard their accusations, He said to them, "Those who are well have no need of a physician, but those who are sick" (Matt. 9:12). In that church with so many needy people, the "no need" people, who were spiritually sick, could not be reached until they humbled themselves and changed their attitude toward the truth of the gospel.

In the church organism, "God has set the members, each one of them, in the body just as He pleased. And if they were all one member, where would the body be? But now indeed there are many members, yet one body. And the eye cannot say to the hand, 'I have no need of you'; nor again the head to the feet, 'I have no need of you'" (1 Cor. 12:18-21). By the church of Laodicea saying, "I have need of nothing," she was also saying to other members in the Body of Christ, including the Head, "I have no need of you."

Collective Pride vs. Collective Humility

Jesus was standing on the outside of that church, making an appeal for an attentive fellowship to "anyone" in the congregation of the church at Laodicea who would listen. The Lord wanted to bring them out of their lukewarm condition into an exciting and enthusiastic relationship with Him.

A church's attitude toward one another individually and collectively is most important. The attitude of the mind and motive of the heart are two essential elements in pleasing the Lord in Christian service. Our prayer should be: "Lord, reveal unto us the motive and attitude of our heart toward You and Your people. We don't want to be a hindrance to the work that You are doing in Your church in these last days."

Jesus' precise function in the church, as the Body of Christ, is the Head. The Laodiceans had lost fellowship with Jesus as her functioning Head. If Christ does not function daily in our lives as the foreordained Head of His church, He does not function at all. In the Body of Christ, an eye must function as an eye and not as an ear. A hand must function as a hand, not as a foot. It is unnatural for a foot to do the work that is intended for a hand to do. For the body to be in harmony, the head must function as the authority over each member in the body. Because He was ignored, the Lord was on the outside knocking on a door that had been closed to Him. He was making an appeal to "anyone" on the inside to receive Him as his or her effectual Head in heartfelt fellowship.

Collective pride can lead to a haughty attitude of disregard, and even contempt, of one church group toward other church groups. The lack of Christian love causes one church group to lack understanding of other members in the Body of Christ. That was true with some in the Corinthian Church that were questioning Paul's ministry as an apostle in the church. Paul said, "But with me it is a very small thing that I should be judged by you or by a human court. In fact, I do not even judge myself." (1 Cor. 4:3). I believe Paul to be a man after God's own heart. He was longing for the day of His appearing when he would be judged righteously (2 Tim. 4:8).

God desires to bless His people, but how can the Father's humble Servant honor haughty humanity? If any church has the slightest wrong attitude toward other fellow-believers in the Body of Christ, she is hindering the unity that is necessary for the Holy Spirit to bring an overcoming church to its predestined glory in maturity or fulfillment.

The Laodicean Church was not a church that is a representation of the overcoming church. One of the most distinguishing marks of His overcoming church is her soul prosperity, where she shows forth her humility toward her Lord and she submits "to one another in the fear of God" (Eph. 5:21). She becomes "poor in spirit" that she might grow rich toward God. The overcoming church exhibits an example of individual and collective humility toward God and His people.

Christ-like humility is something that riches and wealth cannot buy, but it is that "which is very precious in the sight of God." It is a gentle and quiet spirit that comes only at a very high price through sacrificial love. As the future "Lamb's wife," the overcoming church is being trained and prepared as a servant to all for a royal position with the King, known to her as "the Lamb of God," while He rules from the throne of David as "the Lion of the tribe of Judah." A humble attitude, therefore, is needed for such an exalted position in God's righteous kingdom.

A church under the leadership of its functional Head, Christ Jesus, will never have an attitude of "I have need of nothing." As members of one Body of true believers, each church group needs help from one another as each prays for one another. As members of the family of God, we all have need for the spiritual gifts and ministerial callings that are needed to help one another. The challenge is to follow on to know Him in His fullness in humility and commitment in doing the perfect will of God.

Chapter 3

The Greatest Beginning

Seeing the Need to Follow Him until the End

"And to the angel of the church of the Laodiceans write,
'These things says the Amen, the Faithful and True Witness,
the Beginning of the creation of God" (verse 14).

Verse 14 is how the Lord introduced Himself to the church of the Laodiceans. As the Beginning of the new creation of God, He was the beginning of her salvation. Since He was her Beginning in knowledge of the salvation experience, it was also important that He would become her End in knowledge of the fullness of salvation. He was the Laodiceans' access to the riches and wealth of the Godhead. That is why He died on the cross on her behalf. He is the greatest!

Christ is the Beginning and the End of God's complete inheritance for His people. He is the Beginning, the Way and the Finisher to God's full abundance in all things. Start with Him, focus on Him, abide in Him, and conclude with Him. There is no class, race, sex or church distinction in Christ Jesus, for "Christ is all and in all" (Col. 3:11) concerning God's inheritance for His people.

Receiving Him gives believers the right or authority to win it all as members of the family of God (John 1:12). But in their spiritual development, the Laodiceans should have drawn upon the strength and wisdom that comes only from Him. In the building process, all the building material must be of Him. The work is being done and will be completed by the Holy Spirit in Him. The end of the church's complete inheritance is the promise of exaltation with Him. The Father has initiated and predestined all things concerning the church for Him. All things belong to the church through Him. The Bible is a "Him" book! Receiving Jesus is the beginning of salvation. Following Jesus is the way of salvation. Coming to the Father through the Son is the end of salvation. That church had her beginning in Him; now it was important that she would also have her end in Him.

Paul wrote in his last epistle, "For I know whom [not what doctrine] I have believed and am persuaded that He is able to keep what I have committed to Him [not some church group] until that Day" (2 Tim. 1:12b). After many years of Christian service, Paul had developed a personal relationship with Him as the resurrected Christ that few have attained since then.

Yet, no matter how well Paul knew the Christ of the Scriptures, he had a desire to know Him in greater reality. Paul said, "That I may know Him and the power of His resurrection, and the fellowship of His sufferings, being conformed to His death if, by any means, I may attain to the resurrection from the dead" (Phil 3:10-11). After twenty years of Christian service, Paul's focus was still on the God of His salvation. Christ would not only be the Beginning but also the End of Paul's salvation.

Our personal Lord and Savior did not give His life as an atoning sacrifice for any particular Christian system of operation, but He died for each precious soul that might belong to such a Christian endeavor. According to the New Testament, a church is not operating as a true church unless the Authority of that body of believers is abiding in the midst (Matt. 18:20). The church can do supernatural acts on the basis of His authority.

The whole concept of discipleship is a continual moving forward with Him at your side, acknowledging Him, being dependent upon Him, and obeying Him in all your ways. When Jesus said, "Take My yoke upon you and learn from Me" (Matt. 11:29), it means that you are to submit to the authority of His words over your life. Every committed Christian of the end-time church should make a daily effort for the Christ of the Scriptures to be his or her central interest and focus in their thinking.

Before ascending to the right hand of the Father, the resurrected Christ told His future church leaders, "All authority has been given to Me in heaven and on earth…and lo, I am with you always, even to the end of the age *Amen.*" *There is no place in the Bible that says Jesus has transferred that*

authority over to Peter or to any other person in church history. God's people have
authority through being obedient to the unchanging Christ of the Scriptures.

The Importance of Good Church Leadership

The foundation of a church is built upon good Christian leadership. As the resurrected Christ led the way as the Beginning of church leadership, church leaders are to lead the way with His divine authority with them and over them, as they speak on His behalf. That means everything should be done in harmony with the Holy Scriptures.

Church leaders need to continue to persevere in faith in complete dependence upon His promise that the Holy Spirit would lead and guide them into all truth. The Holy Spirit is faithful to enlighten and empower each submissive heart of the end-time church. Even when Christian leaders in the end-time church cannot agree on how certain scriptures should be rightly divided, it is important that they are seeking to develop a loving wholehearted focus upon Jesus and His faithfulness to the church.

The Father's Firstborn has been put in charge of the Father's business in building the church. Church leaders should be in a yielding posture as they think in terms of being His helper alongside His invisible ruling presence. The Holy Spirit has come as a Servant to help church leaders glorify Christ in the exalted position that the Father has placed Him.

Each church leader needs to humbly submit to the help and guidance that only the Holy Spirit can give. Christ, the Beginning, continues to walk with church leadership until all recognize that He will be with them to the end, and then He will become the End to them in all things concerning the church. The Lord had a relationship with the Laodiceans as her Beginning. But she was not "speaking the truth in love" in order that she might "grow up in all things into Him who is the head—Christ" (Eph. 4:15).

Jesus is interceding for the church from heaven, at the right hand of the Father, that she might fulfill her divine destiny in Him. The Holy Spirit is working to lead the church on earth that the Father's ultimate purpose concerning her glorious destiny might be consummated in heaven. The church worships the Father in her newborn spirit by the Holy Spirit in accordance with truth as revealed in Christ Jesus (John 4:23). With divine Leadership leading and guiding human leadership, God's ultimate purpose for the oneness of His overcoming church will be consummated.

Hebrews 13:7-8 gives a scriptural blueprint for human leadership in the church of the Lord Jesus Christ. "Remember your leaders, who spoke the Word of God to you. Consider the outcome of their way of life and imitate their faith. Jesus Christ is the same yesterday and today and forever." What He said yesterday is still true today!

Notice the two phrases: remember your leaders and imitate their faith. Also notice that leadership is to be associated with the unchanging Christ as the supreme authority. Some of the last words that the resurrected Christ said to His church leaders were "Lo I am with you always." The leadership in the Laodicean Church didn't miss His divine presence, only those with ears to hear could hear His voice and His knock from the other side of the church door. Before church members can remember and imitate the faith of their leaders, they need to know three things.

First, notice church leaders were those who "spoke the Word of God." "All Scripture is given by inspiration of God, and is profitable for doctrine, for reproof, for correction, for instruction in righteousness" (2 Tim. 3:16). Instruction in righteousness means that the righteousness of God is to be received by faith in Christ's redemptive work, not by religious works from "the things of men." The only things in heaven that are of the things of men are the scars that are on His hands, feet and side.

There must have been some in that church who had a right attitude toward the Word, like the church at Berea that "received the word with all readiness, and searched the Scriptures daily to find out whether these things were so." There is a need to study all Scriptures in "rightly dividing the word of truth" in order to be "approved to God."

In accordance with the Scriptures, church members should be experiencing spiritual growth and development as an organism within a church organization. Right church leadership, therefore, should teach and live by the Word of God as an example for the rest of the Body of Christ. Each should be submissive to the Son as He submitted Himself to the Father. The outcome of good Christian leadership is providing the faith necessary, through the teachings of the Scriptures, to overcome a captivating world and the deceitfulness of the god of this age.

Second, in order to remember your leaders and imitate their faith, church members need to know the kind of life that they live. Is the life that they live as church leaders in harmony with the Scriptures? The fruit of self-giving love in the sacrifice of Christian duty is serving one another in revealing the fruit of Christian character. No member of the Body of Christ, whose first allegiance is to the Head, should submit to church leadership, at any cost, who are even worse than being lukewarm toward Jesus.

Those who are sent by the chief Shepherd are sent as servants to His sheep. Sheep are to be pointed to the chief Shepherd that He might have the preeminence among the flock for which He, as the good Shepherd, gave His life. Jesus told a repentant Peter, "Feed My sheep!" Church leaders are not commissioned by the Lord to lord it over the flock of God (Matt. 20:25-28). Sheep represent the church organism. He said, "I will never leave you nor forsake you." But a church door had been closed to His loving presence. Repentance was needed to hear His voice and open the door to dine with Him.

Finally, according to verse 8, "Jesus Christ is the same yesterday and today and forever." Christ's authority over church leadership is unchanging. That scriptural fact for church undershepherds is very important, and it should direct the sheep toward the unchanging chief Shepherd. Jesus did not say, "Go therefore," and neglect or forget "that all authority has been given to Me" (Matt. 28:18). The Laodicean Church is one example that the Lord over the church has direct dealing with His people in the church. In the many end-time, historical church organizations, things have changed down through the years by a vote or decisions of men, but the authority of Christ and His relationship to His church organism never changes. What the unchanging Christ said about two thousand years ago holds true today!

Other scriptural rules and discipline concerning human leadership in the church are located in Hebrews 13:17. The writer of the epistle states them as follows:

"Obey those who rule over you, and be submissive, for they watch out for your souls, as those who must give account. Let them do so with joy and not with grief, for that would be unprofitable for you." That scripture is about church leaders who are watching over souls in obedience to the words of the chief Shepherd. When church members submit to God's church leaders, their eternal best interests are being served.

Since the invitation of the chief Shepherd of the church at Laodicea was given to "anyone" who would open the door to Him, He was not honoring the rules of protocol in that church. The Head of the Body was going directly to the members of His Body.

But the Lord could not work through the proud leadership of that church organization. That was an indictment against the leadership of that church. The Scriptures do not require anyone to submit to Christian leaders who lack the integrity and commitment to the authority of the unchanging Christ of the Scriptures over the church. One of the most important revelations of the gospel message is that Christ, as both the Shepherd and the Lamb, deals directly and personally with each blood-bought church member.

Duty to God for both the work and workers in a church is a fact of Scripture. Good church leadership watches over souls of a congregation through bringing them before the Lord in prayer and challenging them to go forward with Christ in being obedient to "all Scriptures." The primary emphasis and focus should be on the Christ of the Scriptures and His importance to the church organism. Being in the church organism means being "in Christ" as a member of the Body of Christ.

A church denomination or an independent local church organization is identified by the office of administration, a specific doctrinal position, Church rules and a system of operation. Can an impersonal, unemotional, complex church organization, which had been identified as a "lukewarm" church by Jesus, repent? Only the lukewarm living organism within that church system could repent. An opportunity was presented to them to experience a restored fellowship with Him with a wholehearted attitude of worship and service.

If there is no fervent, loving fellowship with Jesus, a church system, through its social programs, agenda and church traditions, has church members that think and act no differently than people of the world. If the anointing power of the Holy Spirit is in the ministry where people are hearing and acting on the Word, their hearts, reputation and character will be changed, and God's people will begin to think and act more like Jesus!

On the other hand, Christian leaders need the support and prayers from the congregation of whom they "must give an account." If there are believers who are outside of a deserving church congregation, where leaders are capable and willing to watch over their souls, it would be very foolish for them not to take advantage of it.

The largest church in the last days is made up of unchurched professing Christians that have no church to call their home and no Christian leadership to assist them in spiritual growth and development. They are failing to obey Hebrews 10:25, which says, "Not forsaking the assembling of ourselves together, as is the manner of some, but exhorting one another, and so much the more as you see the Day approaching." Near the end of Jesus ministry, He placed great emphasis upon "the Day approaching."

There should be a continuous dependence upon the Holy Spirit for exhortation, edification and comfort toward one another. That approach to worship would help a church group keep her focus upon Jesus and not on the self-centered thinking of a church system. The Laodicean Church needed to get out of her self-centeredness and into the presence of God. That church leadership needed to learn to lean upon the leading of the

Holy Spirit, which is important to spiritual growth and development in Christian living.

But because of the lack of commitment to God and His Word, some end-time church leaders are full of unbelief and unfaithfulness. Those leaders may be committed to many things in the realm of religion above and outside the authority of the Scriptures. The chief Shepherd does not put excessive and unreasonable legalistic burdens upon His sheep. Jesus said that His yoke is easy and His burden is light (Matt. 11:30).

The kind of leadership that church members are exhorted to follow are those who live the life, and challenge the congregation to go forward with Jesus as the Holy Spirit continues to lead the way. Church congregations need good church leaders to personally watch over their souls. In order for that to be done effectively, the two need a mutual Banner to rally around for battle in spiritual warfare against a common enemy.

Church Traditions Hinder the Work of the Holy Spirit

For a member of a specific church organization, emphasis is usually placed upon having appreciation and concern for the preservation and protection of her historical past and doctrinal position. Church traditions have a tendency to take precedence over the authority of the Scriptures. The nation of Israel is known for their great religious heritage with many religious laws and traditions, not according to the Scriptures.

In His ministry to His own people, the traditions of the elders gave Christ the greatest opposition. Religious traditions deal with the outward appearance and pretense, but the truth, as it is in Christ Jesus, deals with the inward parts and motives of the heart. When too much emphasis is placed on the externals of church traditions, it promotes a reverence for them at the expense of the truth.

If a church is to move forward through present day spiritual experiences by dining with Jesus, she must realize that honoring church traditions, which are the invention of men, comes at the cost of dishonoring the Christ of God. "Because of your traditions," Jesus would tell many end-time church organizations, "you have made the commandment of God of no effect" (Matt. 15:3-6). The commandment to the church is love. In the end-time church, there is an ever-expanding influence of the intervention of traditions within an organizational church system that hinders certain areas of liberating gospel truth.

If His work in the end-time church is in disorder and disunity, it is because the leadership of the Holy Spirit has not been recognized and honored. It is important to notice, however, concerning the church of the Laodiceans, though Jesus was removed to the outside, the Holy Spirit was still striving with her on the inside (v. 22).

Teachers of the Scriptures in the work of the Lord place themselves at a higher level of accountability toward the Lord of the work (James 3:1). An English poet, Alexander Pope, once said, "A little learning is a danger-ous thing." That was true in the teaching and learning of spiritual things where that no-need church was trying to build for God with a little learn-ing in spiritual things. To reach the Father's ultimate purpose for the over-coming church, the learning of more liberating truth is needed, and the more truth that is revealed to a church organization from the Scriptures, the more she realizes how much more there is to learn. That's how God keeps her in the lowly posture of humility.

Teachers of the Bible in the church of the Laodiceans should have taken the study of the Scriptures more seriously (2 Tim. 2:15). If any depth of truth were taught to the Laodiceans, that church leadership would have needed to lean on the Holy Spirit for His help. He resists the proud in heart but He will be there to help the lowly in heart.

Because leaders in that church did not have an ear to hear what the Spirit was speaking to them, He could not challenge them to go forward in "the things of God." That proud church was experiencing resistance from the Head over the church, and she was in no position to receive any assis-tance from the Holy Spirit in the church.

The two things, which are consistent with a lukewarm church system and her church traditions, are having learned to love them more than the Word of God, she has failed to recognize her great indebtedness toward Christ's great love for her. The Holy Spirit is the Spirit of love to the church from the Father and the Son, to empower, direct and guide the church into all truth in becoming maturing offspring of the truth.

The chief Shepherd's rule over the church is a vertical rule. The rule of His undershepherds, with the help of the Holy Spirit working in the church, rules horizontally. The Holy Spirit is continually directing and guiding right church leadership into more truth. Church leaders should speak the words that Christ Jesus gives them to speak where the Holy Spirit anoints them with the ability to speak them.

End-time church leaders, who are being led by the Holy Spirit, are on a much higher level of spiritual enlightenment than the disintegrating, immoral, end-time society of spiritual darkness. In fulfillment of one of the last prophetic scriptures, Revelation 22:11, God's people are changing for the better while people of the world are changing for the worse. There is a parting of the ways in Christian character in the end-time church, where the Lord is separating those who belong to Him away from the ways of this world.

Titles of Jesus

In His introduction to the Laodicean Church, Jesus uses the titles, "Amen," "the Faithful and True Witness," and "the Beginning of the creation of God." Those titles show Christ in a specific way in His relationship to the Laodicean Church. The titles that were given to Jesus in His introduction to all seven churches of Asia Minor were the Alpha and Omega, the Beginning and the End, the First and the Last, and the Amen, the Christ of the past, present and future (Rev. 1:8,11,18). But throughout the Scriptures there are over two hundred different titles and functions relating to Jesus of Nazareth. They all refer to Him as the Eternal One who relates to His people in many different ways in the realm of time and eternity.

The Laodicean Church could have learned to know the Lord through sins forgiven as her Savior, her Healer, her Holy Ghost Baptizer, and her Deliverer. As her Lord Provider, Christ was the answer to the many individual temporal needs of the members of that church. Though many temporal needs might have been met, she said, "I have need of nothing." She had a greater spiritual need to follow Him until the end!

By saying that she had no need, that church was claiming that she had arrived at her divine fulfillment as an imperfect, complete church body. That's a paradox, but she was blinded to the contradiction. Both the physical needs and the spiritual needs should have been provided for that church. Her greatest need was having a restored devoted fellowship with the Christ of the Scriptures.

The Laodicean Church had come to a place where, because of her pride and soulish rebellion, she was found wanting in knowing the Lord Jesus Christ as her Lord Ruler. She needed to become submissive to the functional Head of the church. As her devoted Lord Ruler, His passionate love over her was not being recognized, but ignored.

The title that His overcoming church shall appreciate will be to know Him as her exalted Bridegroom for eternity. As the soon-coming, exalted Bridegroom, Christ deserves all the glory, praise and honor. Jesus gave an open invitation to "anyone" in that church to become a member of the overcoming church. If anyone heard His voice, he or she could open the door and enter into a continual, mutual, loving fellowship with Him.

In coming into the saving knowledge of the Lord Jesus Christ, it is important that each church begins the Christian marathon race with her eyes fixed on the Author and Beginner of faith. In order that she might complete the designated course successfully, as she goes forward in the Christian race, it is important that a church keeps her focus upon the exalted Christ. He is seated at the right hand of the Father as the Finisher and the End of faith.

Complete, exalted soul salvation for the church, which takes place at the resurrection of the dead in Christ (the Rapture of the church), is an objective and goal that needs to be carried out to fulfill God's predestined will and glory for His overcoming church. Exalted soul salvation is consummated in the hope of the physical resurrection from the dead like unto His glorious bodily resurrection.

From the Beginning to the End

Jesus introduced Himself in the book of Revelation and to the seven churches of Asia Minor as the Alpha and Omega, the Beginning and the End, the First and the Last (Rev. 1:8,11,18). That could not be a message referring to relationships in the Kingdom of God, because His kingdom is without end. Neither does the family of God, which spans eternity, have an end.

Jesus introduces Himself as "the Beginning of the creation of God." The new creation of God has its beginning in Him. The old creation had a beginning in Genesis 1:1, and because of sin and rebellion that entered into that creation, it must have an end. It has its complete ending when all things become completely new. Jesus said, "Heaven and earth will pass away, but My words will by no means pass away" (Luke 21:33).

When it comes to the beginning and the end of the Church Age, He is her Beginning and will one day become Her End. Because the work of God's salvation belongs to Him from beginning to the end, nothing is impossible in His complete work of salvation. "With God all things are possible" (Matt. 19:26). Pertaining to His complete salvation, all things begin in Him and all things end in Him.

Christ Jesus had been a Faithful and True Witness to the church of the Laodiceans from the beginning. He wanted to be the love of her life to the end. Because she had a divided heart toward Him, Christ admonished the church of the Laodiceans as her unwavering and devoted Beginning. The church at Laodicea, as a church organism, had her beginning in Him, and anyone who was faithful could be united with Him to the end.

The book of Revelation does not tell the story about the beginning of the Church Age, like the book of Acts, but about its end. It says much about the throne from where God's judgment shall rule in the end time. "Judgment must first begin at the house of God." The first three chapters, therefore, of the book of Revelation introduces and covers the judgment of the church in seven selected cities of that era. He was worthy to judge the seven churches of Asia Minor. Those churches belonged to Him, "which He purchased with His own blood" (Acts 20:28). Each church or churches were to be examples or types in different eras of church history.

As the Beginning of the Church Age, He is the resurrection and life, the chief Cornerstone, the Temple of God of the Father's building program. At the End of the Church Age, the Bridegroom comes for His Bride as the glorious Capstone of the Father's building program.

The Laodicean Church was introduced to Him as her Savior and Lord Provider. Now she needed a revelation of Him as her Lord Ruler. She knew Him as her Justifier. Now she needed to see things in the light of the Scriptures through His eyes as her Judge. She needed to become committed to worshipping the Father wholeheartedly with her whole spirit, soul and body by the Holy Spirit in the name of Jesus.

She had a great beginning with Christ Jesus through His resurrection power with the new birth experience. If she assumed that this would automatically qualify her to experience the grand finale of the Rapture of the church, she was wrong.

The resurrection of the Lord Jesus Christ from the dead is not the end of the story; it's the beginning. Through His resurrection from the dead, as the chief Cornerstone of the Father's building program, Jesus became the charter member of the church as its Living Spiritual Organism. The Christ of His church "has become the firstfruits of those who have fallen asleep."

The first resurrection is complete with a beginning and an end. It begins with Jesus and ends with His church. "But the rest of the dead did not live again until the thousand years were finished. This is the first resurrection. Blessed and holy is he who has part in the first resurrection...and shall reign with Him a thousand years" (Rev. 20:5-6).

The first resurrection, therefore, takes place in two phases. The first phase begins with the resurrection of Jesus, "and many bodies of the saints" were raised after Him (Matt. 27:52-53) as the firstfruits, which took place about two thousand years ago. The second phase ends with the rapture of the church, His Body. The first resurrection had its beginning with the resurrection of His physical body, as the Firstborn from the dead.

The first resurrection will be made complete with the physical resurrection of the spiritual Body of Christ. In a natural birth, the head comes forth first through birth pangs. After the head of the newborn baby comes forth, then you know that the rest of the body will follow. The same is true of the two stages of the first resurrection. Jesus, the Head, was the Firstborn in resurrection glory. The rest of the Body of Christ will follow. The time between the first stage and the second stage of the first resurrection might be two thousand years, but "with the Lord one day is as a thousand years, and a thousand years as one day" (2 Pet. 3:8).

When Paul said, "if, by any means, I may attain to the resurrection from the dead," he had his heart and soul centered on it. Paul did not take qualifying for that resurrection lightly. It is all about getting to know Jesus in His fullness of the Christian experience. Being in the first resurrection indicates being complete in Him from beginning to the end.

The story of Jesus and the church that He died for is like the beginning and the end of story telling. The story begins with "Once upon a time," then they get married and the story ends with "they lived happily ever after." But the story of Christ and His church takes the story out of the realm of time into the realm of eternity. The marriage supper of the Lamb will consummate the Church Age. The Church Age is all about God's Lamb.

A New Beginning

The first verse in the Bible is, "In the beginning God created the heavens and the earth." That was an important beginning, but not as important as the beginning of the new creation of God in a resurrected Christ where "all things are of God" (2 Cor. 5:18a). That is a new beginning with a newly created spirit as the Laodicean Church had experienced new creation life with Christ as her Beginning.

Christ, as "the Resurrection and the Life," "the Firstborn from the dead," was the great true, dependable and faithful persevering witness to the Laodicean Church. Christ's great love for the church of the Laodiceans became evident when He remained a faithful and true witness to the church members fully in view of the fact of her lukewarm attitude toward Him.

In the beginning God created them in His own image and likeness, but through transgression they fell. The heavens and the earth of God's old creation in this space-time world have been corrupted and condemned through Adam's sin. As sin has defiled the heavens through the fall of Lucifer and his angels, sin has also defiled earth through the fall of Adam and his descendants. Now a new creation is needed with a new beginning.

Christ, as the Last Adam, sealed off the evil inheritance by dying as our sin substitute. Through the resurrection from the dead, we have a new inheritance in Him as the Second Man, and as our new Beginning in Him.

The total personality of each individual of the human race is made up of "spirit, soul, and body." Through the saving knowledge of Christ Jesus, Adam's fallen race has an opportunity to become members of God's redeemed race. The old things of Adam's race are passing away and the lust thereof, but the eternal things of God's redeemed race are ever becoming new and precious to them that walk by faith which works by love.

The biological seed of Adam has become a corruptible and mortal seed. Humanity, which experienced spiritual death in Adam, is **a spirit** that is dead to God that needs to be "made alive" because all are "dead in trespasses and sins" (Eph. 2:1). Humanity also has **a corruptible body** that is subject to sickness, afflictions, the aging process and death.

Humanity also has a self-reliant **soul-life** that must be denied before God. By nature, the independent soul-life is proud and rebellious against the plans and purposes of God, especially the ultimate purpose of God for an overcoming, glorious church that will demonstrate His marvelous grace to the whole universe in the ages to come (Eph. 3:10).

"Now may the God of peace Himself sanctify you completely; and may your whole spirit, soul, and body be preserved blameless at the coming of our Lord Jesus Christ. He who calls you is faithful, who also will do it" (1 Thess. 5:23-24). No one will know that they made it until it takes place, but one thing that we do know is the Father's faithfulness will bring it to pass in His foreknowledge and manifold wisdom.

The church of the Laodiceans had a need to see Christ Jesus as the Beginning of everything new in new-creation living in order that she might have a good ending with Him. Jesus invited "anyone" in that church to dine with Him as the Lord over a new creation. "If anyone is in Christ, he is a new creation; old things have passed away; behold, all things have become new. Now all things are of God" (2 Cor. 5:17, 18a).

New-creation living begins with a new-birth experience through receiving the evangelistic message that give repentant hearts access to enter into the saving knowledge of Christ. The Laodicean Church needed to have repentant hearts in order to walk in that saving knowledge. The Lord made His appeal to anyone who would repent, in order that they could hear His voice and open the door and dine with Him.

A large church organization may be built through an effective evangelistic message to the world, but there is a need to go on from there and experience a united effort in seeing the importance of unity in the church organism for the end-time church. But before there can be a strong, united end-time church, there must be a repentant attitude toward an effective teaching message to the church that makes it desirable.

With an unrenewed mind, the church of Laodiceans was glorying in the old "things of men" that should "have passed away." If anyone in that church would repent and come into a renewed fellowship with Jesus, He would lead each one into all the new "things of God" that belong to His new-creation people. When God begins something, He completes it. God's ultimate purpose may be delayed but never nullified—frustrated but never aborted. The same should be true with His people in keeping a right relationship toward Him. We begin in union with Him that should end in communion with Him.

A Greek proverb says that the beginning is one half of the whole. A good beginning, therefore, is very important in the Christian race. The Laodicean Church had received Christ as her Beginning and her Alpha, in His resurrection glory. From past glory they had a great beginning as Christ came to dwell within the life of each church member. But in this story, the focus is on Christ's desire to be the Omega of that church in His resurrected glory. As a church she was not preparing herself to be worthy of Him for the glory and majesty as being a ready Bride to receive an exalted Coming Bridegroom.

The Faithful and True Witness /The Judge

The first chapter of Revelation introduces John to the awesome and majestic glory of Jesus as the Judge over His church. John had been with Jesus from the beginning of His ministry. He had seen His wounded, helpless, suffering body hanging in humiliation on a Roman cross. From the empty tomb, He saw Him in His resurrection glory. But when John saw Him in the brightness of His ascended glory standing in the midst of the seven golden candlesticks, He wrote, "out of His mouth went a sharp two-edged sword…I fell at His feet as dead" (vv. 16-17). What awesome grandeur!

John had never seen the Lord Jesus Christ in that light before. He fell down at His feet in frightened humility. The faithful and true witness was now presenting Himself as the Judge of His church. He was at one time the Alpha, the Beginning, as Lord and Savior to the church of Laodicea. To finish the course on a winning note, He wanted to become her Omega, the End, as her Bridegroom is the consummation of God's ultimate purpose in the plan of salvation.

When the Word of God is expressed as a two-edged sword, discerning the thoughts and intents of the heart, He is judging the things of men in light of the recorded Word of God (Heb. 4:12; Ps. 149:6). Wherever God's truth is being referred to as a two-edged sword, it is discerning or judging. There was the beginning and the end in the scope of God's great plan of salvation to the church of the Laodiceans. He was not only her Justifier; He was also her Judge.

Jesus not only died for the church, but He proved Himself to be a faithful and true witness to each of the seven churches of Asia Minor. "And from Jesus Christ, the faithful witness, the firstborn from the dead, and the ruler over the kings of the earth. To Him who loved us and washed us from our sins in His own blood, and has made us kings and priests to His God and Father, to Him be glory and dominion forever and ever. Amen." (Rev. 1:5-6). If there is any lack or failure on the part of a church not being watchful and ready at His Coming, a lack of faithfulness on His part won't be a factor.

Christ Jesus introduced Himself to the seven churches of Asia Minor as the faithful witness. But in case of the Laodiceans He was faithful to the unfaithful and He was true to the untrue. Though He came to them, through the ministry, as a faithful witness of the Father, they had become unfaithful in being a true witness for Him as a church.

Christ is the Beginning of His church as "the Firstborn from the dead." Through His death, burial and resurrection, the foundation stone of the Father's building program was laid. The Father was the only One who could have laid the foundation in the giving of His only begotten Son. The time of Christ's First Coming and the mystery of the resurrection from the dead of the crucified King of the Jews were foretold in the Old Testament Scriptures, but that mystery was hidden from everyone, including the principalities and spiritual hosts in the heavenly places.

There is an end and completeness to the building plan of the church. God's church is a spiritual building without walls, but one day it will be topped off with Jesus as the Capstone, completing His building program. As Jesus is the Beginning, the Alpha and the chief Cornerstone of the church, He is also the End, the Omega and the Capstone of the church. It is, therefore, important to have a close fellowship with Him throughout the Christian experience, from the beginning to the end.

The church at Laodicea was not making proper preparation for the first resurrection of the dead. Only the Father knows the exact time that the Rapture of the church is going to take place, which must precede His Second Coming. That event is very important because the ultimate title in

Jesus' relationship to the overcoming, glorious church in eternity is "Bridegroom." He is coming to receive His Bride unto Himself.

Toward the end of His pursuit of a church that belongs to Him, He introduces Himself as "the faithful and true witness" to "anyone" who would hear His voice and open the door. Because He cared and knew all about that church, He was a witness that was both faithful and true to her. He overcame the temptation of the enemy through His love and faithfulness to the Father. Now the end-time church must overcome the temptation of the enemy through her love and faithfulness to the Son.

The unfaithfulness of an invisible church organizational system cannot negate His faithfulness toward the church organism for which Jesus died. He is the faithful witness to the truth that will set the captive free from any bondage, even the bondage of an attitude of self-importance and self-sufficiency. As the Lover of the soul, His agape love is a captivating love: a liberating love, an eternal love, and a merciful and forgiving love that was manifested even toward a proud, self-sufficient church called by His name.

Supremacy of Christ over All Things

The resurrected Christ has been given all authority in heaven and earth. *He* has become the firstfruits of those who have fallen asleep (1 Cor. 15: 20). *He addresses* Himself to the Laodicean Church as "the beginning of the [new] creation of God." Colossians 1:15-17 shows the supremacy of Christ over all things in creation because of who He is. "He is the image of the invisible God, the firstborn over all creation." He is "before all things." As Alpha, in Him is the beginning of all new things of God.

The church at Laodicea had a good beginning, but she needed to maintain a hearty affectionate relationship with Him. The supremacy of Christ over all things pertaining to the church should have been emphasized to that church. She had lost the right perspective and began to emphasize only those things that were not eternally important.

As a result, her pursuit in the church world became self-centered. Her church-centered focus had replaced a Christ-centered focus in Christian service. In so doing, she didn't reveal the supremacy of Christ over the church. She was missing out in knowing the true riches of the Father found in the greatness of His Son.

Christ is the Head of all things pertaining to the church organism— "the fullness of Him who fills all in all." Spiritual growth takes place through Him when members of a church "have put on the new man who is renewed in knowledge according to the image of Him who created him…Christ [becomes] all and in all." Outside of the scope of Colossians 1:16-18 we find that the Son must reign till the Father has put all things under Him, "then the Son Himself will also be subject to Him who put all things under Him, that God may be all in all" (1 Cor. 15:25-28). That is in reference to the "one God and Father of all, who is above all, and through all, and in you all."

Colossians 1:18 shows the supremacy of the firstborn Son over all things in new-creation living because of what He did for the church through His redeeming blood. That "in all things He may have the preeminence" in the church is based upon the merit of His atoning blood sacrifice for her. An insignificant doctrine may be overemphasized by a church group that doesn't change lives for the better nor does it bring church unity, but the magnitude of the greatness of Christ to a church cannot be overemphasized.

The blood of Christ is the lifeline of the church. His words are the cleansing redeeming power and authority of the church. The blood of Jesus cries out for the reconciliation of His chosen people unto God. The Holy Spirit reveals to the overcoming church the purity of the Lamb of God through His redemptive power, delivering and keeping power.

That church should have looked to Him as the Personified Word of God for her to feed upon and as the Arm of the Lord for her to lean upon. There is no stronger, convincing right of His Lordship over His people, based not only upon the fact that He is before all things, created all things, and in Him all things consist, but because of what He did through His death as the Justifier of a condemned people. Christ merited His exaltation over all things pertaining to the church based upon what He did for her.

The whole redeemed creation is moving forward toward that one glorious, climatic event in Him. Christ reveals unto mankind the mind of God, the heart of God and the perfect will of God. He is the visible manifestation of the Father's glory. Everything was created by Him and for Him. The resurrected, ascended Christ of glory is to be the central affirmation, affection and allegiance in the thinking of the church.

From the Center Cross to the Center Throne

Christ experienced the greatest humiliation of suffering on the center cross as the benevolent King of the Jews. The greatest exaltation will belong to Him when He comes on the clouds of glory and is seated on the center throne in Jerusalem as the King of kings and the Lord of lords.

Jesus' focus for living was doing His Father's will for His Father's glory. Through His travail in prayer to the Father in the Garden of Gethsemane, doing the will of His Father was His focus for dying the death of the cross.

Fulfilling the will of the Father was Christ's motive, whether it was dying the death or in living the life for the church.

The Christ of the Scriptures was not being taught in His fullness to the church of the Laodiceans. The One who died on the center cross, therefore, was not being placed as the resurrected, ascended Lord of Glory on center stage in the worship services and the teaching messages in that church.

If Jesus had been the focus of the life of the Laodicean Church for living, those church members would have been living the kind of life where He would also be their focus in dying. "For none of us lives to himself, and no one dies to himself. For if we live, we live to the Lord, and if we die, we die to the Lord. Therefore, whether we live or die, we are the Lord's" (Rom. 14:7). The eyes of faith of each church member, therefore, should have been fixed on Jesus, whether in life or in death. The same should be true to each church member in his or her relationship to the soon-coming King.

The exalted, resurrected, ascended, coming-again Christ of glory, therefore, should be the focus for Christian living. His "throne of grace" at the right hand of the Father should be at the center of thinking for the church in Christian living, for His judgment seat will be the center stage in our dying (Heb. 9:27-28).

There are phrases in the Scriptures that are referred to as "in that Day," "the Day of Jesus Christ," or "the Day of our Lord." That is the time when the Father gives His Son the center stage among His people. "You are worthy, O Lord, To receive glory and honor and power; For You created all things, And by Your will they exist and were created" (Rev. 4:11). Soulish Christianity falls short in giving to Christ the preeminence in all things pertaining to the church that He deserves. He is worthy!

As the sun is the center of the solar system, the Christ of the Scriptures is becoming the nucleus, and the rallying point and Banner for unity of the end-time church. But the Laodicean Church thought she was the center of the solar system and everything should encircle around her.

The Lamb of God died on the center cross as the central attraction for the world to see. The resurrected Christ provides new-creation living for all those who believe in Him. He is now the Head over all things in new-creation living that belong to Him by right of redemption. One day, as the Lion of the Tribe of Judah, He will rule from the center throne with a rod of iron, as the center of attraction for the world to see.

The Holy Spirit is bringing forth an overcoming, glorious church through the Word by a creative act, followed by a creative process in Christ Jesus. The whole natural creation "groans and labors with birth pangs together until now" (Rom. 8:23). The rest of creation is waiting for God's new creation in Christ to be brought to completeness.

Not once but three times, Jesus prayed to the Father in the Garden of Gethsemane saying this prayer, "If it is possible let this cup pass from Me, nevertheless, not as I will, but as You will." That was the most difficult time for Him, but Jesus totally gave Himself to do the will of the Father for His overcoming church. The Father will never forget that, and neither will His overcoming church. In eternity she will forever be grateful in being known as "the Lamb's wife." His self-denial before the will of the Father at Gethsemane was necessary in order for Him to bear the cross for the church on the cross.

On the day of His crucifixion in the historical past, He was hanged on the center cross for the world to see. In His agonizing death, He was on center stage. There is coming a day in the future where He is coming with the clouds in all of His glory and splendor and "every eye will see Him" (Rev. 1:7). At that time, He will be on center stage.

But in the meantime, in churches like the lukewarm Laodiceans, He is not at the center of things in the lives of professing Christians. He was standing outside wanting to dine with anyone in that church. Union with Him would become the dining hall in feasting and meditating on His words, and the learning center of prayer and worship to the Father through Him. He was giving an invitation to anyone that desired for Him to be at the center of Christian fellowship and activity.

The overcoming, glorious church is where Christ is given center stage, individually and collectively, for the world to see. From the beginning until the end, He is becoming more and more at the center of things in Christian worship. The climax is at the end of the story of the church, not at its beginning. A tested and tried people are looking forward to a matrimonial relationship with the tested and true Head of a new race of people, the Emmanuel race. She will be called His Bride, the overcoming church, with whom He will share His throne (v. 21).

The total picture of Him who died on the center cross for the world to see was not a pretty picture, whether viewed from the natural or the spiritual perspective. His body was mutilated beyond recognition, but what about His sinless soul? "He poured out His soul unto death" for the ugly self-centered, independent, sinful soul-life of proud humanity.

The church life of the Laodiceans, as a church family, could be called an egocentric family. As a collective church body, she was only one church family among many in the Father's family that encompasses heaven and earth. Her self-worth (riches) gave her an attitude of self-importance (wealthy). That gave her an opinion of being self-sufficient: "I have need of nothing." That caused an attitude of self-conceit that led to self-deceit where she became self-contented in her own self-gratification.

That's an ugly self-portrait of one church family in the vast family of God. That picture contained only the self-serving church of the Laodiceans. Being a self-sufficient church did not make her stand out as a special church among all the others. Instead of humbly looking forward to the exalted throne of His grace in heaven's glory, she was sitting upon a disgraced throne of earthly self-glory.

Chapter 4

The Greatest Appeal

See the Need to Accept His Challenge

"I know your works, that you are neither cold nor hot. I could
wish you were cold or hot" (verse 15).

The Lord begins one of the most interesting appeals in the Scriptures
to a lukewarm church with the words, "I know your works." His appeal
to the church of the Laodiceans is introduced in verse 15, where He is
very displeased with her works of halfhearted Christian worship and service. The appeal is concluded with verse 21, where the ultimate reward will
be given to the overcoming Christian who opens the door to dine with
Him.

The Lord gave a merciful but stern, decisive rebuke and admonition to
a church that was proud and boastful in her self-centered material prosperity. Every one of the seven churches had works that were judged, and the
Lord knew each of them in detail. Each work varied as the personality, tests
and characteristics of each church varied.

God is a God of detail. He is concerned and knows the smallest detail
of every work in each church. Some church members think that if they do
something in secret, God won't know about it. Nothing is hid from an all-
knowing God. The Lord said, "I know your works." He not only knew what

she did, but how she did it and why she did it. Only God knows the hidden motives of the heart.

Each church that bears His name should be wholehearted before Him in fulfilling His will, as Jesus was wholehearted before His Father in His ministry to do the Father's will. He is just as thoroughgoing and complete as a Judge in His judgments as He is a Savior in His work of justification and redemption.

God has two creations and He knows the works of both. The first creation was in Adam; the new creation is in Christ. The natural creation in Adam came first; then, the new creation is brought forth in Christ Jesus. It is now in the spiritual realm but shall be brought forth in the physical realm when Christ comes to set up His visible kingdom on earth. The new creation in Christ Jesus is more interesting and important because "all things are of God," who rewards abundantly.

God is a God of detail in both creations. The Lord gives illustrations in the natural to show His concern over His people. Not even an insignificant sparrow falls to the ground without His knowledge. Even the irrelevant hairs on the head of an aging man are all numbered. Jesus said, "You are of more value than many sparrows" (Matt. 10:31).

The Lord is very interested in how we relate to one another in each church congregation and between church congregations for which He died. It can be concluded that the work of the church, for which He gave His life, is personal and of supreme importance to Him. He loves the church with fervent tenderness and respect.

Rebirth of the Fires of Passion

The works of that church could be understood from the words that she spoke. Her spoken words identified her with a desire toward self-centered love and works, and not with self-giving love toward Him and His work. Because the church at Laodicea became all wrapped up in herself, she lost her fires of passion for Him. The wholehearted love that she once had toward Him needed to be rekindled.

Each one of the seven churches had works. They were all different, some right, some wrong, but the Lord knew each one of them individually. Only the Lord truly knows the fullness of the work of a church, and whether the church is right or whether she is wrong.

The right church is moving in spiritual growth and development for mature love toward the Head of the Body and for each member in the Body. Under the new covenant, there is no stationary place such as the

Tabernacle or Temple with its outer court, holy place or holy of holies. Under the new covenant it is important to be moving in the right direction with a proper spiritual perspective toward Him. The Holy Spirit having come to lead and guide into all truth denotes movement. The right spiritual movement has a goal where a daily personal walk with the Christ of the Scriptures challenges each believer to become more like Him.

In order for a church to grow into the likeness of Christ and have the mind of Christ, she must empty herself of all personal ambitions and complete the work that she has been sent to do. When that is accomplished, all personal glory will be abandoned and Jesus' prayer, "Father, that they may be one as we are one," will be answered for the glory of the Father. Rebirth of the fires of passion could have come only through a change from a church-centered focus to a Christ-centered focus.

The church of the Laodiceans had been part of the initial Christian movement that had a wholehearted zeal and passion for Him. The early church of the Apostolic Era had the "good works" of the message of the gospel of the kingdom flowing through her because of her devoted focus upon the victorious, resurrected Christ.

Every church movement throughout church history that sought God with a whole heart of gratitude and recognition has been used effectively by God. Those were movements that moved forward with God such as the Lutheran revival movement, the Wesleyan and Holiness revival movements, the Pentecostal revival movement, and the Charismatic revival movement. But when the fiery passions and excitement toward the Lamb of God begins to smolder and fade, where will the Holy Spirit light the fires of passion toward the Lover of her soul for the next revival movement?

A Disturbing Judgment

Jesus is very interested in the works of a church. In each of the seven churches of Asia Minor He says, "I know your works." To be pleasing to the Lord it is important, therefore, to accept the challenge to enter into the good works that new-creation life provides for the church.

"I could wish you were cold or hot" indicates the type of problem that was confronting the Lord. That is what made the judgment and rebuke against that church so painstaking. Love would rather commend and reward than condemn or rebuke, but the Lord had nothing to commend or endorse in regard to that lukewarm, self-centered church. Because His commandment of her having love toward others was being ignored (John 15:12), His heart of love was aching. Open rebuke is true love. "Open rebuke is better than love carefully concealed (Prov. 27:5).

The coldhearted church, though she identifies herself as a church, will not be judged with the rewards for the church but with the condemnation of the world. Christ deals primarily with the organism in a church organization and there is no living organism in a "cold" church in which to judge. The Christ of the church is looking forward with anticipation and delight in rewarding the hot or wholehearted church. But this lukewarm or half-hearted church was living on the edge, and she was blinded to that fact.

It was necessary for Jesus of Nazareth to speak harshly against the religious leaders of His own proud, stubborn people, the nation of Israel. Now it was necessary for Him to deal harshly with His own people, the church. The Father gave His Son for the world, but the Son gave Himself for the church. The church at Laodicea had a self-serving and egotistical attitude toward the things of God. Developing a wrong motive in a church organizational system cancels any right that she might have done in her work in the past.

The religious leaders of the nation of Israel wanted glory from the people more than from God. The leadership in the Laodicean Church desired glory from the membership in the church more than the glory from the God of the church. Honor toward the brethren and reverence toward God should be in agreement, with God always receiving the glory. The reward from seeking glory of men lasts for a little while. The reward from seeking glory for God is forever. The Lord said, "My glory I will not give to another."

Because they have zeal to please Him, a reward waits for those who deny themselves and practice being a cross-bearer in the process of pleasing Him. The Laodiceans' lukewarm, halfhearted love toward Him was not in harmony and agreement with His wholehearted love toward her. Her works were self-seeking—for self-glory and not for God's glory. She had forsaken God's will and was trying to do the work of God in self-will. She became so busy doing what she thought was the work of the Lord that she neglected the Lord of the work.

What led her to a halfhearted love toward Him? She had compromised her emotions toward Him with the love for riches and wealth of this temporal world. "The love of money is the root of all kinds of evil." Jesus told His disciples, "Children, how hard it is for those who trust in riches to enter the kingdom of God!" (Mark 10:24). It was heartbreaking for the Lord to be confronted with the fact that the church of the Laodiceans' love for Him had developed into a halfhearted love.

At the beginning of conversion, the newness of life gives birth to His love from a repentant soul. The zeal of new-creation life is present, but the knowledge and understanding of His ways must be learned. Paul's prayer for both the church at Colosse and Laodicea was that they might be "filled with the knowledge of His will in all wisdom and spiritual understanding" (Col. 1:9). That covers a broad scope in understanding His will for daily living. Loving Jesus means loving His teachings and God's way of doing things. God's ways are not man's ways. For what is highly esteemed among men is an abomination in the sight of God (Luke 16:15).

The faithful and true witness was now making an appeal to a church that had become unfaithful and untrue because of her change of attitude toward the Body of Christ. The Resurrected, Ascended, Soon-Coming Lord was still working in the capacity as a servant to His people. He was making a humble appeal to rekindle a mutual love of the past.

The Laodicean Church had become arrogant and she was lifted up in her own eyes. Because she was rich and had become wealthy, her eyes became focused on her own self-importance and self-glory. Her focus needed to be changed, with a thankful heart, toward the importance and glory of Him who had redeemed her with His own precious blood. His *agape*, self-giving love, not only takes the initiative in giving out God's love, but that love was also pursuing the church that had lost her commitment of love toward Him.

Wrong Kind of Zeal

Paul said that the Jews had a zeal that was not according to knowledge. They would not receive God's righteousness in Christ Jesus by faith, but they went about trying to establish their own righteousness by their religious works. Christian zeal should be pointed toward Him. Christ is the righteousness of God for the church.

As a result of the sin of spiritual pride, the Lord called the Laodicean Church to repent. "As many as I love, I rebuke and chasten. Therefore be zealous and repent" (Rev. 3:19). The Greek word, *zeloo*, translated "zealous" could also be translated "full of emotional desire, hot with passionate love for a closer fellowship with Jesus." She needed to rekindle her passion of love and devotion to Him. People will diligently pursue that which they passionately love. If that church loved Him the way that He deserved to be loved, she would always have been ready and willing to give attention to His voice. Jesus said, "My sheep hear My voice."

In many church groups today, displeasing God comes primarily from dealing with the carnal nature. But one of the strongest temptations comes from the emotions, the seat of passion of the soul. If love for family, church, friend, job, or self is stronger than the love for Christ, one cannot be a true disciple of Christ (Luke 14:26). The hardest love to overcome in order to love Christ the way that He should be loved is the love of self. That was the primary problem and predicament of the Laodicean Church. She was full of religious contentment, but she did not have Christ abiding in her midst.

The Lord said, "I know your works." His love for the church should be the motivating factor for Christian service, and not selfish ambition for self-glory. The self-centered thinking of the church of the Laodiceans had made her think that because of who she was, and the way that God had blessed her with material prosperity, God had approved her works. But that church was the only church of the seven churches that was not commended for doing anything right, and her rebuke was more severe. The Lord went directly to the heart of her problem—collective spiritual pride. Her heart of devotion and admiration was not upon Him but upon herself and her material wealth.

God's great love for His new-creation people in Christ is the motivating power behind His so-great salvation in Christ. We do not come to God in order that He may learn to love us in the end. He has loved us from the beginning. Believers belong to the family of God. Obedience to Him is not primarily based upon being servants to the church, but in being sons and daughters in serving one another in the Father's family.

That church had been called into a work of self-denial and self-giving love in Christian service, and not into a work of religious obligations and church duties. A Christian life lived in self-denial and cross-bearing is to be the result of the work and leading of the Holy Spirit. The letter kills but the Spirit gives life.

An Appeal to See His Greatness

Because of the great compassion and mercy of the Lord who made it, and the grave consequences for refusing it, the appeal to the church of the Laodiceans should have been taken thoughtfully. Christ's love for that church should have made her realize His eternal greatness to her. But her promotion of self-glory was robbing the Lord Jesus Christ from being glorified in the midst of the services of the church. Self-centered love for that church had blinded the people from being aware of Christ's self-giving love for the whole church. Christ laid down His life for each individual in that church organism and not for the impersonal, unemotional organizational system itself.

What did Jesus truly mean to her? Here was a church that owed it all to Jesus, but at the same time; she was resisting the work of the Holy Spirit to reveal the greatness of Jesus to that congregation. Instead of promoting self-importance as a church, she should have been emphasizing the crucial role that He was to play in each life.

That egocentric church organization had taken away an indwelling personal Christ in her midst. By seeking her own greatness through her self-centered thinking and speech, she was neglecting to promote His greatness. She was not being submissive to the Holy Spirit to authorize Him to reveal the greatness of the Lord Jesus Christ to her.

The Lord knows the works of His church, but the Laodicean church needed to know more about the work of His great love toward her and His complete redemptive plan for her. The church has been bought with a price! As the bride-elect sets her eyes more upon His greatness and the works of His hands, the attraction and glitter of the riches of this world will grow strangely dim.

"Great is the LORD, and greatly to be praised; and His greatness is unsearchable…Men shall speak of the might of Your awesome acts, and I will declare Your greatness" (Ps. 145:3, 6). God's greatness is unsearchable. Who can search it out, understand it or explain it? If that church had only let the Holy Spirit direct her toward "the unsearchable riches of Christ" (Eph. 3:8), she would have had no need to repent from preaching a gospel of misplaced emphasis.

The Old Testament Scriptures show the greatness of God's love toward His wayward chosen people. But the religious leaders of the nation of Israel drew the attention and devotion of the people away from the greatness of the God of Abraham, Isaac and Jacob toward their own greatness. They were not prepared to receive His obedient Son.

The magnitude and greatness of the divine Lover of her soul had become very small and insignificant to the church at Laodicea. She had become unaware how much her love for Him would have meant to Him. As the greatness of God's love draws the church closer to Him, the church will see more clearly how much her love means to Him.

"For if we are beside ourselves, it is for God; or if we are of sound mind, it is for you. For the love of Christ compels us, because we judge thus: that if One died for all, then all died" (2 Cor. 5:13-14). That church congregation, therefore, should have lived and promoted a life for His glory and not for self-glory.

Magnitude of His Greatness

A mountain looks small from a distance, but the closer you get to it, the more you realize the enormity of its great size. The same is true in knowing Christ' great love that motivated Him to die for the church. The Christ of the Scriptures is like a mountain rising from the floor of the desert. The closer you approach Him, the more you realize the enormity of the magnitude of His greatness.

A photograph might be taken of a church and its congregation, built at the base of a mountain. To get more of the magnitude of the mountain into the picture, the photographer must back up farther from the base of the mountain. The farther that the photographer backs up from the church building and its congregation to get more of the magnitude of the mountain into the picture, the smaller the image of that church becomes at the base of the mountain.

The Laodicean Church's self-centered thinking was nourished along with her spiritual ignorance of the ultimate purpose that the Father has for the church. Her perception of the goal of what a church should be was very narrow compared with the Father's goal of the church's ultimate greatness with her Bridegroom.

Because of her spiritual laziness and spiritual blindness, she did not know the magnitude of the Father's ultimate destiny of the church according to the Scriptures. Her zeal for self-glory had replaced the zeal necessary to rightly divide the Scriptures in order to see what was necessary to advance God's glory.

If the photographer backs up far enough, the image of that church congregation at the base of the mountain becomes so small that it is lost in the magnitude of the mountain. Since the purpose of the Holy Spirit is to exalt and glorify the Christ of His church, the photographer could be called a type of the Holy Spirit.

The end-time church is identified by a countless number of church labels. Out of the many different church organizations, each functional member in the Body of Christ is willing to lose his self-identity in the Head of the Body. A church organization might have many godly leaders, but the church organism can only have one Head.

The photograph of the magnitude of His greatness is an illustration in the physical realm to better understand the greatness of the Lord Jesus Christ as the Holy Spirit reveals Him to the church. "He must increase, but I must decrease," said the forerunner of Jesus (John 3:30).

Here is one divine, eternal principle of the universe that has even affected the angels of the heavens: "For whoever exalts himself will be humbled, and he who humbles himself will be exalted" (Luke 14:11). Because of the exaltation of the Son of Man, who humbled Himself to the death of the cross, the greatness of His humbled Bride before Him will be the reflection of the greatness of her exalted Bridegroom by the Father.

I don't believe John the Baptist understood the depth of that statement when he said it. He was introducing Jesus of Nazareth as more than the King of the Jews. Jesus Christ of Nazareth, the one Mediator between God and men, is the Head of a new covenant between God and the church. The Baptist was introducing the method for living a new-creation life, where old things would be passing away and all things would become new. The Lord of the church would present a new and living way upon which His people would learn to walk.

The church of the Laodiceans had a very high opinion of herself. Not only did that cause her to have a low opinion of others in the Body of Christ; it also caused her to have a low opinion of His greatness. Because of her appetite for the riches and wealth of the world, she lacked the appetite and thirst for His righteousness that was needed for her to overcome the love of "the world or the things in the world" (1 John 2:15; 5:4).

Riches and wealth gave her power, prestige and privilege in the world. But it robbed her of having a fervent love toward Jesus and a persevering faith in the leadership of the Holy Spirit. Having a faith that works by love is necessary to serve God effectively and do those things that are pleasing in His sight. The more the glory of her self-life is denied for His sake, the clearer her spiritual vision will become in seeing His glory for her sake.

One of the reasons for Paul's disapproval of the church at Corinth was her building on the foundation of human personalities, which was causing disunity in the Body of Christ. But that is a prevailing condition in the Body of Christ in these last days. Church leaders, with all of their human frailties, should not be put on a pedestal to such an extent that they overshadow the greatness of the Christ of His church. Human personalities may form a church system, or on a smaller scale, social cliques within a local church that conceal the greatness of Christ. The Holy Spirit has come to reveal Christ in the fullness of His greatness. The primary work of the Holy Spirit to the church is to proclaim and promote the invisible Christ over every aspect and function of the church. Many carnal things get into the way of His work.

Misplaced emphasis in the church of the Laodiceans had led her to develop into a church system that no longer had a passionate and enthusiastic love for Jesus. As with the church in other cities of that Church Age, the outpouring of the Holy Spirit during the Feast of Pentecost in Jerusalem had given birth to that church. But she had cooled off to a lukewarm position toward the Christ of the Scriptures. The story of His greatness, consequently, had been lost in her own eyes because the Lord was now standing in the shadow of her own greatness, knocking on her door to receive the love and attention that belongs to Him.

Greatness of Love's Appeal

The story of the greatness of the Lord is an ever-expanding story. There is so much more to tell about the story and so much that has yet to be heard. Only that portion that has been revealed by the Holy Spirit can be told. His kingdom is one without end, and so is His ever-unfolding story that is still being revealed by the Holy Spirit for the Father's glory. Through His amazing grace, His love is without end. The church of the Laodiceans was being challenged to a commitment of a fervent love toward Him until the end; whereas, His great love toward her had been from the beginning.

The Scriptures make it quite clear what the church means to the Lamb of God who gave Himself for her. The question is: "What does He mean to the church?" The church of the Laodiceans was so wrapped up in the glitter of her riches and wealth that she became blinded to the Lord who had prospered and blessed her with so many good things. If she had the proper focus instead of "I have need of nothing" attitude, her thinking would have been changed to "Thank you, Lord, for Your great love, mercy and grace toward us."

The story about the prospective bride of Christ is about one who has her focus upon the greatness of the One who "loved the church [so much that He] gave Himself for her" (Eph. 5:25b). In giving Himself for the church, Christ is given the title, "the Lamb of God." Not every church member will truly appreciate the depths in the meaning of Him being a sacrificial Lamb to the church, but His Bride will forever be thankful. For in eternity the Bride of Christ will be identified as "the Lamb's wife" (Rev. 21:9).

The Bible pictures the bride-elect as humble and lowly like her Bridegroom. She does not focus upon herself or on the glamorous world around her. Because she has eyes only for Jesus, she is maturing more and more into having single-mindedness with a hearing heart toward her beloved Redeemer. As a double-minded man cannot have the steadfast faith that is necessary to acknowledge God's faithfulness toward him, a *luke-warm* church with a divided heart cannot recognize God's great abiding love toward her.

The focus for the bride-elect is "looking unto Jesus, the author and finisher of our faith" (Heb. 12:2a). Her focus, therefore, is not an inward self-centered focus or horizontal focus of what the world around her might think. Her focus is a vertical focus on pleasing her Mediator and Intercessor who is sitting at the right hand of God.

The focus of the bride-elect is not on her self-importance, but on His faithfulness, importance and eternal worth. She knows that wealth and abundance in material things will not give true, permanent satisfaction. This earth is not her permanent dwelling place; she has heard about and she "desires a better [country], that is, a heavenly country."

The focus of the end-time church needs to be more upon God's eternal blessings that are waiting for her than the temporal blessings that He has provided. The bride-elect does not have a limited focus of working only for the temporal blessings of this life. She is not contented with the treasures of this earth like the church of the Laodiceans. Her heart is set on "those things which are above where Christ is." "For where your treasure is, there your heart will be also" (Col. 3:1; Matt. 6:21).

Story of His Greatness

The pride of the Laodiceans caused her to seek greatness for herself in self-will. Christ, who loved that church with an everlasting love, is greater than all things. Christ had identified Himself with that church organism in the death that He died in order that each member of that part of the Body of Christ might be identified with Him in the fullness of His life. Christ had laid down His self-life in death for that church in order that she might lay down her self-life in living for Him.

There are many interesting stories in the sense-knowledge realm, but the whole story cannot be told and much is left to the imagination of the mind. Though you have been entertained for a time, there is no lasting comfort from the story. Because it is a story involving insight and intellect on the temporal level, there can be no everlasting satisfaction in knowing the details of the story. Mankind is more than body and soul. The basic element of the human personality is an eternal spirit that belongs to its Creator.

The story of His greatness is based upon who He was and what He did. "God so loved the world that He gave His only begotten Son." Many true stories end in the death of the hero. But the Hero of the gospel story does not end in death. The story of the church's identification with Him began with His death. The church "has been crucified with Christ." He died the substitutionary death of the sinner on the cross in order that the church might qualify to live like royalty on a throne through His resurrection power.

The greatest story ever told began with a single life, which is about the greatness of the most wonderful person who ever lived and died. But the story of His solitary life on earth lays the groundwork for a greater story of a united church family in Him through His resurrection from the dead.

The resurrection from the dead of God's firstborn Son becomes a greater story because He no longer abides alone. His church (the Body of Christ) becomes one with Him, and she is identified with Him forever. He is Lord over a new-creation people. As the old creation is identified with the sin of Adam's transgression, the new creation is identified with the righteousness of God through Christ's redemptive work.

His resurrection life is a life that is identified with His people who are called "the ecclesia," the called-out assembly. She has been called out of the world, as a church organization, in order that the church organism might be set apart unto God for His eternal glory. That remarkable story covers both realms of time and eternity. He became the planted "grain of wheat" that would no longer "remain alone" (John 12:24).

Before going to the cross, everyone, including His own disciples, did not understand the purpose of His First Coming. But the Father would raise Him from the dead in resurrection power and glory with an ultimate purpose in building His church. He has become the source of new-creation life where the Holy Spirit would bring new-creation people into fellowship with His loving, abiding presence.

Now He is no longer the misunderstood, lonely Man of Galilee. He fellowships with the church that is willing to come into His loving presence. Now, it is easy to get excited with a flaming desire and passion for Him. Because the church of the Laodiceans had her focus totally on her own self-worth, she had lost her focus of His great worth to her.

Christ identified Himself with our death and burial that we might identify ourselves with His resurrected, ascended glory. The purpose of the Holy Spirit is to lead God's people into a mutual knowing in courtship between Christ and His church. Because Christ died a worthy death in being identified with an unworthy people in His death, He has made the church worthy in being identified with Him through His resurrection from the dead. Based upon becoming one with Him in His death, the church has a new identity of becoming one in Him through the resurrection of the dead. Worthy is the Lamb!

No matter what kind of label a church may prefer to call her self, that ego identification is not as important to God as she might think it is. What is important is that the church belongs to Him, and He belongs to the church. According to the Scriptures, you cannot separate the two, and "the Scriptures cannot be broken." The church is one in Christ Jesus. The church owes it all to Jesus. He no longer abides alone; the church is being challenged by the Holy Spirit to be identified with Him more and more in His fullness.

The bonding of the church's spiritual relationship with Him can become closer than any human relationship in the realm of time. Because the oneness of the church with Jesus begins with a new-creation spirit, it is an eternal spiritual relationship. He is alive forevermore living for the benefit of His church. The church of the Laodiceans, therefore, should have been living her life for His sake and not for her own self-glory.

Christ is not only the chief Cornerstone of the church; He is also the church organism itself, which is called "the Body of Christ." The Head cannot operate independent of the Body. The Head needs the Body and the Body needs the Head. If that church had placed her focus on the importance of the Organism, there would have been no "I" problem.

Understanding His greatness is recognizing His oneness with the church. The church belongs to Christ who is over all things. Because of your identification with Him, you can proclaim that "all things are yours" (1 Cor. 3:21b). Because you are one with Him, you are being created in Him, as workers together with Him, for good works. That church needed a wholehearted love toward the One that gave her newness of life.

Christ gave Himself for the church that He might redeem her from every lawless deed. He is purifying for Himself "His own special people, zealous for good works" (Tit. 2:14). The purification of His own special people is God's *poiema*, a creative masterpiece as recorded in Ephesians 2:10. God's ultimate purpose for the church is a progressive creative workmanship, "created in Christ Jesus for good works, which God prepared beforehand that we should walk in them."

God's eternal work of art in Christ will be taken out of Christ in eternity and "made known by the church to the principalities and powers in the heavenly places" (Eph. 3:10). The unseen world in heavenly places is interested in what is taking place in the end-time church on planet earth in these last days. The prophecy of the Bridegroom rejoicing over His Bride will be fulfilled in accordance with God's one ultimate eternal purpose that He has for the church in Christ Jesus (Is. 62:5).

When it comes to the Lord dealing with a church at any time, He can say, "I know your works." The Lord, who knows all things, has a special interest in His church. As Adam's bride was made from a rib—"the rib" closest to his heart—taken out of Adam, Christ's Bride will be taken out of His Body, closest to His heart.

The bride-elect should live a life as a church "after God's own heart." As the woman was presented to Adam as his bride in earth's paradise, the church will be presented to Christ as His Bride in heaven's paradise. As the woman was the crowning glory of Adam, the church is to be the crowning glory of Christ.

Fanny Crosby wrote *Blessed Assurance*, which tells about her love for Christ. "This is my story, this is my song, praising my Savior all the day long. Perfect submission, all is at rest, I in my Savior am happy and blest, Watching and waiting, looking above, Filled with His goodness, lost in His love." The story of His great love has become the great story of the church and Fanny Crosby told it long ago in song.

Knowing Him in sins forgiven will put an eternal song in your heart. There is no other story like His story. He is the believers' Blessed Assurance, who will bring peace to a discouraged and disturbed soul. Because the church, as the Body of Christ, is maturing toward identification with His greatness for time and eternity, the church is becoming a part of the story of His greatness. Because the Lover of her soul possesses all things, He is willing to share His inheritance with a church that shares in His benevolent love.

You Play an Important Role in God's Story

It is one thing to be entertained by an exciting story. But when you become an important part of the greatest story that is still being told, then the story begins to take on a new dimension with a new meaning. The story of His greatness is being played out on the stage of church history.

The faithful will play an important part in God's glorious story of His salvation by grace through faith. The Father is the Source of self-giving love. He does all things by the Spirit of His *agape* love. Christ is the Object and Nature of the Father's love that was manifested as God's substitutionary Sacrifice for lost humanity.

That is the Father's story, and the Son of God merits center stage in the story. The story of His great worth and His importance to the church through His bodily resurrection from the dead is a story that needs to be emphasized to a church like the Laodiceans. But the story is still incomplete; it is still unfolding in the annals of church history toward the consummation of the Church Age.

The story concerns the person of Christ as He is related to His redeemed people. The significance of the oneness that is between Christ and His church organism becomes an indescribable uniqueness. We can endeavor to keep the unity of the church, as the Body of Christ, but no power in heaven and earth can decapitate the Head from the church organism. Each believer, therefore, becomes a very important part of the story of His greatness, which is still developing. That is what makes the story so exciting and delightful. That story is great because of the excellence and worth of the Person to whom it relates.

A book was written about the Christ of the Gospels that covered the period of time from His birth to His resurrection entitled, *The Greatest Story Ever Told*. It is a story of the greatest solitary life that ever lived. Now through His resurrection from the dead, He is the Vine and the church, as the branches, are abiding in Him. The resurrected Christ no longer lives a solitary life, and neither should any member of His church. The church organism and Christ are one, and He is the Head of the Body with its many different functioning members.

The Son of God lived His life on earth in complete obedience to His Father's will, but there was no fullness of fellowship with His disciples because of their unbelief and lack of understanding of why He came. The lonely, misunderstood Man of Galilee prayed to His Father in the Garden of Gethsemane in preparation to laying His life down for the church, as His disciples were fast asleep. They had no idea of the gravity of the moment. He would be faithful to the Father's plan for Him as the one grain of wheat that had life within itself. Christ had life within Himself, but that life would become "a life-giving spirit" (1 Cor 15:45) to anyone who believes in His resurrection from the dead.

Jesus is no longer the incorruptible grain of wheat that abides alone (John 12:24). He has been planted as God's immortal Seed in death and burial and has come forth in resurrection glory for the benefit of the church. He no longer abides alone. Christ and His church organism are one Body, but He was standing on the outside of that church organization with a closed door dividing Him from His people on the inside. He was abiding alone without having a loving fellowship with anyone in that "lukewarm" church.

Christ shouldn't be related to a church that is called by His name, standing on the outside, separated by a closed door. He belongs at the center of the life of His people, whereby the Father is glorified. His identification with His new-creation people, who are growing in newness of His life in mutual love and understanding one toward another, is an exalted position. If the church of the Laodiceans only knew that in Him is where true riches and wealth may be found, she would have been in hot pursuit for a loving fellowship with Jesus. "He who did not spare His own Son, but delivered Him up for us all, how shall He not with Him also freely give us all things? (Rom. 8:32b).

Christ, therefore, came that His incorruptible life of immortality would not abide alone. He desires to share His life and His victory over the devil with the church. He will receive anyone who is a captive to the misery of the devil and will deliver him to enjoy the mercy of God. He desires to abide in human hearts. It is the Father's desire that His resurrection life might grow and develop into maturity in His people by faith. "Faith comes by hearing, and hearing by the word of God" (Rom. 10:17).

The importance of the story of His greatness continues with Christ and His church as she walks with Him in the Spirit. The Father sets the church apart unto Himself in order to do a complete work that the "whole spirit, soul [mind] and body be preserved blameless at [that moment] the coming of the Lord Jesus Christ" (1 Thess. 5:23).

The church is joined together with Him as one spirit (1 Cor. 6:17), and over a space of time, she is being transformed by the renewing of the mind until she matures in becoming as one mind with Him (Rom. 12:2; Phil. 2:5). The church is one spiritual body, but through the resurrection from the dead, our present corruptible, mortal body will put on incorruption and immortality in order that we might become one in likeness with His glorified resurrected body.

In these last days, "because lawlessness will abound, the love of many will grow cold. But he who endures to the end shall be saved" (Matt. 24:12-13). Endurance is an important ingredient and virtue in experiencing complete salvation in the church world in these last days.

What makes the story of Christ and the church so different from all other stories? Entering into His story belongs to the meek and lowly who walk by faith and not by sight. There is no other one like the Father's first-born Son. The more a church's interest centers on Him, the more of His greatness is revealed to her and through her.

The church of the Laodiceans had a hunger and thirst after self-glory. In order that God could receive glory in her midst, she needed to humble herself. To remind her of that truth, a strong rebuke from the Lord of the church was necessary. Following the example of Christ in humbling Himself is the way to true exaltation for a church. It is in eternity where the meek, modest Bride will be presented to her exalted Bridegroom.

In telling the church of the Laodiceans to repent, the Lord takes some sting out of His severe chastening rebuke by expressing His love for her. But her lofty pride was what caused the door to be shut, and only the lowly in heart will be able to hear His voice and open it. Then He says," I will come in to him and dine with him, and he with Me."

Jealous for Jesus

Because of His great love for her, the Lord was making an earnest appeal to the church of the Laodiceans. God is a jealous God. His possessiveness is a justified one. That church had been bought with a price. She truly belonged to Him and to none other. As a result He was zealous and vigilant in having deep concern over His investment that He "had purchased with His own blood." Because Christ was no longer having a loving fellowship with that lukewarm church, members of that church couldn't experience any joy in Jesus or develop a zeal for Jesus. If committed Christians ever visited that church, they might leave the church service with a "jealous for Jesus" feeling.

As a jealous God, the Holy Spirit does not want Jesus to be in second or third place in the lives of church members. He is the One who is always worthy of first place in the hearts and lives of His people. That was the attitude of a spiritual man like Paul when he wrote, "For I am jealous for you with a godly jealousy" (2 Cor. 11:2a).

The Laodicean Church was making her riches and wealth an idol. God's opinion toward idolatry is, "You shall not bow down to them nor serve them. For I, the LORD your God, am a jealous God" (Deut. 5:9). The Father's love is a jealous love over His whole family. The Holy Spirit, which abides in you, is jealous for Jesus! Like Paul, Jesus is jealous over His church. The Laodiceans should have been jealous for Jesus. The Holy Spirit should have been allowed to work freely in that church to place Jesus on center stage in worship and Christian service. Jesus' redemptive work authorizes Him to be acknowledged as having first place in the lives of His redeemed people.

"You shall have no other gods before [or beside] Me" is the first and key commandment of the Law of Moses. If the Laodicean Church loved Him the way that He should have been loved, He would have been Number One in her life in everything. That basically is the foundation and challenge of the discipleship message.

Among the Corinthians, Paul was fearful that they would be deceived by the simplicity that is in Christ, and he was jealous over them with a godly jealousy. He said, "For I have betrothed you to one husband, that I may present you as a chaste virgin to Christ" (11:2b). There was a need for pastoral and ministerial training. That church should have been learning how to better serve others. No one needs to attend three years in seminary training to learn how to love Jesus wholeheartedly. Let a humble and contrite heart become submissive to the leading of the Holy Spirit.

The Father has loved the church in Christ Jesus before the foundation of the earth. Her obedience to Him is not primarily based upon her servitude to Him as King. Because she loves the words that come forth from His lips, she obeys Him. The King came to set the example in obedience to His Father of being a servant to all. That is the basic discipleship principle of the gospel of the kingdom.

The objective of the church is the brotherhood of all believers and learning to yield to Him as the promised beloved Bridegroom. A church is called into His work of self-giving love, not primarily a work of obligation and duty, but submitting to His loving care. To the loyal and amenable "Lamb's wife," the throne that He shares with her will be remembered eternally as a throne of grace. She will never forget the great price that was paid for her being brought out of spiritual bondage to an exalted position with Him.

The indebtedness of that church to her beloved Master for her complete redemption should have produced a faithful servant. The Laodicean Church should have developed an attitude of servitude in Christian service. They were God's servants, first to God and His people, then to all people. Humble Christian service, which promotes church unity, should be through love toward the Christian brotherhood in serving the Master.

That calls for the church to be sanctified and cleansed "with the washing of water by the word" from the world and all of its fleshly endeavors. What is it that really counts at the end of life's story? How closely will you be related to the Lover of your soul?

"Him we preach," Paul wrote to the Colossians, "warning every man and teaching every man in all wisdom, that we may present every man perfect in Christ Jesus" (1:28). Notice the goal of Paul's preaching; he recognized that his apostolic ministry couldn't do it alone. The Holy Spirit uses all the saints to present the church perfect in Christ. The five-fold ministry is "for the equipping of the saints for the work of ministry, for the edifying of the body of Christ" (Eph. 4:12).

It's clear that the church of the Laodiceans did not get to know the loveable Christ the way that He can be known. Because of the direction that the Laodicean Church was headed, Christ would eventually become to her nothing more than the Babe-of-Bethlehem Jesus or a "picture-on-the-wall" Jesus. She would never know the living reality in experiencing daily fellowship with a loving resurrected Christ.

Would she continue on a halfhearted, self-centered course in becoming absorbed only in her own prosperity and continue to neglect the whole-hearted personal fellowship that the Christ of the Scriptures has to offer? The invitation to open the door of fellowship with Him shows that He wanted to become to her a personal, living, loving, resurrected Christ. He is the One who has won the hearts of the faithful.

He has not only become the subject matter of the songs that are being sung in the worship service, but He is also becoming the subject matter of the sermons that are being preached from the pulpit in many areas of the end-time church. He is becoming the pivotal point and center focus of believing hearts and lives. He is the Champion of the souls of the redeemed where He personifies the centerfold of the Book of books as the perfect Example in righteous and holy living.

A Christ-centered focus should have been at the heart of the thinking and the basis for Christian living of the church of the Laodiceans. She needed to continue to learn of Him until she knew Him as the Christ of the Scriptures in all His fullness. The priority and primary position of many members of the end-time church needs to be changed from temporal earthly things to eternal heavenly things.

From the center cross, the resurrected Christ is to become the center of all things pertaining to the church. "That in all things He may have the preeminence" should be at the top of the list, and that church needed to study the Scriptures to see what it takes to place Him at the center. When He is not at the center of the activities of the church called by His name, the Holy Spirit in you becomes jealous for Jesus. The things and ways of religious people can take center stage away from a loving fellowship of the Christ of the Scriptures with His people. That was why the lukewarm church of the Laodiceans was being judged by her Redeemer because "the LORD your God, [is] a jealous God."

The Drawing Power of His Appeal

The ultimate purpose of Christ's appeal to that church was to create an overcoming church through fellowship with Him. "That which we have seen and heard we declare to you [a relationship with a personal Lord and Savior], that you also may have fellowship with us; and truly our fellowship is with the Father and with His Son Jesus Christ (1 John 1:3). Coming into a oneness in fellowship with the Father and the Son through the work of the Holy Spirit in the church is the end purpose for Christian living.

God is directing His overcoming church to be conformed to the image of His Son, "that He might be the firstborn among many brethren." A believer's life with Him is the greatest story ever told because it is unlike any other story ever told. Believe that you are an important part of the overcoming church in the Father's predestined plan. It is included in Christ's total victory over the devil that He has won for the believer.

Now this story is not in the realm of sense-knowledge reasoning. When a church has her spiritual senses properly fed and nourished with God's Word, she will have the discernment necessary to learn and understand spiritual things. Revelation knowledge comes by the transforming power of the Holy Spirit through God's Word, which makes this story a walk of faith that works by love. God's ultimate purpose for His church is for her to get her eyes off temporal things and have a steadfast heart, "looking for the blessed hope and glorious appearing of our great God and Savior, Jesus Christ" (Tit. 2:13).

Christian maturity is needed for the matrimonial union of the church with the Christ of the Scriptures to be consummated in eternity. As the mature woman made the first man complete in matrimonial union in the creation story in the Garden of Eden, the overcoming, glorious church will make the Second Man complete in matrimonial union in the Eden of Heaven.

Christ, therefore, is the focal point of interest in the story of hope concerning the church. The story is not only about who He is and what He did for the church, but why He did it. Because of His love for the church, He is faithful and just to bring her unto Himself as a glorious church through spiritual growth and development.

What should be a church organization's response to God's "so great a sacrificial love" for her? Christ's great love for His church presents "so great a challenge" to His church. That challenge comes to an end-time church that has been blessed with an extraordinary abundance of material blessings and sensory pleasures.

The present-day church of America has experienced prosperity and blessings in the material realm like no other church generation before her. She lives in a world of darkness that is accustomed to being highly entertained with the finest entertainment in the history of civilization, but God is not in the entertainment business. The Father that never changes is in the changing business. His church is becoming more like His firstborn Son.

Living in a generation that has been entertained more than any other generation that has ever lived, the world with its influence and glitter to the realm of the senses makes Jesus' appeal to a lukewarm church a difficult appeal to overcome. Can church members who are ruled by the reasoning of the senses assemble themselves together and embrace the great challenge where "true worshipers will worship the Father in spirit and truth; for the Father is seeking such to worship Him?" (John 4:23).

To fulfill His purposes under the old covenant, many times God ended up having to work with a remnant of the faithful. To the Laodiceans the Lord gave the invitation to "anyone who hears My voice and opens the door," providing a spiritual environment with Him that would enable an obedient church member to overcome. Under the new covenant, the Holy Spirit is working with an "anyone" remnant that will be granted the reward with the overcoming church.

Fellowship with Jesus would prepare repentant church members for the Day of the Lord where Christ Jesus will be glorified. Man has had his day throughout the ages of time, but His Day is coming to earth, and the overcomer will be identified with Him in that Day. That glorious Day will last throughout His millennial reign. Then "the earth will be filled with the knowledge of the glory of the LORD, as the waters cover the sea."

Unlike the halfhearted love of the Laodiceans, the church that Christ is coming for loves Him with a whole heart, with all her soul, with all her strength, and with all her mind (Luke 10:27). God didn't give that greatest commandment to His people to obey as a recommendation or a suggestion. Christ fulfilled the commandment of God's love through His atoning work on the cross in order that God's love might be revealed through the church to a world that is passing away.

In the appeal to the Laodicean Church, the problem was stated before the solution was given. The solution was making a decision to come out of self-love into a fervent mutual loving fellowship with the Savior of her soul. Being a joint heir with Christ makes God's overcoming, glorious bride-elect a sharer of all things with Him in that day.

The Father is creating a workmanship that is His masterpiece in Christ Jesus. The Father knows that His Son, the Bridegroom, deserves the best Bride that can possibly be formed. In that daily transforming process in Christ, the free will of the individual is involved. If that weren't true, Christ would not have been required to die. The God of excellence would have already done away with Adam's fallen race, and He would have begun all over again with another perfect creation as He did at the beginning in Adam before the fall.

The Father is bringing forth an overcoming, glorious church through a creative process as a new creation in Christ Jesus. Christ, as the Lamb of God, was committed to the will of the Father to the end while He was dying on the cross saying, "It is finished." The Lamb's wife will be eternal living proof of the Father's commitment to His Son to her quality and excellence through His great plan of salvation in the creation of an overcoming, glorious church in Christ.

Chapter 5

The Greatest Test

A Need to See Herself as He Saw Her

"So then, because you are lukewarm, and neither cold nor hot,
I will vomit you out of My mouth" (verse 16).

The judgment of the Laodicean Church was a test in the realm of the emotions. There are three emotional measurements toward God in the church—lukewarm, cold and hot. There are two judgments according to the Scriptures; one judgment is for the church in rewards, and the other judgment is for the world in condemnation.

When it comes to the judgment of the church, there are two categories. "For we [the church] must all appear before the judgment seat of Christ, that each one may receive the things done in the body, according to what he has done, whether good or bad" (2 Cor. 5:10). There is no third category between good and bad. The different levels of good are based upon Christian fruit-bearing through faith. The good that is being done through spiritual growth and development until the end will cancel out the bad that was done through the years of growing pains.

In association with Him, there is no acceptable middle ground between right and wrong, being for Him or against Him, or being hot or cold. In the church setting of the Laodiceans, the Lord regrettably declares the category of the lukewarm, which is a halfhearted commitment toward Him in response to His wholehearted, benevolent love toward her. That church had lost her zeal as worshippers of God in Christ. Because He literally gave Himself for the church, she should have had a loving heart toward Him. She had set her heart on earthly riches and wealth. Because of her independence toward Him, she was forfeiting the privileges of knowing the true riches of His grace.

There can be no spiritual life, relationship or commitment from a dead-cold church. Because of false security and false hope, a spiritually dead church is worse off than the unbelieving world. No church can receive truth from God until they first humble themselves and recognize that they have a need to feed upon the Bread of Life. Because He is not alive to them, cold churches have no consciousness of or affections for Jesus. That kind of church doesn't fit into the category of judgment for Christian rewards.

The right church category is where there is a wholehearted commitment to Him. That becomes a mutual commitment between the Lord and His people, because He loved the church before she loved Him. There is no heartbreak in rewarding fervent fellowship with Him, which the Scripture calls "hot." That is the result of heartfelt fulfillment!

The church of the Laodiceans was having services, but the Head of the church was not in the midst. Jesus said, "For where two or three are gathered together in My name, I am there in the midst of them" (Matt. 18:20). What does it mean to do something in Jesus' name? Jesus set the example in His relationship to the Father. He came in His Father's name, which meant He said and did everything according to His Father's will in order that the Father would receive the glory. Anything that is not done for the glory of God is not being done according to the will of God.

Halfhearted Christianity

The Lord rejected the Laodicean Church's halfhearted zeal in her personal service in representing Him. All other loves, including her love for material riches, should have been secondary to her supreme love for Him. That love relationship begins with a one-to-one relationship as a sheep to a shepherd. From the standpoint of a church's commitment to the One who died for her sins, there should be no straddling the fence. On one side are the things of God, on the other, the things of this world. Jesus said, "You are either for Me or against Me."

In the Laodicean Church, those in Christ had become "lukewarm" toward Him. Why would it be difficult to make a successful appeal to a lukewarm church? Lacking the fires of passion for Jesus necessary to be ready for Him at His Appearing, she developed a sense of false security in her lukewarm attitude and concern for the need of drawing close to Him. Instead of seeing a need to draw closer to Him, she was drifting away from Him. She saw no purpose or need for gaining and maintaining a passionate love relationship with a compassionate Christ.

To have never known Jesus is most unfortunate, but to have known Him and then have drifted away from walking with Him without a yearning, searching heart to know Him better is heartbreaking. The deceitfulness of riches was choking out the fervor and passion of the spiritual life of that church for Him.

Why the strange preference of being confronted with a church being cold over the need to judge a lukewarm church? Those who are cold are not in the Body of Christ; therefore, there are no emotions involved from the Head of the Body. There is a great difference between being one who professes having Bible knowledge and practicing it. Those who are spiritually emotional cold toward Him are "dead cold." They have not entered into a know-so salvation and cannot be responsive toward the things of God.

The lukewarm profess Christianity with the self-satisfaction of being and belonging. These are more difficult to reach for wholehearted worship than are those who make no Christian profession at all. To have arrived at a place of self-complacency is not accepting the Bible challenge of continuing to follow Jesus all the way in revealed truth.

The "lukewarm" do not inspire or motivate those who are cold and indifferent, and their influence of holding back might become a hindrance to those who are in hot pursuit of a closer walk with Him. The pathway is set before us and there is still much to learn, but the lukewarm can go no further. The Laodicean Church had come to a spiritual plateau and her spiritual pride made her unable to go to the next level in the Christian experience. Because she was not reaching out with others to go forward in Jesus, as a church she couldn't be an inspiration to those who were looking for Christian reality.

The Laodicean Church needed to recognize her problem in the light of God's Word. Recognizing the problem is the first step, and spiritual pride would hinder her taking it. It is the halfway point toward the solution. She needed to take the first step and admit her problem. If you think you have light when you are in darkness, how great is that darkness? If you think you have no problem, how can there be a solution? She not only thought she didn't have a need, but she actually spoke it: "I have need of nothing!"

The answer to halfhearted Christianity is repentance. John the Baptist proclaimed the basic need to receive the gospel message to a religious people. "Repent and believe for the kingdom of heaven is at hand." He was a voice crying in the wilderness to prepare the way of the Lord. Another Voice followed John the Baptist.

But Jesus was more than a voice! As the Resurrection and the Life, He is the only way to the Father. Eternal Truth is found in Him; everlasting Life is in Him. The voice of John the Baptist has faded into Bible history like all other voices of godly men, but the voice of the resurrected, ascended Lord of Glory is ever fresh and alive to those who hear and respond to His voice. It was important that "anyone" in that church that had a hearing heart toward Jesus would respond to His voice. Though being lukewarm toward Jesus caused many problems in that church, loving Him would be the answer.

Loving Him Is the Answer

People who have a fiery passion for Jesus are setting an example before the world of the true reality of the Christian walk. They have accepted Christ's challenge to follow Him all the way to the end. They have a desire to obey the words of Jesus: "Let him deny himself, and take up his cross daily, and follow me" (Luke 9:23b).

It is not that He needs to learn to love the church. His love for her motivated Him to die for her! But a church needs to learn to love Him the way that He deserves to be loved. The more a church walks with Him, the more she, as a church, learns to love Him.

Loving Him means that she is willing to endure the sacrifices that are necessary to continue to follow Him. To know Jesus in the power of His resurrection glory is to know His loving kindness and tender mercy in a heartless world of religious hatred and strife. As they hated and rejected Him without a cause, the more the true church becomes like Jesus, the more the religious world will reject her.

God's great love for His new creation in Christ is the motivating factor behind His so-great salvation in Christ. We do not come to God in order that one day He may learn to love us. We are drawn to Him by His love for us. We are introduced to Him as the Savior who died for us because He loved us. A church's fellowship becomes delightful as she takes up His yoke and denies the selfish, carnal nature in the Christian walk. He becomes altogether lovely to those who persevere to know more of Him in His fullness.

To be passionate toward Jesus as a bride toward her bridegroom is an emotional attitude of love and devotion toward Him. His church is in pursuit of a loving relationship with Him. To have an enthusiastic, enduring, fervent love of the Bride toward her Bridegroom is the goal of Christian maturity. That is what makes His church "a glorious church" (Eph. 5:27). The Bridegroom loves the church with all His heart, and the more she matures the more she will be able to reciprocate that love.

Being a persevering follower of Jesus puts Christ on center stage in Christian living where no other Christian label is absolutely necessary. The glorious mature church has endured in Christ, and she will be taken out of the side of "the last Adam" as a completed creative work of God, just as a mature woman was taken out of the side of the first Adam.

By being "lukewarm," the Laodiceans were not warming up to a closer walk with Jesus. On the contrary, it was a departure from the original position of their first evangelistic love for Him. At the beginning, they were on fire for Jesus, but they had gone through a cooling-off trend and now they were in a lukewarm condition. Church history speaks of church movements that began with revival fire. They began to grow and prosper in evangelistic fervor, but over a period of time there was no longer the fervent appeal to keep their eyes on Jesus.

So by being "lukewarm," the church at Laodicea was dwelling in the sphere of personal convenience and physical comfort as good church members. They were not following on to know Him more in His fullness through self-denial and cross-bearing. By their attitude toward other members in the Body of Christ, that church had developed "a form of godliness but [she was] denying its power." She was denying the power of the gospel message that was needed to keep her passionately in love with Him.

She wanted to be identified with His name without being obedient to His words. The church people could tell you that their names were on the church's membership roll, but there was no evidence that any change was taking place in their hearts and lives.

Reaching the Lukewarm for Jesus

"So then, because you are "lukewarm," and neither cold nor hot *I will vomit you out of My mouth*." Why was that statement of Jesus so harsh and unpleasant relating to this lukewarm church? Her attitude of self-rule for self-glory separated her from the rest of the Body of Christ. Members of the Body of Christ cannot function independently of the Head of the Body and still remain spiritually hearty and healthy.

A church must humble herself in order to come under His rule. Since that church organization represented a system of thinking that was irreversible, the appeal was to anyone in that lukewarm church organism to accept His invitation for divine fellowship through a contrite act of obedience. A church organization cannot lead and direct wrongly without going wrong herself.

Our attitude toward God and our fellow believers is very important. The meaning behind the word church (*ecclesia*) is "a called-out assembly." The church is God's believing people who are a called-out assembly from the world of unbelievers. God's people are to be separated unto Him through love for Him and not separated from one another through spiritual pride and self-righteousness. His church is not being built for self-glorification or self-gratification but for the glory and delight of the Father.

The church at Laodicea had a collective ego problem because of her collective self-worth (I am rich) and self-sufficiency (I have need of nothing). There is nothing wrong in being prosperous. God blessed Abraham "in all things," which included his abundant living. Though Abraham valued the temporal blessings, he esteemed more highly the hope of His eternal blessings than the temporal riches of this world.

The fullness of the blessings of salvation through Christ Jesus is the church's objective and inheritance. Israel's inheritance is the Promised Land that was given to the seed of Abraham through Isaac according to the prophetic Scriptures. The church's inheritance is found in a land of promises given to the spiritual seed of Christ Jesus. Like the nation of Israel, the church has enemies to battle and overcome, but the church's battle is against the invisible enemies of the kingdom of darkness, and she fights a spiritual warfare against them through prayer and by putting on the full armor of God.

In addition to being unlike the nation of Israel's combat against the enemy, the church's battle is the good fight of faith. She takes her inheritance through the righteousness of God in Christ from the enemy stage by stage, "from faith to faith" (Rom. 1:17). The full inheritance of the church in Christ Jesus comes from the Father by the work of the Holy Spirit through the finished work of Christ at the cross.

Three Emotional Levels of the Church

Cold, hot and lukewarm are the three classifications that the Lord gives to the expression of emotions of a church's identity toward Him. The cold represents church people who have never experienced new-creation life. Those people conduct church services, but they could not be vomited out of His mouth because they are not in the Body of Christ. The cold would have a pseudo relationship with the Christ of Christianity. There has never been any awareness of worshipping and serving a living God here. No heartbreak through having to confront the dead cold or lifeless.

The "cold" church has a preference to be more in the political arena of the world than the spiritual arena of God. She knows more about the affairs of the world than being able to qualify in discerning things that are of spiritual value in the church. After chapter 3 in the book of Revelation, only two churches are pictured: the bride and the harlot. The harlot church loves and is committed to the political arena of this present evil age; she has no commitment to the Christ of the Scriptures.

Using the emotional term "hot" indicates that self-love has been set aside in order to come under the authority of His self-giving love. He enjoys the fellowship that He is having with those who love Him with all their heart. No heartbreak toward the hot!

That fellowship with Him is leading the wholehearted into a transforming experience of being changed more and more into the same image and likeness of the Firstborn Son. The emotionally "hot" church is being transformed from glory to glory that she might become qualified for the bride class. A continual passionate pursuit of a loving fellowship with the Lord Jesus Christ raises a need for a prayer-conditioned church atmosphere of worship.

If all people speak well of a church and she has developed creditability and respectability in the world community, she will be tempted to become self-complacent and self-satisfied. The focus of the Laodicean Church should have been based upon the standard needed to please Jesus and not upon the standard of this world's riches.

Three Levels of the Soul-life toward Him

The trichotomy of human life is spirit, soul and body. The trichotomy of the soul-life covers the will, the mind and the emotions. All three areas of the soul-life are to be denied from the direction of self-will (I want), self-glory (I think), and self-love (I feel) and committed toward the direction of doing God's will for His glory through self-giving love. Jesus said, "Whoever loses his *psuche* (soul-life) for My sake will find it."

The three levels of the mind (I think) of church members are the natural or soulish mind of newborn Christians, the renewing process of the mind of maturing Christians, and then having the mind of Christ as the goal for Christian maturity (Phil. 2:5). The mature Body of Christ, as a church organism, will have the mind of Christ.

The three levels of the will of God, which may be experienced through the process of the renewing of the mind, cover "the good, well pleasing and perfect will of God" (Rom. 12:2). The church of the Laodiceans began in "the good will" of God, but she was even falling short on that level of good works.

The three levels of the emotions of a church are cold, lukewarm and hot. Christ said to the Laodiceans: "That you are neither cold nor hot. I could wish you were cold or hot. So then, because you are lukewarm, and neither cold nor hot, I will vomit you out of My mouth." The Lord rejected the half-hearted effort of the church of the Laodiceans personal service to Him. The relationship always begins as one sheep to its Shepherd. Then something or someone comes between the sheep and the chief Shepherd. In the case of the Laodiceans, it was her riches and her material success.

Why is it so difficult to appeal to a lukewarm church congregation to acquire an enthusiasm and excitement for Jesus? The Laodiceans lacked the fires of excitement and enthusiasm toward the One "who loved the church and gave Himself for her." She would not have been ready to receive Him at His Appearing. In her lukewarm condition before the Lord, she had developed a false sense of security in the eyes of the Lord. Though the Lord had declared the Laodicean Church wrong, they undoubtedly believed in their heart that they were right.

God's people who have a passion for Jesus are setting an example before the world of true reality concerning Christianity. No rebuke is needed here. The right church has accepted Jesus' challenge to follow Him until the end.

Jesus told His disciples, who had followed Him up to a given point, but who had no understanding of the meaning of true discipleship; "If anyone *desires* to come after Me, let him deny himself, and take up his cross daily, and follow me" (Luke 9:23b).

Three steps, therefore, are needed to follow Jesus in complete discipleship. First, a desire is needed to come after Him. The Laodicean Church could not get pass the first step or test. Next, a desire to become closer to Him leads to the denial of self-will in order that His will may be done. Finally, His disciples must become cross-bearers in their daily contact with other people for His sake.

To be passionate toward Jesus, as a bride toward her bridegroom, is an attitude of love and devotion that means being emotionally passionate toward Him. To be in pursuit of the fervent love of the Bride toward her Bridegroom is the goal for Christian maturity. That is what makes His church "a glorious church" (Eph. 5:27). Being a follower of Jesus puts Christ at the center of Christian living and no other Christian label is necessary for those who are following Him unto the end.

One of the symptoms of a lukewarm church is that the challenge of a commitment to the Christ of the cross is no longer being preached. The preaching of the crucified life will challenge believers to put off the old things, which have not passed away in the lives of church members. The old ways of living are the old lifestyles that make no room for the new things of God in new-creation living where church members worship God with "clean hands and a pure heart" (Ps. 24:4). That means doing the work of the Lord with a right motive.

So by being "lukewarm," that church was dwelling in the sphere of personal convenience and physical comfort as good church members. She was not willing to follow on to know the Christ of the Scriptures more and more in His fullness. She wanted to be identified with His name without being obedient to the fullness of the gospel message of pressing forward toward spiritual maturity. "For as many as are [continually being] led by the Spirit of God, these are [the mature] sons of God."

Three Kinds of Tests, Growth and Materials

Three emotional levels were used in comparing the three kinds of relationships that church members might have with Jesus. Elsewhere in the gospel message are given three levels of tests in building materials, and growth that leads to harvest maturity. Why are tests necessary for those who build for God? Types and parables are used to show God's objective and steps given in fulfilling His ultimate purpose for His church.

In the Old Testament, the Tabernacle of Moses in the wilderness, which later was built as the Temple of God in Jerusalem, had three compartments: the outer court, holy place and holy of holies. The function of the service of the priesthood in the holy place involved three pieces of furniture: table of shewbread, golden lampstand and altar of incense, which represent the will, intellect and emotions of the soul-life.

What are also the three different kinds of materials that are found in God's building program under the new covenant? In building for God, two categories of building materials are used, and the two building plans are very different. One is the building plan with "the things of God," and the other plan is building with "the things of men."

"The things of God" begin with a believer being crucified with Christ. Those materials will stand the test of the purifying fiery trials within the Christian experience. It follows the pattern of God's building process and procedure of priestly service in the Temple of God with gold, silver and precious stones, which will stand the test of fire and receive an eternal reward (1 Cor. 3:12-15). The number "three" is the endorsement mark of the Godhead that represents levels of yield and the full measure for His building program in experiencing the provisions of the fullness of His salvation.

Paul also refers to "wood, hay and straw" as three different types of building materials that would not stand the test of judgment fire. The category of right materials was being compared with wrong materials, which are of "the things of men." That category, which is against a life of self-denial and becoming a cross-bearer, will not stand the test of fire.

After a time Jesus began to teach in parables. His disciples questioned that method of teaching (Matt. 13:10). In teaching how the Word of God might become fruitful in understanding the end-time harvest yield, He taught the parable of the seed and the sower, and the importance of the soil where the seed would be planted (vv. 2-9).

The seeds of the fullness of God's truth are more available to the end-time church than ever before, and those who sow the seeds are available, but what about the soil? When Jesus taught the truth, He did not fail as a Teacher. It was the failure of the multitudes that did not profit by His message. It depends upon the nature of the soil where the seeds are being planted. "If anyone has ears to hear, let him hear." That means that there is a hearing that keeps the message of truth outside of our understanding.

The seeds that fell by the wayside in today's vernacular could be the asphalt payment, concrete sidewalk and hard-beaten pathway where the seeds could not take root in soil. That refers to the worldly-minded and the high-minded that would not receive His words so that the birds of the air fed on them. Since the seeds were never planted, the wayside could not be considered as soil. The three different kinds of soil where seeds of God's Word are sown and take root are the rocky soil, the thorny soil, and the good soil.

Seeds planted in rocky soil were received with joy, but they had no depth of earth. When the hot sun of trouble and adversity arose, the plants withered, for there were no depth of roots. The seeds planted among the thorns took root, but the thorns grew up and choked the fruit-producing life out of the plants. The thorns are representative of the cares of this world and the deceitfulness of riches that grew up and choked the Word from yielding any fruit.

To churches, like Smyrna, which are tested with trouble and persecution on account of the Word, things could become too hard and hinder their endurance. To churches that are tested with the cares of the world and the deceitfulness of riches, things could become too easy. That was the test category that the lukewarm church at Laodicea was experiencing. That test is typical of many end-time churches in modern America.

But the example of the three levels of harvest yield of the seed planted in the good ground was a three-level increase of a "hundredfold, some thirty, some sixty" (Matt. 13:23). The hundredfold yield is greater than the thirty and the sixty combined. The thirty, sixty and hundredfold increase can be compared to Jesus' parable of the Vine and the branches, where each branch might be on one level of a possible three-level yield: fruit, more fruit, and much fruit. Before the Father can be glorified, a branch must bear much fruit (John 15:8). When the complete ultimate purpose and plan of the Master Architect of the church is fulfilled and realized, then the Father will be glorified.

When the seeds of God's Word are planted in the good ground, Jesus teaches that the growing and developing process comes in three stages. Jesus presents the growing seed as "the earth yields crops by itself; first the blade, then the head, after that the full grain in the head" (Mark 4:28). The harvest yield comes after the crop has matured. The three stages in the ripening process to mature fruit is first the bud, then the blossom; and finally, the green fruit that takes time to develop into mature golden ripeness.

Three is the signature of the Godhead's authorization to the completeness of the growth and development of new-creation life in Christ Jesus that is representative of God's building program for the church. "A threefold cord is not quickly broken" (Ecc. 4:12). The leadership in a Christian home, with husband and wife and with Jesus at the center, becomes a strong threefold cord in the realm of time.

Jesus prayed to the Father concerning the church, "that they may be one just as We are one" (John 17:22). That will become an answered prayer that involves the unity of the Father, the Son and His Bride, which will become a mighty, impressive, unbreakable threefold cord in the unity of the Spirit in the realm of eternity. The glorious, overcoming church needs to learn to think in oneness of heart toward the Godhead right now.

The relationship of Christ to the church in the emotional realm is either having a right fellowship or having no fellowship with Him. A jealous God will not accept a lukewarm fellowship in between. The right church becomes more like Jesus by being transformed from a self-centered love of the emotions to a self-giving love toward Him.

God's Ways vs. Man's Ways

The temporal material riches of the world have always been a test or temptation for the people of God from the beginning of Old Testament history. Riches and wealth that give financial security and self-glory in a transitory, fleeting world continue to be the top priority of the masses in these last days. But the church has been commissioned to present the eternal riches of God in Christ Jesus, which are found in God's great plan of salvation.

People usually do not see themselves the way other people see them. The Laodicean Church unquestionably did not see herself the way the Lord saw her. She did not see her need to have union and communion with the highly esteemed Beloved of the church. Like the church of the Laodiceans, collective self-centeredness through an attitude of self-importance causes an end-time church system to become lukewarm toward Jesus. This is one of the greatest obstacles to spiritual development of newborn Christians.

God's thoughts and ways were not the thoughts and ways of the Laodicean Church. She should have developed a more meek and contrite spirit toward the Lord in being obedient to the fullness of His teachings. Her self-worth and egotistical attitude hindered her from having a tender, devoted fellowship with Him as the meaningful and unique One, as of special great worth and significance to the church. That church should have been magnifying His name with gratitude and praises for having an opportunity to be identified with such majesty and greatness.

The specific value of that church congregation was the overemphasis that was placed upon her temporal material prosperity. To the Laodiceans, the witness of her prosperity was a witness that she had become a privileged church with the God of her prosperity. But the main issue and principal emphasis should have been a need for a proper and personal response to the revelation of Christ's great love toward the church. His great love for the church is not to be ignored! It is to be reciprocated.

The world has no love for God and functions independently of God. The church (Gk. *ecclesia*) means the "called out" assembly. The church is called out and separated from the ways and the thoughts of the world. God, therefore, needs to sanctify her, which means she must be "set apart unto God." When believers are set apart unto God, they do the will of God. When they do the will of God, they glorify God. God's will and good pleasure need to take precedence over self-will and selfishness in the life of a church. The pride of life is one basic sin against God that leads to a countless number of sins against our fellowman.

Her Divided Heart

As in any era of human history, fortune and fame are twin sisters of success in the eyes of the world. Fortune can become very impressive to the world and give birth to fame. The church of Laodicea had obtained the riches and wealth of the world. Though that may have given her a distinguished status in the eyes of the worldly-minded, it didn't make her any more favored with Jesus. Because the world represents a social order that operates independently of God, the Bible says that the world is an enemy of God. The world highly esteems those who become independently wealthy.

The riches and wealth of the Laodicean Church motivated her to seek fame like the world as "the church." She had need to worship and serve God with a whole heart, but she said, "I have need of nothing." That kind of thinking led her to move on an independent course away from God, where she developed a feeling and a heart toward the importance of the riches and wealth of this world. At the same time, being a church organism that belonged to the Body of Christ, she had some feelings toward knowing and experiencing the importance of the things of God. She had a divided heart.

Christ loved that church and gave Himself for her. The Lord has proven His love for the church through the death that He died for her. He just doesn't tolerate her; He wholeheartedly loves her and desires to have fellowship with her. Christ's pivotal relationship with the church is the love relationship.

Christ was jealous over that church; He rebuked a divided heart. He desired to have the fullness of that church's attention and devotion. He wanted her for His very own. His love is an everlasting love.

The Laodicean Church had grown lukewarm toward Him, but He had not forgotten her. He was standing outside of that church knocking on a door that had been closed to Him. He was trying to persuade anyone in that church to become committed to His love by dining with Him.

As success may give rise to celebrity status and fortune may give rise to fame, the Laodiceans had a personal ambition to be the greatest. Their selfish ambition was void of self-giving love, and it is one of the works of the flesh that cause division in the church (Gal. 5:20). Having a desire for personal greatness often comes at the expense of others—lifting oneself up by putting the other guy down. According to the gospel message, he who serves is greater than the one who is served. "But he who is greatest among you shall be your servant. And whoever exalts himself will be humbled, and he who humbles himself will be exalted."

When does exaltation come in the work of the living God? Self-exaltation is opposite to the way God exalts a person. Jesus, as the living Example for the church, "humbled Himself and was obedient unto death, even the death of the cross." Through His death, burial, resurrection from the dead and ascension, God has highly exalted Him above all others (Phil. 2:5-12). But self-exaltation, if not corrected with the help of the Holy Spirit, will lead to spiritual ruin and loss.

His exaltation was not based upon who He eternally was as the only begotten Son of God, but upon what He accomplished for the church as the sinless Son of Man. In other words, Christ merited His exaltation by what He did for the church. He gave Himself for the church! One day He shall become the exalted Bridegroom to the church.

Because she wants God's best, the Bride will pass the test of loving Him more than all others and all things. God will have a tried and tested church. The purpose of many tests will be answered through the test in how much the organism of a church organization loves Jesus. As a lukewarm church, she was not expressing her heartfelt devotion toward Him in the enthusiasm and excitement as it should have been expressed.

The Laodicean Church had an "I" problem toward her self that led to a "heart" problem toward Him. She could not understand that her zeal for the work of a church, such as her own, was not in harmony with having a zeal for the Christ of the church. She took greater delight in her riches and wealth of earth than she did in Christ, the Father's Treasure House of heaven.

After Eve was deceived, Adam had to make a choice. Eve was the love of his life, but she had eaten the fruit from the forbidden tree. Adam was the love product of a loving God, and he reciprocated that love. He must not transgress against the commandment of the One who created him in His own image and likeness. Adam loved God but He also loved his bride who had transgressed against God. As a living soul, Adam had to make a choice. He did what his wife asked him to do. Adam had a divided heart!

As soon as Adam disobeyed God, he had a change of nature and heart toward God. Before God confronted Adam for his act of transgression, He "and his wife hid themselves from the presence of the LORD God among the trees of the garden" (Gen 3:8b). And then, Adam indirectly blamed God for giving him the woman in the first place. "The woman whom you gave to be with me, she gave me of the tree and I ate" (v. 12). Adam experienced spiritual death, and as a result of the fall, and through spiritual pride, he and his descendants have become rebellious souls toward God and the things of God. A new life and nature is needed in Christ Jesus.

The nature of traveling an independent course away from God was the nature that every individual in the church of Laodicea had inherited from Adam. God didn't tell Adam that he had nobody to blame but himself. Pride is the result of a corruptible nature that produces rebels against the things of God. Adam was now a proud man; and he now also had the same rebellious nature as Satan. That soulish nature has a desire to live a life independent of God (Is. 53:6). To become a disciple of Christ, Jesus said that one must have a desire to come after Him, and "deny himself, take up his cross, and follow Me" (Matt. 16:24).

There are certain church rules that are supposed to tell church members how to live righteously, but the righteousness of God is revealed through faith in hearing the gospel message (Rom. 1:17). There are no church rules dealing with the pride of life that separates God's people from having fellowship with their Creator. The Laodiceans' "divided heart" was between the God of her salvation and the ways and riches of this world.

Building for God

Pride produces rebels against God's authority. That fallen nature has a desire to live a life independent of God. This breaks down the unity in the Body of Christ in the end-time church. "All we like sheep have gone astray; we have turned, every one, to his own way; and the LORD has laid on Him the iniquity of us all" (Is. 53:6).

God had a purpose when He told Noah to build the Ark, but He did not tell the builders of Babel to build their tower. The builders were building the tower of Babel for the purpose of self-glory. God came down and caused disunity among the workers by changing their language so that they couldn't understand one another or fulfill their self-appointed purpose. Because they now spoke many different languages, they could not communicate to finish the work and were dispersed to all parts of the earth.

Before unity can be restored in the church, all churches need to learn to speak the same language, the language of faith that works by love. "Therefore, if anyone is in Christ, he is a new creation; old things have passed away; behold, all things have become new. All things are of God." The fullness of God's new creation has been predestined in Christ before the foundation of the earth.

God is now in the creative process of transforming the church more and more to bring her forth in the image and likeness of His firstborn Son. God's creative process brings forth a new heart, a new mind and a desire to learn to speak the new-creation language of faith and love that will unite new-creation people together in oneness toward the fullness of spiritual maturity.

In other words, born-again believers have been given birth to new-creation life in order that they may do new-creation deeds, thinking and learning to speak a new-creation language, which is a language of faith. Because of what she has become to the Father in Christ Jesus, the church is able to do the good works of God.

Because of God's work in preparing the Bride for the Bridegroom, only the Father can make the Bride worthy of the Bridegroom. The foundation for the structure of God's workmanship in Christ is by the grace of God.

Paul said, "By the grace of God I am what I am." The grace of God did a work of love in Paul for the benefit of others. He became a servant to others for the cause of Christ.

Paul had his heart set on winning the Prize, and he was willing to pass any test necessary to obtain it. His longing was to win Christ in all His fullness, in all His glory. Unlike the church of the Laodiceans that boasted, "I have need of nothing," Paul had a need to the very end to fight the good fight of faith and finish the predestined course that was laid down before him (2 Tim 4:7). At that time he was a member of the Body of Christ, but he had his focus on the Lover of his soul. "If, by any means," he wanted to qualify to become a member of the Bride of Christ through the bodily resurrection of the dead like unto His glorious bodily resurrection.

The Goal and Results of Good Works

"Where there is no revelation, the people cast off restraint" (Prov. 29:18). The church of the Laodiceans needed a revelation from God to go forward as a people with God. She needed to be a vital force in God's building program in working out the good works by grace, but her self-sufficient attitude and pride hindered her from any further spiritual progress. Since her thinking revealed self-centered small talk, she was coming up short according to God's complete building objective for His church as stated in the Scriptures.

Those church members were saved by grace through faith, "not of works, lest anyone should boast." Paul said that as workers together with Him, based upon Christ's atoning sacrifice, they should "not receive the grace of God in vain." Because of the pride of life, the church people at Laodicea were boasting in their religious works.

Because Christ, as the Bridegroom, merited His exaltation in giving Himself to fulfill the Father's will through the death that He died, His Bride will humble herself and be united with Him in His exaltation through sacrificial obedience. She receives His grace and walks in it until the end. To walk in the truth of God's Word, "anyone" in that church could open the door and dine with Him as God's "Grace and Truth."

The eternally begotten Son of God could do what He did for the Father because He was the Father's only begotten Son. God's children born into the Father's family through the Spirit of adoption by faith in Christ's atoning death for them are to become God's "workmanship created in Christ Jesus for good works." The Holy Spirit is directing the end-time church, being created for good works, for the glory of the Father as He matures the Father's creative masterpiece in Christ for the deserving Bridegroom.

After laying down the divine principle and example of how Christ humbled Himself as the Son of Man to achieve the Father's highest-ranking position in the universe on behalf of His church (Phil. 2:6-11), Paul challenges the Philippian Church with these words: "Therefore…work out your own salvation with fear and trembling." Christians are able to act upon that command based upon the grace that God gives to the faithful. "For it is God who works in you both to will and to do for His good pleasure" (2:12b, 13).

An end-time church saved by grace shows her works through her faith. "As the body without the spirit is dead, so faith without works is dead also" (James 2:26). A church may give thanks for the free gift of faith that provides for all temporal physical needs. But the spiritual fruit of faithfulness to the Lord, where He is developing growth in new creation living, is eternal and it takes time and testing to cultivate. There is no room for the boasting of the flesh while developing the fruit of the Spirit. An attitude like Paul's is needed, who said, "if, by any means, I may attain" to that ultimate purpose that God has planned for the church.

God's good pleasure that He is working in the heart and life of each individual believer is the same as His ultimate purpose for the church. The Father desires to create a new-creation masterpiece called the Bride of Christ out of the Body of Christ in order that she may become worthy of His Son, the Bridegroom. The result of that devoted work is a heart full of love that is only for Him—"do not love the world or the things in the world"—the crowning feature that the Bridegroom is looking for in His waiting Bride.

The Laodicean Church had entered into the saving knowledge of Christ, but they had become lukewarm toward Him. Church members who are born again know that salvation comes "by grace through faith." Nobody needs to tell them that they have had an experience with a living God. There was a point in time when God saved them.

Believers don't need to work for their salvation. It comes by the free grace of God. The only cost involved to the initial seeker of God is laying down pride and self-effort, giving up self-will and saying "God be merciful to me, a sinner." It was God's will to save the lost by giving His Son for them. No works are involved except His work at the cross. The humble act of repentance is all that is required for the initial experience with God on the part of the forgiven. Born-again believers have a know-so-salvation. "We know that we have passed from death to life, because we love the brethren."

The Bridegroom achieved His exaltation over all things by humbling Himself in doing the will of the Father by fulfilling the prophetic Scriptures for His life. Near the beginning of Jesus' ministry, He read from the book of Isaiah in the synagogue of His hometown of Nazareth. "He began to say to them, 'Today this Scripture is fulfilled in your hearing'" (Luke 4:21). It is important to notice in the gospel story the many references concerning Jesus "that the Scripture might be fulfilled" for His life at that given moment in time.

Jesus Christ of Nazareth highly regarded the Scriptures, and He taught from the Scriptures. He spoke the words that His Father gave Him to speak, that has been recorded as the gospel message, and He also came to fulfill all the prophetic Scriptures of the Old Testament that concerned His life. Many are yet to be fulfilled. His bride-elect, likewise, honors the Scriptures, lives by the Scriptures and will fulfill all the prophetic Scriptures concerning her life, and many have yet to be fulfilled.

The Bride's exaltation is her identity as one with the exalted Bridegroom. It is by the outworked grace of God where she humbles herself with the help of the Holy Spirit in fulfilling the will of the Father and the Son. She will pass the tests in fulfilling all the Scriptures concerning herself as the bride-elect.

That would even include Ephesians 5:27 where it says, "that He might present her to Himself a glorious church, not having spot or wrinkle or any such thing, but that she should be holy and without blemish." That doesn't seem reasonably conceivable with the many weaknesses and divisions that are so prevalent in the end-time church, but "the Scriptures cannot be broken." Jesus is preparing an overcoming church with whom He might share His reward as an Overcomer. The overcoming church is another description of the Bride of Christ.

The scripture pertaining to the Marriage Supper of the Lamb is waiting to be fulfilled with great expectation and excitement of heaven. That event should also be anticipated with the same great expectation and excitement by the end-time church. The Lamb of God has need for a Bride that is passionately in love with Him for the marriage to take place. A lukewarm church, like the Laodiceans, could never qualify. Christ Jesus is the One who is "worthy to receive glory and honor O Lord," and His bride-elect says, "Amen."

Chapter 6

The Greatest Deception
A Need to Focus on God's Eternal Riches

"Because you say, 'I am rich, have become wealthy, and have need of nothing'—and do not know that you are wretched, miserable, poor, blind, and naked" (verse 17).

Verse 17 is the key and pivotal verse in the story of the church of the Laodiceans. Both chapter 2 and chapter 6, therefore, have been given to that key verse. The attitude and character of not having any need, as a church, are the theme, thread and pattern throughout the book. Since "the love of money is a root of all kinds of evil," then the love of riches can become one of the greatest deceptions for a Christian institution as well as for an individual. The root of the problem of that church, therefore, was not only the sin of self-sufficiency and pride but also her "love of money."

Spiritual pride caused her to say, "I am rich, have become wealthy, and have need of nothing." Pride, which is the root sin of rebellion, is the sin that brought warfare among the angels in the heavens. The angels of light are warring against the angels of darkness in heavenly places. Spiritual pride, which brought rebellion against God in the heavenlies through a fallen angel named Lucifer, was also the primary sin that Christ had to face from the religious leaders of the nation of Israel.

119

When the Messiah came to His own people, it was not the heathen Gentile world that gave Him the most problems. It was the religious leaders of God's chosen people, the nation of Israel. In the incident with the Laodicean Church, it was the lukewarm church causing Him the problem and not the spiritually dead secular world. If the world was to be blamed, it was the world's influence upon the thinking of that church.

No doubt that church had preached against drunkenness, sexual immorality, thievery and other vices. Against the background of those sins, her statement of pride and self-sufficiency seemed so natural and harmless. But in light of the fullness of the total picture, Lucifer's pride and self-exaltation led one-third of the angels in heaven to rebel against God. Lucifer's name was changed to Satan, which means "resistor."

The self-righteousness and spiritual pride of the scribes and Pharisees gave birth to the envy that caused their rebellious false accusations and acts against Jesus. Self-sufficiency and self-exaltation of the Jewish religious leaders against the God of the nation of Israel led them to have their Messiah crucified upon a Roman cross. The Laodicean Church was not a church full of gross immorality, neither was she in the realm of doctrinal heresy, but in her lukewarmness she was a church that was deceived in thinking that she had a right relationship to the Christ of Christianity, which was not true.

She, as a church, had a need to be challenged that the Christ of the Scriptures would become the center of her life. The church at Laodicea was headed downward toward a lower level, a religious social club with high moral standards. It takes Christ dwelling in the center of things to make a religious gathering truly Christian. At that moment, Christ wasn't dwelling in the midst of that church.

One whole chapter in the book of Job is given to the description of a sea creature by the name of Leviathan. The chapter ends with the words, "He beholds every high thing; He is the king over all the children of pride (41:34). Leviathan was a dragon-like creature of the sea that was a type of the devil. That great dragon was cast out, that serpent of old called the devil and Satan, "who deceives the whole world" (Rev. 12:9). False christs and false prophets are going to "show great signs and wonders to deceive" many in the last days. "If possible, even the elect" would be deceived (Matt. 24:24).

"The king over all the children of pride" is working very hard in trying to deceive end-time churches, and he is the master of deception. The devil is a defeated foe. He has been stripped of all his weapons through the death, burial and resurrection of Christ according to the Scriptures.

Deception is the only tried and tested, effective tool that Satan has left. But the light of truth will penetrate and absorb the spiritual darkness of his lies and deception.

When people put on a front that they are the greatest, it is usually a cover-up. In fact, they feel inferior; they have a void and emptiness on the inside. God's deep settled peace is missing, whether they will admit it or not. If they do not submit to the God of love, their hearts will be empty of the true reality of God. The Holy Spirit works in our hearts as the Spirit of Love, "who was given to us," and it is up to the end-time church to submit to Him until the end.

The Laodicean Church needed to walk in the Spirit and begin to learn and understand things in the spiritual realm. She wanted to appear as the right church to the world, but at the same time, she was becoming more like the world. She was deceived through her self-complacency and self-sufficiency. She had developed an exalted mind-set to her own greatness as the church.

Counted Unworthy

The Lord over the church was counting the church of the Laodiceans unworthy. What does it take to be counted worthy? God's eternal riches are in Christ Jesus. "Watch therefore, and pray always that you may be counted worthy to escape all these things that will come to pass, and to stand before the Son of Man" (Luke 21:36). Where can the label "worthy" be placed? It cannot be placed on a church encampment, like Babel, that is building for self-glory. It is the church that is devoted to Him with all her heart, worshipping Him, and proclaiming Him as worthy.

The church of the Laodiceans needed to become meek and contrite at heart in the sight of the Lord. The overemphasis of her self-worth became a hindrance to the Holy Spirit's revealing the great work and the true worth of Christ Jesus to her. He is absolutely worthy! Without Him, mankind is bankrupt! Church members have no worth outside of His work of grace (John 15:5b). God had blessed her with riches and wealth, but she got her eyes on the material riches and ignored the true riches of God's grace in Christ Jesus.

The Holy Spirit has come into the world to prepare a worthy Bride for the Father's deserving Son. That is one of the chief functions of His work in the end-time church. The Holy Spirit is exalting the Christ of the Scriptures and taking the things that are His and making them real in the hearts and lives of His people (John 15:26a; 16:14-15).

The bride-elect is fixing her eyes more and more on the work and worth of her beloved Bridegroom. Her focus will not be on her self-worth but on Him who is truly worthy. For anyone who accepted Jesus' invitation to open the door would exchange her self-love, to be replaced with a passionate love for Him who is entirely worthy.

As more emphasis is being placed upon Christ Jesus, His great worth and importance will increase in the eyes of the bride-elect. It is not what a church is worth in her own eyes, but that she has been identified with Him who is truly worthy. He is the only One who can satisfy the eternal thirst of a thirsty soul and give the fullness of His Word to a hungry heart.

A church should not have a lofty attitude of her worth to God measured in material wealth like the Laodicean Church. If she concludes that she is solely the right church on that basis, she is surely wrong. The self-satisfied hunger for material prosperity of that church revealed that she didn't have a heart of passion or hunger for Jesus.

Before a Christian begins the new journey *in Christ*, the old life, by faith, must be identified with Christ at His crucifixion. It is His resurrection power that provides a new life from Christ. The focus on finishing the journey is looking unto Christ. The Holy Spirit provides the way for a believer to walk by faith, which is of Christ. He is altogether worthy!

The "I Am" Church

The Laodicean Church thought that she was a great church, but she was not a church under the rule of the great "I AM." The term "I am" exhibits her collective ego problem. That term was a representation of her collective arrogance and self-worth that was brought about by her self-will. Anyone in that church that heard His voice and opened the door would change her focus from a "How great I am" church to "How great He is." The Holy Spirit makes a church great according to her fellowship with Christ, as Head of the church. A wrong attitude made that church a very small "I am" church.

Because she was completely ignoring the great "I AM," that "I am" church was growing even smaller. When Jesus gave the great commission, He told His disciples to go into all the world and teach "them to observe all things that I have commanded you." Then He ended the great commission with these words, "*I AM* with you always even to the end of the age" (Matt. 28:20). He was passionately working with that church.

The church of the Laodiceans' thinking was so self-centered on "I am rich, have become wealthy," that the loving presence of the great "I AM" was no longer being recognized or honored as her functioning Head. Jesus desires to be in the midst of a church gathering to rule and reign over it. But He was on the outside seeking for hungry hearts on the inside that would hear His voice and open their hearts' doors to Him. That one "I am" church needed to forget about her material riches and wealth and open the door to Him who proclaimed the seven "I ams" of Himself in relationship to His church as recorded in the gospel according to John.

The book of Acts was the first church movement built on the foundation of revival fires. Beginning at Jerusalem, the Holy Spirit had given birth to the church located in different cities from those revival fires during that period of time in church history. Each local church, set in order by the early apostles, was on a good foundation by the power of the Holy Spirit, having a passionate, wholehearted love toward Christ Jesus.

But over a short period of time, the church at Laodicea had quickly cooled off to becoming lukewarm toward Jesus. She no longer had any enthusiasm or excitement toward the things of God with regard to the Christ of His church. She had become a self-centered and self-serving church concerning the work in Christian service.

People in that church organism had an initial life-changing experience where they met Christ who became the first love of their heart. But now they were attending a lukewarm church where there was no longer any loving fellowship with Jesus. The Lord continues to give life-changing experiences to those that have an ongoing loving fellowship with Him. The Christ who never changes is still in the changing business.

The church of the Laodiceans might apply as an example to many Fundamental, Evangelical, Pentecostal, Charismatic and denominational churches of the end-time church. These movements of God owe their existence to the revival fires of the past that brought spiritual birth, spiritual power and enlightenment to those who were experiencing His passionate love. But in most of these movements, the revival fires have flickered out long ago. The "lukewarm," rich and wealthy church systems, however, still exist during this climacteric era of the end-time Church Age.

The thinking of many people of the world may be, "If I am rich, I have need of nothing," but that should never be the thinking of a church. In the Laodiceans' thinking, being rich with material resources and having experienced God's blessings of past history was the only evidence needed that she had God's approval upon her church life.

The overcoming church is the future reigning queen of the earth with a meek servant's spirit as a helper to her King and His subjects. That overcoming church will inherit a new identity with her King who said, "For I am meek and lowly in heart." All the proud, self-seeking, greedy grabbers for great gain, who are now on earth, are going to leave it empty-handed. But "blessed are the meek, for they shall inherit the earth."

The Woman as a Type of the Church

At the beginning of creation, the woman was a type of the church in two ways. First, the woman was a type of the church in the way God brought her forth out of Adam, creating her in the likeness of Adam, to be united to Adam in matrimonial oneness with him. Second, the woman was a type of the church by the method that Satan used to tempt her. Satan led her to disobey God by deceiving her about the true nature of God.

The woman became related to Adam as a complete mature bride. God saw the need and made the decision that Adam needed a bride, like him, made in the image and likeness of God. God said, "It is not good that man should be alone; I will make him a helper comparable to him" (Gen. 2:18).

The other way that the woman was a type of a church was the way the devil tempted her. Satan purposed in his heart to deceive the woman to get to Adam, and he spoke through the serpent to tempt her to disobey God and His Word. Satan has not changed from using that manner of attack on the thought life in deceiving a church, whether it is the church of the Laodiceans or an end-time church.

The battleground is in the mind, and church members are exhorted to cast down every stronghold or high thing that exalts itself against the knowledge of God and bring "every thought into captivity to the obedience of Christ" (2 Cor. 10:4). Church history attests to the fact that Satan's tactics of lies and deception are the prime reason why the end-time church needs to rest more and more upon the faithfulness of the Holy Spirit to lead and guide her into all truth.

1. Right Pattern as Identified with Adam

Notice the unique way in which the woman was created. "And the Lord God caused a deep sleep to fall upon Adam" (Gen. 2:21). The woman was made from a rib taken out of Adam's side, and she was presented to him in holy matrimony as his bride in the paradise of God's garden. I believe that Adam had a scar in his side to remind his bride that she had come out of him.

The church, as the Bride of Christ, is in Christ, and she will be taken out of Him and presented to Him in the paradise of God's heaven. We know that the Bridegroom has a scar in His side to prove and remind His Bride that she belongs to Him. Therefore out of Adam, God created one of the same kind. Then God brought the two together and they became one in union in holy matrimony.

The woman was a perfect "rib" in Adam before she was perfectly created out of Adam. Because our Creator God is the God of excellence as well as the God of detail and completeness, I believe the first woman, as God's special creative masterpiece, was a very beautiful and mature bride for Adam.

Picture this scenario as Adam looked upon one of God's greatest accomplished works of creation. When God brought the woman to Adam, Adam did not tell God, "Is that the best you can do?" Nor did Adam say in a disappointed tone, "Father, why did you give me someone like that as a helper?"

No, Adam said, in a tone of admiration and appreciation, "This is now bone of my bones and flesh of my flesh." Because the woman was a part of Adam, she was identified with him and shared in everything that belonged to him. She shared equally in a mutual reign with Adam over all things in the Garden of Eden. The woman was made a quality bride to rule and reign over the garden as a helper with her grateful bridegroom.

The woman became the object of Adam's love just as the Son is, always has been, and shall forever be the object of the Father's eternal, unchanging love. Christ's giving Himself for the church shows that His church is the object of His love. His love for the church is something precious that lasts forever! Now Christ shall become the ultimate objective of His glorious church's love. "We love Him [fervently] because He first loved us [fervently]" (1 John 4:19).

Adam had received a glorious prize in his bride. Being a gift from God, Adam's bride was a product of God's grace. The woman, being of Adam's own kind, could reciprocate Adam's kind of love. Their love for one another was an important element in the consummation of God's creative process.

At His Second Coming, Christ's bride will become "members of His flesh, and of His bones" (Eph. 5:30). His Bride will be known throughout eternity as "the Lamb's wife." What a beautiful spiritual, eternal, love story! He is the Lover of her soul.

In her purity before the fall, the woman had no name. After the fall, Adam named her Eve. As the church has no individual identity outside of Christ, the woman had no identity outside of Adam. "Male and female created he them; and blessed them, *and called their name Adam*, in the day when they were created" (Gen. 5:2, KJV).

From the beginning the bride didn't need any identity; her ego identity was lost in her bridegroom. The church at its early beginning had no identity other than the church of the city where it was located—the church at

Colosse, the church at Ephesus, the church at Laodicea, etc. Because the end-time church is described by so many ego identities, it becomes detrimental in creating a disunity problem for the church.

2. Wrong Pattern in Giving an Ear to the Tempter

The woman knew not to eat the fruit from the forbidden tree because Adam had told her what God said. The woman's faith in God's Word was based upon what her husband had told her. The woman, therefore, became the target for Satan's scheme to deceive her about what God had said.

The woman should have told the tempter, "My husband told me what God said!" Jesus, as the church's right pattern in temptation, told the tempter, "It is written!" On another occasion Jesus asked the question. "Have you not read?" (Matt. 19:4). The end-time church should also stand upon all that has been written in the Holy Scriptures.

Satan began tempting the woman by first casting doubt on the Word of God. He questioned her, "Has God indeed said?" Then Satan counteracted her reasoning based on God's Word by telling her "the big lie," "You will not surely die!" In giving an ear to the devil, her doubt led to disbelief. Then, the next step was to disobey and partake of the fruit from the forbidden tree. Satan had accomplished what he set out to do. He had purposed in his heart to deceive her. "Adam was not deceived, but the woman being deceived, fell into transgression" (1 Tim. 2:14).

So the great dragon in Revelation 12:9 "deceives the whole world" but his prime target is the accusation that he makes to God against the church. At some future time this prophetic scripture will be fulfilled in verse 10. "Now salvation, and strength, and the kingdom of our God, and the power of His Christ have come, for the accuser of our brethren, who accused them before our God day and night, has been cast down." After Satan deceives church members, he then accuses them before our God day and night. Satan is in the condemnation business, and he seeks to make God's people feel guilty.

In His work of deception, Satan's tactics have never changed. He uses the same steps in deceiving the end-time church as he did the woman at the beginning. First, he gets the church to doubt God's Word. After doubting the Word, then comes disbelief; then disobedience to God's Word follows, which results in deception.

After the woman partook of the forbidden fruit, Adam had to make a choice. Would he go the way his Creator had made him, or would he choose to go the way of the beautiful bride that God had made for him? Adam had a divided heart and he had to make a choice. Since the Lord told the Laodiceans, I could wish you were cold or hot, I wonder if the Lord would rather deal with almost any kind of problem other than having to deal with His own people who have a divided heart?

After they transgressed God's commandment, Adam and Eve became rebels toward God. They tried to cover their nakedness with the works of their own hands. They tried to hide from God, and in their pride and rebellion they made excuses to God. Their rebellious souls would not take responsibility for their act of transgression against God and His Word. Adam blamed the woman that God gave to Him; thus, indirectly blaming God. The woman blamed the serpent for deceiving her.

Poor in Spirit / Rich toward God

That church must have thought being rich and wealthy was a high efficiency rating with God. But Jesus' direct response toward that church was an exact opposite account. Jesus said to her, do you not know "that you are…*poor*." She might have been rich to those who could see only with the senses, but she was poor to Him.

The Scriptures teach God's people to "walk by faith and not by sight," with complete confidence and dependence upon Him. A church organization that is "poor in spirit" represents the passion of the spirit that desires a *need* for a closer relationship with the Lover of her soul.

Riches and wealth provided the means for becoming a self-contained church. Paul spoke about the church in some locations that had a need of material subsistence. Going her own way led to selfishness where everything revolved around her. She did not see the need for serving other members in the Body of Christ.

You don't need to be poor in the things of this world to become "poor in spirit" (Matt. 5:3). The poor in spirit know they have many spiritual needs. But it is more difficult for those who are rich in material things to cultivate an attitude of complete dependence upon the Lord over all things.

A church may be rich and wealthy in material things and still be "poor in spirit" to the things of God. It is not easy, but it can be done. Proud people are full of unbelief and rebellion. Only the humble heart can have the faith that is needed to be submissive to the direction and guidance of the Spirit of Truth.

The Laodicean Church had a spiritual infirmity called "self-conceit" that had led her to a place of self-deceit, and Christ Jesus, who used to be the Lord and love of her life, was addressing the issue. She had become a useless joint in the Body that could no longer supply the needed help to other connecting members in the Body of Christ. The Lord Jesus Christ, as the Head over that spiritual organism that gave life to the Body, was the authority that determined the direction that the Laodicean Church should have taken.

She was not only spiritually poor, but Jesus stated that she was spiritually destitute, being "wretched, miserable, poor, blind, and naked." Jesus' desire was to instruct her in such a way that she could become rich toward Him. Jesus told her, "Buy from Me gold refined in the fire, that you may be rich; and white garments, that you may be clothed, that the shame of your nakedness may not be revealed; and anoint your eyes with eye salve, that you may see" (verse 18).

The Great Deception of God's People

The nation of Israel under the old covenant experienced deception many times in her long history as the chosen people of God, but the greatest deception was when she rejected her Messiah at His First Coming. Because religion deals with eternal values, the greatest deception to humanity is in the realm of religion.

There are all kinds of deception in the realm of the church. The church is Satan's favorite arena for his deceptive work. Religious cults, going under the banner of being Christian, believe that they are absolutely right when they are totally wrong. A deceiving religious spirit forms a mind-set in people's thinking toward not having a desire to rightly divide the Scriptures, and it is working with great effectiveness in the end-time church.

The Laodicean Church felt comfortable in her short but orthodox Christian tradition that she had inherited, but a church must keep her heart right toward God. "The heart is deceitful above all things, and desperately wicked; who can know it?" But the Lord was searching her heart and testing her mind (Jer. 17:9-10). In her self-complacency she got her eyes and heart away from the Lover of her soul.

The greatest church deception is a collective self-deception of being "the" church. Why? Because Christ has so much to offer the church, and the church of the Laodiceans, in her self-centered plans and agenda, was not taking advantage of it. She was not walking along the pathway of God's righteousness in Christ Jesus. Because of her feeling of self-importance through her inward self-centered thinking and reasoning, she sought for self-glory. Spiritual pride kept her from being nurtured by the Lord of the church into spiritual growth and development as a church organism.

Because it deals with the realm of eternity, religious deception is the greatest deception. The church has been commissioned by Christ to deliver people from a perishing, judgment-bound world and be set apart unto

God. One tactic that the enemy uses is an evil religious spirit that causes church leadership to compromise their personal Bible-based convictions in their faith, fervor and zeal toward the Christ of the church.

The enemy knows that he has but a short time to do his work of deception. He is sowing and multiplying religious error and Christian deception in any soil made available in the planting of his seeds of distrust, dissension, dispute and discord.

Since the world has more sparkle and glitter in these last days, an end-time church might be tempted to find a middle course. The command to obey the first and great commandment to "love the Lord your God with all your heart, with all your soul, and with all your mind" (Matt. 22:37) is a great challenge to the end-time church.

Though the enemy comes in like a flood, the Lord will raise up a standard against him. The Spirit of Truth is moving mightily in the end-time church. He is speaking to listening, sanctified hearts that have been called out of the world and are being separated unto God.

In the good fight of faith, there is no comfort zone, only boot camp and the battle zone. Spiritual food is the pure milk of the Word for those who need strong spiritual bones for Christian health. Solid spiritual food is for growth and development for those maturing to "have their (spiritual) senses exercised to discern both good and evil."

The church of peacemakers, ministering the gospel of peace and exalting the Prince of Peace, must fight the spiritual warfare of the soul-life against a common enemy where the mind of Christians becomes a battleground in enduring hardship as good soldiers of the Lord Jesus Christ. The Lord gives His soldiers "the sword of the Spirit, which is the word of God" (Eph. 6:17) to fight the battles in spiritual warfare.

Every person who has ever lived among people has been manipulated or deceived by someone. Little children want their own way, and by nature, they learn to become better at manipulation as they grow older. The con artist delights in deceiving people. But the greatest deceiver is the devil. He is "the great dragon" that deceives the whole world (Rev. 12:9).

Those who lose out on eternal life have become the victims of the greatest deception. But the devil's deception doesn't stop with the world. The Laodicean Church was allowing the thinking of the world to splash over into the church; thus, she was being deceived. It is right for the church to be in the world, for she is like a ship in the sea. But when the world gets into the church, it becomes like the sea in the ship, and the more water that gets in the ship, the more likely she will sink.

Riches as a Temptation for Selfishness

Money can be put to good use and open many doors in influencing spiritual pursuits and advancement in Christian service worldwide. In case of the church of the Laodiceans, wealth closed the church door to the influence of the Lord Jesus Christ, who was standing outside the door knocking. It was as if the closed door between Jesus and that church typified her attitude toward riches and wealth that was standing between her and the riches of God's grace in Christ Jesus. Her riches had become a dark cloud that overshadowed the church from enjoying the sunshine of God's love.

When any church thinks and declares, "I am rich, have become wealthy, and have need of nothing," she fits into the category of selfishness. Her focus becomes how she can use her riches for self-promotion and self-glory. The enemy uses riches as a temptation and God's people begin living more for the pleasures and glory of the present temporal kingdom of this world than the future joy and glory that the Bride is to have with her Bridegroom in the kingdom to come. Living only for the visible temporal blessings will cause a church to forget the invisible Lord who provides the blessing. The Bible says that Moses "endured as seeing Him who is invisible" (Heb. 11:27).

The church of the Laodiceans forgot about the debt of love and devotion that she owed to the Lover of her soul. Her heart and mind became fixed on temporal values over eternal realities. She began to measure her success as a church with the same method of evaluation that the world measures success—with visible, temporal values and benefits.

The deceitfulness of riches directs God's people down the pathway of misplaced emphasis, leading them to a sense of false security. If emphasis is placed upon living the good life, based solely upon material abundance of this world, it becomes a temptation to abide in self-indulgence and self-satisfaction in contrast to the message of the gospel of self-denial and cross-bearing.

If everything were put into proper prospective, Christ would receive the recognition and the honor in the midst of the good life. Is there a middle ground that a church can find between self-denial and self-indulgence? Is there a middle ground between going the way of the cross and serving Him at our own convenience and comfort? The middle ground between a wholehearted love for Jesus and not knowing Him or having any love for Him at all is a halfhearted love. The church of the Laodiceans found that middle ground, and the Lord had to judge her on the basis of being a "lukewarm" church.

Self-deception

Jesus told Peter, "You are not mindful of the things of God, but the things of men" (Matt 16:23). Sometimes we understand that which is right by seeing what is wrong. The things of men are the basis for the glory of men, where the self-life is at the center. Jesus said, "He who speaks from (of) himself seeks his own glory" (John 7:18a). A church seeking self-glory robs God of His glory in the midst of the end-time church.

Because the pride of life is the fleshly nature of "the old man," there are multitudes of proud, poor churches in America compared to the very few humble, rich churches. The things of God, as opposed to the things of men, are the basis for the glory of God. "But He who seeks the glory of the One who sent Him is true, and no unrighteousness is in Him" (v. 18b). Nothing by any means should rob God of the glory that belongs only to Him. The Lord said, "My glory I will not give to another" (Is. 42:8). The church of Laodicea exchanged the glory of God in her midst for the glory of gold in her boasting.

The ultimate purpose for Christ suffering our shame and rejection at Calvary is our sharing "all things" with Him (Rom. 8:32). The church, as an excited and ecstatic Bride, will one day be rewarded to share the glory with her exalted Bridegroom. The end-time church's prime objective should be to become God's humble servant in serving people for the glory of the Lord who commissioned her.

The Lord had blessed the church of the Laodiceans with financial blessings, but she had not gone very far in the spiritual journey of having fellowship with Jesus to the end. The Holy Spirit no longer was leading her into all truth. She had a beginning in the walk of faith, but she saw no need to go any further. That is indicative of a spirit of compromise against receiving the fullness of the gospel message as "revealed from faith to faith."

Her self-sufficient attitude brought about by an erroneous opinion of her self-importance before God indicated that she saw no need to diligently seek God. She saw no need to diligently study to rightly divide the Scriptures with the motive of presenting herself "approved to God." Pride seeks self-approval rather than approval from God. More attention was given to self-glory among one another within that church system than learning what was needed to give the glory to God.

Like the prodigal son, that rich church needed to "come to herself." She needed to rise up out of the pigpen of self-centeredness and become excited about finding the way back to the Father's house through fellowship with Jesus. A continual promotion of self-sufficiency led her along an independent course that led to self-deception.

Pride makes people think of themselves as being better or greater, whether anyone else agrees with them or not. She thought she was rich. The Lord didn't think so. He told her that she was "poor." Although she declared self-fulfillment, she was empty on the inside. Although she declared self-satisfaction, the Lord said that she was "miserable." She appeared to be self-sufficient in the material realm but she was full of insufficiency in the spiritual realm.

Pride is very deceptive to the self-life. Why would she say that she had arrived in the Christian journey when she had only begun? That is why the self-life should be denied in order to follow the Christ of the Scriptures unto the end. The purpose in continuing to pursue Him is that she might learn from Him and of Him, for He is the perfect Example to the church.

The gospel message presents a phenomenal challenge that takes more than a lifetime to fully understand. "Now I know in part, but then I shall know just as I also am known" (1 Cor. 13:12). If any church compares her self with Christ, as the true Example for Christian living, she would become submissive to His teachings, and there could be no room for spiritual pride. If she loved Him wholeheartedly, she would have kept His commandment to love one another, and not think of her self more highly than she ought to think. Only the proud in heart would take the challenge of the gospel message lightly.

The Deceitfulness of Riches

Things looked good from without for the Laodicean Church. In the parable of the seed and the sower, good seeds of God's Word were sown among the thorn seeds of the world. When both the wheat and the thorny tares sprang up, they both looked like strong young healthy plants for a while. But the thorny tares as "the cares of this world and the deceitfulness of riches choke the word, and [a church] becomes unfruitful" (Matt. 13:22).

The deceitfulness of riches caused that church to say, "I have need of nothing." The thorn-life of uncertainty in the deceitfulness of the riches can choke the life out of any healthy-looking plant. That's how the deceitfulness of riches manipulates God's people. It provides a lifestyle that is not one of self-denial, but one that caters to excessive self-indulgence with its different forms of self-centered living.

There is the test of worldly cares and riches that can promote a life in the comfort zone with its many material conveniences. When things become too easy, a believer has a more difficult time bringing the body under discipline. Then a halfhearted attitude and devotion toward the Christ of His church begins to take control.

Many things can delay God from reaching His ultimate purpose in Christ for the church, but few have more power to frustrate than the deceitfulness of riches. The end-time church has much to overcome, but the ease and comfort of life in the time of abundance and prosperity present a difficult barrier to overcome in meeting the requirements in receiving the promise that is waiting the overcoming church.

The Laodiceans' attitude toward the works of her own hands had taken her eyes and heart away from the finished work of Christ on the cross on her behalf. Like Aaron's golden calf at the base of Mount Sinai, the works of her own hands had become her idol, coming between her and the Lover of her soul.

"Anyone" in that lukewarm church organism was given an opportunity to overcome the deceitfulness of riches. After hearing His voice, they needed to open the door of their heart to the Lord. Coming before the Lord in a meek and contrite spirit would be going the opposite way from where the Laodicean Church was headed.

Jesus would share His reward of being an overcomer with anyone in that church that would accept the challenge of overcoming the deceitfulness of riches. There is only one true throne of authority in the universe and that is the throne of the Father. The Father shares His throne with His Son who overcame a God-rejecting world, and His Son shares His throne with His church who is overcoming a Christ-rejecting world. The reason the overcoming church may share it with the Father and the Son is because Christ's prayer in John 17:22 will be answered, "That they may be one just as We are one."

The unity of the church is based upon and designed after the unity of the Godhead. For unity, therefore, to become a reality for the end-time church, it must be accomplished by the work of the Godhead. The loving Father will answer the prayer of the Son of His love in motivating each church to lose her self-love by perfecting a wholehearted love toward the loveable Bridegroom by the work of the Spirit of love.

The value of something is the price that someone is willing to pay for it. Now the church organism that Christ purchased with His own blood (Acts 20:28) is more important to God than anything in the whole world. Every child of God in each church organization is of measureless value to the Lord. It might be compared to the value of a priceless antique vase, but the vase will only keep its value if it is not damaged in any way. That is why the unity of the church is so important.

Example of Solomon

The story of Solomon covers more than just the deceitfulness of riches. Solomon was king of Israel when she was at the peak of her power and glory. Solomon is a good example of a man that had everything this temporal, materialistic world could possibly offer; yet, he had become a skeptic and a despondent man according to the book of Ecclesiastics.

Like the Laodicean Church, Solomon had turned his eyes away from the eternal to things in the realm of the temporal. Yet he spoke of the futility of it all. He found no true satisfaction in the riches, wealth and fame in the temporal realm. The book of Ecclesiastes opens in verse 2 with these words: "Vanity of vanities," says the Preacher; "Vanity of vanities, all is vanity." The word "vanity" or "futility" occurs five times in that scripture. The book contains only twelve chapters and the word "vanity" or "futility" occurs thirty-six times.

The reason for everything being meaningless or senseless in life is found in the next verse of the book. "What profit has a man from all his labor in which he toils "under the sun?" (v. 3). The phrase "under the sun" occurs twenty-nine times in the book. So the book of Ecclesiastes covers those things in the materialistic, temporal, transitory realm.

Solomon, like the Laodicean Church, had taken his eyes off the God of eternal spiritual things, and he began to focus only on the temporal things under the sun. In spite of all of his riches, wealth, fame and privileges as a king to God's chosen people, Solomon could find no true satisfaction in the temporal, the transient materialistic world.

So much depends upon the focus of the heart. Solomon and the Laodicean Church had a heart for the temporal realm. Both had lost a wholehearted love toward the eternal God. Jesus taught, in His Sermon on the Mount, how God cares for and watches over the lilies of the field that have nothing more to do than to look beautiful in their own time.

Jesus went on to say that "even Solomon in all his glory was not arrayed like one of these" (Matt. 6:28-29). God has made everything beautiful (under the sun) in its time (Ecc. 3:11). Furthermore anything meaningful under the sun has its time which is like "a vapor that appears for a little time and then vanishes away" (James 4:14).

Through all the lofty opinions of the Laodicean Church's self-worth, ability and attainments in riches and wealth, merciful Jesus was on the outside, knocking on the church door. He was willing to give anyone in that church an opportunity to change his or her thinking away from the material and temporal realm and focus on the spiritual and the eternal realm in dining with Him in the Word. Only the meek and lowly that loved Him more than the opinions of men would hear His voice and respond by opening the doors of their hearts to the Savior of their soul.

Deception / Truth

As light is the only thing that can absorb darkness, truth is the only answer for lies and deception. Christ Jesus is the Truth that was sent from God as the light of the world. "In Him was life, and the life was the light of men. And the light shines in the darkness, and the darkness did not comprehend it" (John 1:4-5).

The opposite of truth is falsehood, dishonesty, distortion and deception, which are so prevalent in the realm of the religious world in these last days. This present evil age of darkness is saturated with remarks, sayings and statements that are misleading and untrue. Only the light of God's truth can penetrate and absorb the spiritual darkness in the hearts and minds of people in these last days. Liberating truth is found in the Scriptures; it is not out of reach of anyone. The unchanging Christ stood and knocked on the door of that church and said, "If anyone hears My voice…"

The devil is pictured in the Scriptures as one who deceives the whole world. What is deception? Those who are deceived will believe the lie over the truth. The lukewarm Laodiceans were in the twilight zone. The church was losing her love for walking with the Truth and walking in the truth. She thought that she had arrived at the right place, but she was going the wrong way.

If anyone in that church desired a right interpretation of the Scriptures, everything depended on having the right attitude of the heart toward the Christ of the Scriptures. There was a way that seemed right to that church, but she was headed the wrong way. The Laodicean Church proclaimed that she had need of nothing, but she needed to have a desire and a heart to please Jesus.

Salvation costs the church nothing. Each member comes into the saving knowledge of the Lord Jesus Christ by the free grace of God. *Christ paid it all.* But if that church is to walk in the saving knowledge of the Lord Jesus Christ, she must come to know Him as Truth. And truth has a price tag. Proverbs says, "*Buy* the truth and sell it not" (23:23).

As a whole, mankind, because of a soulish nature, opposes God's truth as revealed in His written Word, according to His Living Word, and by the Spirit of Truth. Followers of Christ will humble themselves and submit to the power and ability of the Spirit of Truth who is the Author of the Scriptures. He will lead and guide into all truth.

The messages from the pulpit to the rich Laodicean Church should have been a challenge for her to have a proper and personal response to the revelation of Christ's great love for her. That church should have continued to love Him, and not let anything of this world hinder that love, because He first loved her. That church needed to grow in the newness of love from the new birth to becoming full of the Holy Spirit. The more a church walks in His love for her, the more she enters into His passionate love toward her.

The Balance of Soul Prosperity

Though riches and wealth deceived the church at Laodicea, it is God's will that His people prosper in all things. "Beloved, I pray that *you may prosper in all things* and be in health, just as your soul prospers" (3 John 1:2). Like John, the elder, a church may pray for people to prosper in all things and be in health in this temporal life.

When God's people, however, enjoy the blessings of prospering in all things and have good health, they also need soul prosperity in order that they don't get puffed up in being God's privileged people by being blessed in the realm of the temporal.

When a church enjoys the privileges of God, she needs to humble her soul and be thankful to a compassionate and merciful God. Therefore, nothing is wrong with being prosperous in the Lord, but it should be "just as your soul prospers." A prosperous soul not only receives "the truth that is in you" where you are in Christ, but also "just as you walk in the truth" where you are moving on your foreordained course in Christ (v. 3). The truth of God's Word transforms the soul-life to walk humbly before God in health and prosperity in all bodily needs. The soul is to yield to the leading of the Spirit in truth.

Soul prosperity is needed on the side of the scales that represents eternity to balance out the temporal, material and physical blessings from God in time. "For what profit is it to a man if he gains the whole world, and loses his own soul? Or what will a man give in exchange for his soul?" (Matt. 16:26).

The Laodicean Church definitely was not representative of the glorious church that is depending upon the guidance of Holy Spirit to help her overcome the world. But anyone within that church that could hear His voice from without would open the door of a heart full of love toward Him. By dining with Him in fellowship, each would be headed in the right direction in becoming a member of the overcoming church.

One of the most distinguishing marks of the overcoming church is her soul prosperity. If God's people are "submitting to one another in the fear of God," they are experiencing soul prosperity, where souls are submitted in humility before the Lord. The overcoming church is "poor in spirit" but rich toward God. She exhibits an example of individual and collective church humility toward God and His people.

Christ-like humility is something that money cannot buy and it is that "which is very precious in the sight of God" (1 Pet. 3:4b). It is a gentle and quiet spirit that comes only at a very high price through sacrificial love. As the future Lamb's wife, the overcoming church is being trained and prepared as a servant to all for a royal position with the Lamb of God for eternity. A humble attitude is needed for such an exalted position in Christ. A prosperous soul, therefore, is a humble soul that is walking in the truth.

A church under the leadership of her functional Head, Christ Jesus, will never have an attitude of "I have need of nothing." As members of a Body of true believers, let us receive help from one another as we see the need to pray for one another. As members of the family of God, we have need for the gifts and callings that are needed to help one another. Everyone in that church had an opportunity to come before Him in wholehearted worship and fellowship in doing His will, but not everyone would answer His call to open the door.

"Blessed are the poor in spirit, for theirs is the kingdom of heaven...Blessed are the meek, for they shall inherit the earth...Blessed are the merciful, for they shall obtain mercy" (Matt. 5:3-7). Even though that church had no lack or no need in the realm of temporal, material things, that attitude should not have been carried over to her needs in the realm of eternal, spiritual things.

Nothing should prevent a church from achieving the complete redemption that has been provided for her in Christ Jesus. The Laodicean Church needed to have a greater realization of the reality of Jesus functioning in the life of each church member. Experiencing a close fellowship with a resurrected Christ is enjoying the eternal riches of God in Christ. Jesus in His tender mercies and loving kindness was offering those riches to anyone who saw a need for them and would open the door to Him.

Chapter 7

The Greatest Riches

A Need to Learn the True Riches of His Grace

*"I counsel you to buy from Me gold refined in the fire, **that you may be rich**; and white garments, that you may be clothed, that the shame of your nakedness may not be revealed; and anoint your eyes with eye salve, that you may see"* (verse 18).

The Lord points to the problem of the church of the Laodiceans in verse 17. The first half of the verse is what she thought about her self. "Because you say, 'I am rich, have become wealthy, and have need of nothing.'" The last half of the verse is what the Lord thought about her. "Do (you) not know that you are wretched, miserable, poor, blind, and naked."

Those two opinions are at opposite ends of the right and wrong spectrum of the thinking of the Lord and the thinking of a church called by His name. "Can two walk together unless they are agreed?" (Amos 3:3). Because the Laodicean Church was definitely not in agreement with Him, she could not be walking together with Him. How many churches are walking together as one with God in these last days? The Voice of Personified Truth gave the commandment to love one another and the Spirit of Truth helps the end-time church with the means and ability to do so.

Of the innumerable church organizations, each church group should have a desire to walk with God. Out of that desire, each group would then become one church organism while walking together with Him. But that was not happening with the Laodicean Church. That church thought that she was absolutely the right church and had need of nothing to prove her claim. Because of her self-sufficiency and pride, that church was at the bottom of His approval rating as a lukewarm church. But in the Laodicean Church organization there must have been humble members within the church organism that would repent, hear His voice, and open the door.

Receiving Christ begins the walk into the saving knowledge of Christ. "But as many as received Him, to them He gave the right [authority] to become children of God" (John 1:12). The Laodicean Church knew that the unchurched had spiritual needs, but she was a church that thought she had actually arrived. She, without a doubt, did not understand the depth and challenge of the gospel message for she said, "I have need of nothing."

Resisted but Not Forsaken

The Laodicean Church is a prime example of how God resists the proud and lofty. It should be recognized that Christ hadn't forsaken that church that was full of self-conceit, but He was rightly resisting her. In reading the Scriptures, sometimes so much rests upon just one word. "God resists the proud." It does not say God forsakes the proud.

Because God resists the proud, the spiritual problems of many end-time churches are too numerous to tell. I appreciate the fact and I'm thankful that the Father of mercy does not forsake the proud. If He did, most of us would be in terrible trouble!

At one point in the wilderness journey, God wanted to forsake the proud and rebellious nation of Israel, but Moses interceded for her. The Laodicean Church was full of self-centeredness and self-conceit. But merciful Jesus, as the mediator and intercessor of a better covenant, would bring a remnant of repentant hearts to comply with the Father's ultimate objective and destiny for the glorious, overcoming church.

The problem was a question of relationship—the relationship between Christ and one rebellious church. That relational problem corresponds to, and resembles in appearance, the problem that Jesus had with the nation of Israel. Jesus came to His own people who had a lofty opinion of themselves as the chosen, privileged people of God. The nation of Israel rejected her Messiah in His First Coming. Though there is no mutual relationship between the nation of Israel and her King at the time of this writing, the prophetic Scriptures of God's old covenant people, Israel, with her promised Messiah in her Promised Land shall one day be fulfilled.

The nation of Israel had rejected Him, and the Laodicean Church was neglecting Him. Because of her lofty, independent attitude, the church of the Laodiceans ignored her mutual relationship in the eternal worth of the Lover of her soul. She had a halfhearted, lukewarm devotion toward Him compared to His wholehearted love for her.

The solution to her problem is given in verse 18. It is not the proud in heart but "the poor in spirit" that becomes rich in God. Her inward thoughts that were directed toward her own merits had turned her thinking away from the worth of her Lord, who was standing outside knocking on that church door. Apparently that church was successful from all outward appearance, but God always rewards the faithful, and not necessarily what religious people might call success. "For what is highly esteemed among men is an abomination in the sight of God" (Luke 16:15).

In worshiping the goddess of success before the eyes of the church world, there are some Christian ministers who believe that the end justifies the means. If they can obtain what they think is a "good" end, it matters not what kind of unrighteous means that they might use to achieve that end. Like the Laodicean Church, they are deceived.

Paul compared the Christian life in the church with an athletic contest. If you do not play the game according to the rules, you will be disqualified. You cannot wear the winner's crown unless you obey all the rules for running the Christian race (2 Tim. 2:5). The many rules can be summed up in the one all-inclusive rule of true Christian love.

Jesus pointed out in the Sermon on the Mount that the religious leaders, who perform religious duties to be seen of men for self-glory, have already received the temporal reward that they were seeking. The Laodicean Church did not know her own proud, deceitful heart, and that is true of many today that think they have a mandate from God to do His work, no matter by what unscriptural method or unchristian character they are doing it.

Riches of His Grace

Attitude is most important because it is decisive. The attitude of that self-sufficient church was not being "poor in spirit." The "poor in spirit" recognize a continual need for a fuller knowledge of God and the things of God. Because she saw no need for a continual walk with Him, Jesus rebuked that church in a very blunt and direct manner. Her rebellious soul had not been put under His control. She needed an experience of the working power of God's marvelous grace!

Paul said that "by the grace of God I am what I am" and he laid down his life in commitment to Christ. According to 2 Corinthians 5:21-6:1, it was important to Paul that God's people would not receive the grace of God in vain. For the good work of the church together with Christ is based upon His precious sinless life that became "sin for us, that we might become the righteousness of God in Him."

Paul is saying that salvation is based upon Christ becoming sin with our sinfulness, and there is nothing that we, as the church, can do to merit God's righteousness in Him. But based upon God's righteousness in Him, different church groups can become "workers together with Him" proving the value and usefulness of having a working knowledge of their indebtedness toward God's grace.

The Laodicean Church needed to know her accountability toward God's grace. A good theological acronym for God's grace is **G**od's **R**iches **A**t **C**hrist's **E**xpense. Living the abundant Christian life on Christ's unlimited expense account makes the church a limitless debtor to Christ's great sacrificial love toward her. We are born to die, but Jesus came to die and be resurrected from the dead in order that we might be born again to everlasting life.

Because the church is indebted to God's great plan of salvation that He has provided for her, she should keep a faithful, steadfast heart toward Him from the beginning to the end of the Christian journey. The Laodicean Church was falling short in her loving obligations of appreciation toward His loving kindness and tender mercies.

Jesus taught His disciples to lose their soul-life for His sake (Matt. 16:24). By her not denying or losing her soul-life (her self-will for God's will, her natural mind for the mind of Christ through a renewing process, and her self-centered emotions for God's self-giving love) for His sake, the church at Laodicea was found wanting. Jesus told her that she was "wretched, miserable, poor, blind, and naked" (v. 17b).

Jesus was telling that church with her self-sufficient attitude that she was inadequate and lacking in many areas. Calling her wretched was the Lord's resistance to her self-exaltation. True greatness is found in true riches. The true riches of God are the eternal riches of His marvelous, matchless grace.

Though in her pride she boasted of self-fulfillment, she was miserable and empty on the inside. Self-satisfaction does not give anyone true satisfaction and contentment. She was poor because of self-glorying, and her temporal self-worth made her worthless in the eyes of the Lord. She became destitute in not accepting, regarding or becoming accountable to the riches of God's grace.

"For the grace of God that brings salvation has appeared to all men, teaching us that, denying ungodliness and worldly lusts, we should live soberly, righteously, and godly in the present age" (Tit. 2:11-12). The grace of God, therefore, is teaching the church to deny the affections toward the things of the world in order that she may walk in a committed loving relationship with the Lover of her soul.

The church at Laodicea had become poor in eternal values because her heart was in the pursuit of riches and wealth of temporal values. Gold and silver are corruptible things. They will perish with the using. That church was "not redeemed with corruptible things, like silver or gold." The cleansing and purifying power of "the precious blood of Christ, as of a lamb without blemish and without spot" are the riches of His grace.

Good spiritual eyesight is important in the work of the Lord, but she had become spiritually "blind." Jesus said, "You shall know the truth and the truth shall set you free." She had to know some truth from the Scriptures, but she knew nothing of the truth about her self. Pride seeks self-approval rather than seeking to be approved by Him.

She was blinded and in bondage to her self-importance, which happened to be a church system of operation that only functioned for self-glory. The invitation that Jesus gave to the Laodicean Church in verse 20 was to those with repentant hearts in that lukewarm church organism.

The church of the Laodiceans' spiritual pride is what led to her self-righteousness. Her self-righteousness revealed her soulish nakedness. Only God can adequately clothe the nakedness of a sinful soul with His holiness, as He separates church people unto Himself. She had a need to be clothed with God's righteousness, but she did not know it. She saw no need to seek "the kingdom of God and His righteousness."

1. Buy from Me

Where are true riches found? If a church wanted to have true riches, the Lord would say, "Buy from Me." Only in Christ can the eternal riches of God's grace be found. Only a church that is "poor in spirit" will see the need to purchase what God has to offer—true riches in Him.

The Lord could have made her rich with His riches. The eternal spiritual riches of God in Christ are more challenging and exciting to obtain than the fleeting material riches of this present, temporal world. Jesus' desire was to fellowship and instruct "anyone who would hear His voice" and become rich in Him by dining with Him.

Because Christ has already paid the account with His blood sacrifice, all blessings become as a gift from the Giver of all good things to the believer.

But when it comes to cultivating the fruit of Christian character, we must come to God and pay the asking price of having a wholehearted love for Him. Before we can enter into that love, loving like He loves, we must pass the tests and trials with the attitude "that all things work together for good to those who love God, to those who are the called according to His purpose."

In the parable of the wise and foolish virgins in Matthew 25:1-12, the Bridegroom delayed His Coming, and "they all slumbered and slept." That meant that all ten bridesmaids were caught unaware at the moment of His return. But He said that He was going to come at a time that the church would not expect Him.

What was the difference between the wise and the foolish—only one thing? The foolish did not have the supply of oil necessary to keep their lamps burning. Oil is a type of the Holy Spirit. Only He can keep the fiery passions of love burning in the waiting bride-elect, watching for her coming Bridegroom.

"Then all those virgins arose and trimmed their lamps. "And the foolish said to the wise, 'Give us some of your oil, for our lamps are going out.' But the wise answered, saying, 'No, lest there should not be enough for us and you; but go rather to those who sell, and **buy for yourselves**.' And while **they went to buy**, the bridegroom came, and those who were ready went in with him to the wedding; and the door was shut." Truth has its own price tag. Now is the time to "**buy the truth** and do not sell it" (Prov. 23:23).

Committed Christians live a life different from the world, which does not know the grace of God in Christ Jesus. Christians, therefore, should so live their life by the free grace of God so that the world does not look upon the grace of God as being something cheap. "Christ loved the church and gave Himself for her" (Eph. 5:25). What should be a church's free-will response to that kind of love? That poor, rich lukewarm church was a debtor to Christ's self-giving love toward her.

Now is the time to act upon the veracity of His words. God says, "Buy from Me," for there will be an hour when it will be too late to buy from Him. God stills honors all of heaven's credit cards of grace endorsed and sealed by the blood of Jesus. The amount of credit is unlimited to what God's people might charge on God's credit card of grace through faith. God works everything out according to the riches of His grace.

Christ Jesus, as the Grace of God, has already paid the price for the fullness of our redemption. Buying from God is not only about the new things received but it is also about the old things that a church is able to put off. God is selling the eternal riches of His grace for the price of putting off the poor, old corruptible fleshly nature.

Paul wrote to the Ephesian Church telling her that she needed to "put off the old man" (Col. 3:9). The reason was that old soulish nature inherited from Adam is a nature "which grows corrupt according to the deceitful lusts" (4:22). All fleshly, deceitful lusts are a product of Satan's lie to Eve, "You shall not surely die." The old nature is identified with a condemned life, which is the corruptible soulish life of the first man, Adam.

Paul further explains to the Ephesian Church that it is through the renewing process of "the spirit of your mind" that she would be able to "put on the new man which was created according to God, in true righteousness and holiness" (vv. 23-24). Putting on the new man is putting on the newness of His resurrection life, which is the product of truth. The new-man nature, therefore, is also identified with a life, the incorruptible, resurrected (zoe) life of the Second Man, Christ Jesus.

The Holy Spirit is always ready to clothe the meek and lowly with the righteousness of God in Christ Jesus. That church needed to hunger and thirst for God! A "hunger and thirst after righteousness" is a hunger and thirst for Christ as God's righteousness. He gives true meaning to the Christian life. He is the objective for Christian living. In Him are the eternal riches of God. Without Him, that poor, rich church was spiritually bankrupt. Justification or true satisfaction cannot be found in self-righteousness.

Christ was looking out for the eternal best interests for anyone in the Laodicean Church who could respond to His voice. It may come forth as a paradox in our thinking, but the free riches of His grace can only be purchased from God. Any good works that a church may do are done by the grace of God through faith. Only people that God has made "good" in Christ can do good works by faith toward Christ.

The Laodicean Church needed to buy daily from Him that which He was selling. The five foolish virgins waited until it was too late to buy. Their lamps were going out, and the Greek word for "going out" in verse 8 is the same word translated "quench" in "do not quench the Spirit" (1 Thess. 5:19). Though the Holy Spirit had not forsaken the church of the Laodiceans, the work of the Holy Spirit had been resisted, grieved and quenched from exalting Christ to and through that church.

The Holy Spirit was the One who was able to prepare the five wise virgins to be ready for the Lord's coming. When death is at hand, this world's riches are unimportant. When the thought of the Lord's quick return is at hand, there is a need to have the right focus. "O Holy Spirit enlarge our hearts for Jesus. May we have a whole heart directed toward the Lover of our soul."

The close encounter of the five wise bridesmaids almost missing it shows the weakness of the flesh at a time of darkness when He appears. But the Bride of the wedding needs to be ready. She is the one that gives the signal that it is time for the wedding party to begin. "Let us be glad and rejoice and give Him glory, for the marriage of the Lamb has come, and His wife has made herself ready."

There won't be a wedding until the Bride is ready. Heaven's focus is upon the work of the Holy Spirit in the preparation of the church. Why is it taking the Bride so long to get ready? Jesus said to His three sleeping disciples at an intense moment during His time of prayer in the garden of Gethsemane, "The spirit is willing but the flesh is weak."

That church needed a new focus where her eyes and heart would be steadfast toward Jesus. She needed a new understanding of Him as the glorious Bridegroom to the overcoming church as revealed in the Scriptures. She needed to buy from God what is needed to have fellowship with the Lord over the church, the coming Bridegroom. She was a very needy church!

Attitude Means Everything

There is nothing wrong with being wealthy. It's the attitude that usually goes along with it that is wrong. When the Israelites were delivered from Egyptian bondage, God saw to it that His people left Egypt as a wealthy nation. But God warned Israel of the importance of having a right attitude toward her wealth. "And you shall remember the LORD your God, for it is He who gives you power to get wealth" (Deut. 8:14-18). God's people do not need to become the servants of mammon.

The Lord wanted the nation of Israel to have an attitude of gratitude toward Him for the way that He protected her and cared for her in bringing her out of Egyptian bondage through the wilderness journey. If a prosperous church doesn't express her thankfulness to the Lord, who gives all good things, she, in her ingratitude toward God, will forget God's goodness to her, as did the nation of Israel. She will become a "lukewarm" church.

The Laodicean Church's attitude expressed that she was trusting in her riches more than she was trusting in God. The attitude of the world toward the rich varies from hate to envy. Hate and envy appeared as ugly and vile twin sisters against Jesus. The religious leaders of the nation of Israel were filled with hate and envy toward Him. They had a heart problem toward God that caused an attitude problem toward Jesus of Nazareth. They rejected their Messiah!

The Laodicean Church's selfish attitude toward riches and wealth gave her the glory, rather than the Lord who provided the riches. God resists the proud that trust in their riches. The right focus, however, is not upon the material riches of this world but upon the true riches of God's grace in Christ Jesus.

Her interest and attention should not have been on her material self-worth, but on the greatness and importance of His eternal worth. The focus of the bride-elect is "looking unto Jesus, the author and finisher of our faith" (Heb. 12:2a). The bride-elect's attitude, therefore, is not one that is self-centered but a self-giving horizontal commitment toward other members in the Body of Christ. Her primary and supreme interest that makes all of this possible, however, is her vertical focus on the church's Mediator and High Priest who is sitting at the right hand of God.

2. Gold Refined in Fire

If that church wanted to become truly rich, God would bring her forth as pure gold refined in fire. The Laodiceans took pride and had confidence in their riches, but the Lord would show her how to obtain true riches. "These [trials] have come so that your faith—of greater worth than gold, which perishes even though refined by fire—may be proved genuine and may result in praise, glory and honor when Jesus Christ is revealed" (1 Pet. 1:7 NIV). God's true riches will be purified through trials and testing that is of greater worth than gold that perishes. Do you look on a trial and test as greater riches than gold that perishes or "count it all joy when you fall into various trials?" God has a purpose for bringing His church through the wilderness of trials and testing.

True Christianity is not just another religion among the many religions of the world. Christianity should make God's redeemed people aware of their union with the oneness of the Godhead in Christ. But it takes the melting power of the fire of God's Word in testing and trials to make this happen. All things may be justified before God through the cleansing and purifying fire of His Word. All things are accountable to God through the justifying and judgment fire of His Word.

Elijah challenged the prophets of Baal and the people of Israel on Mt. Carmel. He said, "You call on the name of your gods, and I will call on the name of the Lord; and the God who answers by fire, He is God...the fire of the Lord fell and consumed the burnt sacrifices" (1 Kin. 18:24, 36). The fire that justified that Elijah served the true God was the same fire that condemned the false prophets of Baal.

The God that answered by fire under the old covenant is the same God that will also respond by the purifying and refining fire of tests and trials under the new covenant. The Laodicean Church could be purged from her self-centeredness through experiencing the fiery trials of life, which Peter calls being much more precious than gold that perishes though it is tested by fire.

The Lord is waiting for a purified treasure that has been refined in the fire of trials and tribulations. Relationships that have been refined by holy fire become precious, prized and permanent relationships. That includes the greatest relationship of all, which is the relationship of the church with her Lord. Concerning His people, God said that He would "refine them as silver is refined, and test them as gold is tested" as He would bring them into the fire (Zech. 13:9). Shadrach, Meschach and Abednego were not saved from the furnace of fire. They were saved and brought through in the test of the fiery furnace.

Comparison of His Word with Refining Fire

The benefits and advantages of God's Word are too numerous to tell, but some benefits may be told through the properties of fire. There is an abundance of sanctified energy in the fire of God's Word. "Is not My word like a fire?" (Jer. 23:29).

Since the Word of God is like fire, it has two sides. It is either friend or foe. The church of the Laodiceans had a need to take God and His Word seriously. One time the preached Word saved the people in that church and served them well; now that same Word of God was judging the church and challenging her to repent and change her presumptuous ways.

Fire can be one of man's greatest friends, and it also can be one of man's worst enemies. Fire can purify and cleanse or fire can purge and eliminate. The fire that warms our homes and cooks our meals is also the same fire that can destroy and annihilate us. The same Word of God that justified the Laodicean Church from her sins was also judging her for her sin.

What are the distinctive features of fire in God's Holy Word? The Laodicean Church tried to find a middle ground with emotions divided between love for God and love for this world's riches and wealth. Her emotions were no longer set on fire by the Holy Spirit for Jesus. She was a lukewarm church and she did not realize or recognize it.

The church of Laodicea had been confronted and rebuked because of her divided heart and rebellious soul by the God of her salvation. God's riches are refined through acting on the Word of God in the fiery trials of life in becoming pure before God as gold ore is refined in fire to make it pure.

God refines and purifies each soul to the image of Christ through the fire of His transforming Word. Since true riches come through the fiery trials of being obedient to God's Word, comparisons can be made between the properties of fire and the exercise of God's Word. God's Word, like fire, can mold and transform a soul for the glory of God. God's Word can also penetrate, discern and judge the soul-life.

The same divine fire that was working with the prophet Jeremiah in the purifying of his soulish nature was working against the nation of Israel in judgment against her rebellious nature. In his discouragement, Jeremiah was tempted to forsake the work that God had called him to do—but he couldn't! Jeremiah understood the message. He said, "But His word was in mine heart as a burning fire shut up in my bones." Jeremiah was experiencing cleansing and purging by the fiery trials of life as a minister of God's Word. That was the purifying and purging fire of God's Word that dwells within, and it burned within Jeremiah's heart until he had discharged the mission that God had called him to do. God "makes His angels spirits, and His ministers a flame of fire" (Heb. 1:7).

The church of the Laodiceans was not taking the God of His Word seriously. That was Eve's mistake in the Garden of Eden. In reference to the end-time church, Jesus said, "Remember Lot's wife!" The more a church respects and loves the Word of God, the more she respects and loves the God of His Word.

The same heat that softens the clay also hardens the clay. That church had become like hardened clay in the Potter's hand. The members of the church needed to humble themselves and be changed by the transforming power of God's unchanging Word. The Living Word of God said, "He who is not with Me is against Me, and he who does not gather with Me scatters abroad" (Matt. 12:30). There is no "lukewarm" middle ground in the relationship of loving worship and Christian service to Him.

The church of the Laodiceans should have maintained a steadfast heart toward the truth of God's Word. There was no need for her to suffer the consequences for neglecting it. She had a need to experience the true riches of God through the refining fire of His spoken words. The gospel message that justifies the repentant is the same message that judges and condemns the unrepentant.

The mind and heart of that church had been drawn away from dining with Him on the food of God's Word. There was a need for her to learn to live "by every word that proceeds from the mouth of God." From the mouth of God come His words through His breath into the newborn spirit of the believer.

Christ Jesus, as the *Logos*, "who is in the bosom of the Father," is the totality of God's Word, which is forever settled in heaven. But the *rhema* is that portion of God's total Word that has been empowered by the Holy Spirit to do what it was sent to do. With a repentant heart and a right attitude, anyone in that church could have received overcoming faith through dining with God's Living Word. It is faith in the Word of God that transforms the soul-life. The clay is not holding God's truth in its grasp. In reality, it is Truth, as the Potter, that molds the clay for God's glory in His grasp.

Likewise, the resurrected Christ spoke the Word to two of His disciples along the road to Emmaus. When He disappeared out of their sight, they concluded, "Did not our heart burn within us...while he opened to us the Scriptures?" There is nothing lifeless about fire. It clearly declares the enthusiasm and vital force of spiritual life through the energy of His inspiring flaming Word. The love for God's Word supplies the spiritual energy needed to bring God's people through every trial. The love of that church for Christ needed to be hot like fire, which burns on but never burns out.

Fire can be fascinating. God appeared to Moses and Ezekiel, to their amazement, as fire. The New Testament apostles in the book of Acts witnessed the revival fire of God's Word in their ministry. Revival movements, which have been experienced through the Word of God, have come and gone down through church history; "but the word of our God stands forever" (Is. 40:8). His truth is marching on through the revival fires of His end-time church.

Wherever the Word of the Lord is received in humility and acted upon in faith, there is revival fire. Whether it was under the old covenant or the new covenant, the fire of God's Word is not only significant for its illuminating power but also for its purifying, justifying and transforming power. The glowing fire from the altar of incense that was located in the holy place before the second veil in the Tabernacle represents our sanctified emotions. The incense from that altar represents heartfelt love for Him. The aroma of a smoking coal of incense was taken from the altar by the high priest as he went before the presence of God into the Holy of Holies once each year.

The glowing heat of God's spoken Word has set believing hearts aflame toward God down through the centuries. The hearts of the prophets under the old covenant and Christians under the new covenant still beat in response to the call of God. The church at Laodicea needed that kind of heartbeat toward God's call. The Lord was not behind the pulpit. He was on the outside, knocking on a door of a church that had been closed to Him, where anyone that heard His voice might dine with Him as God's Truth.

Though the Lord over the church was standing on the outside, the Holy Spirit as Lord in the church was on the inside working to convict repentant hearts. Jesus will only come in and reign over a repentant heart that accepts His invitation. The Holy Spirit strives with a lost world and a lukewarm church in order that each might experience "repentance toward God and faith toward our Lord Jesus Christ" (Acts 20:21).

A fire may not put out much light or heat; it may just crackle and pop. But there is still something amazing about the energy of fire. A spark indicates life, and all it takes is a spark of God's anointed Word to set a soul aflame for God. There was hope for repentant hearts in the lukewarm church of the Laodiceans.

There is a corresponding relationship between justifying light and judgment fire. As God is Light, He is also a consuming fire. Fire illuminates; fire purges; fire purifies or fire consumes. It depends upon how a church relates herself in conformity to the Holy Scriptures. If used aright, Bible fire will purify and set the repentant heart in any church on the right pathway.

Going through the Purifying and Refining Process

Why does a church need to go through the purifying and refining process? Why did God, whose very nature is love, create a people that He knew would transgress His commandment? Why did He foreordain a plan for redemption in Christ before the fall took place? Jesus of Nazareth was the Lamb slain from the foundation of the world.

God did not create evil. He created a beautiful and gifted angel named *Lucifer* that became proud and rebellious before God. The name of that fallen angel was changed to Satan; he is the source of all evil in the universe. Through the foreknowledge of God, He allowed it. But if it were not for the existence of evil, the church would have never come to know and appreciate the kindness, mercy, grace and goodness of God. The Father uses the devil to bring forth His masterpiece in Christ Jesus by the power of the Holy Spirit.

In an evil setting, the church experiences suffering for the cause of Christ. Agape love "suffers long and is kind." God's suffering Servant of Isaiah 53 was predestined to take center stage in the course of human events, from the center cross to the center throne, for the glory of God. As the Father's predestined, perfect Example to the church, Jesus Christ of Nazareth showed the divine paradox that the way up is down.

That church organization thought of God as an isolated being who is totally immune to poor, suffering humanity. Her self-sufficient attitude had closed her church door to the Lord. What touches God's people touches the Son. And what touches the Son and His people touches the Father. "For he who touches you touches the apple of His eye," says the Lord (Zech. 2:8b). The Son of God has identified Himself with two different people under two different covenants: first, He is the King of the Jews and then, He is the Head of His church, the Body of Christ.

Jesus' work with the church has caused God much suffering, sorrow and grief. But "in the ages to come He might show the exceeding riches of His grace in His kindness toward us in Christ Jesus...For we are His workmanship, created in Christ Jesus for good works, which God prepared beforehand that we should walk in them" (Eph. 2:7, 10).

God will make known "to the principalities and powers in the heavenly places, according to the eternal purpose which He accomplished in Christ Jesus our Lord" (3:10-11). But the Father's masterpiece in Christ Jesus could not have been brought forth without pain and suffering. God needed to add the ingredient of endurance through suffering in the complete transforming process for the overcoming church.

Knowing Him "in the fellowship of His sufferings" is where the church gets to know Him in His tender loving care as she walks with Him in the purifying process of refining fires. Mutual suffering with Him will draw the church closer to Him.

> I walked a mile with pleasure,
> She chattered all the way,
> But left me none the wiser
> For all she had to say.
>
> I walked a mile with Sorrow,
> And ne'er a word said He,
> But, O, the things I learned from Him
> When Sorrow walked with me!

In times of sorrow, you would like to find words that would comfort the discouraged, the dejected or the devastated, but many times there are none that can help. But when you feel the loving presence of the "Man of sorrows and acquainted with grief" walking with you, it makes a difference.

The church of the Laodiceans had a need. In the physical comfort, leisure and pleasure of her riches and wealth, she saw no need for His comforting power through suffering. Her attitude of self-sufficiency had shut her away from the Lord who can "be touched with the feeling of our infirmities [weaknesses]" (Heb. 4:15 KJV).

That church's purity of faith toward Him would have been "much more precious than gold that perishes, though it is tested by fire." The refining riches that come from God transform the lives of people who are precious in His sight. True riches come from being refined through the fire of God's Word that the church might be more like Jesus.

Like the church of the Laodiceans, many Christians in these last days are holding dear to their hearts this world's temporal riches that perish. 2 Timothy 3:1-4 lists eighteen moral defects that would be very noticeable in the end-time church. Out of the eighteen moral defects, at least five that were apparent in the church of the Laodiceans were "love of self, love of money, boasters, proud" and "lovers of pleasures rather than lovers of God." That would indicate that God must oppose and resist sinful pleasures for the love and devotion of His people in these last days.

Nothing is suggested in regard to love of pleasure in the statement of that church, but the love of self is the soil for the seeds of the love of money to take root. Out from the leaves of the money tree, the love of different kinds of pleasure can be found.

3. White Garments, That You May Be Clothed

The Lord was offering the kind of clothing needed for the overcomer to qualify "for the marriage of the Lamb." For the Laodicean Church to be clothed with white garments, she first needed to rid herself of the filthy rags of her self-righteous acts, which would dry up and fade away as fast as Adam and Eve's fig leaf covering.

"White raiment" refers to the purity of the spotless and clean nature of the linen wedding garment. "That He might present her to Himself a glorious church, not having spot or wrinkle or any such thing, but that she should be holy and without blemish" (Eph. 5:27).

There won't be any spots, wrinkles or stains of sin on the wedding garment of the Bride of Christ. God's ultimate purpose for the church is awesome. Only our heavenly Father, who foreordained it through His manifold wisdom, is capable of putting forth a masterful plan for creating such a glorious workmanship in Christ.

"The fine linen, clean and bright, for the fine linen is the righteous acts of the saints." Each righteous act will be a spiritual thread of fine linen holding the wedding garment together. The heavenly hosts are also clothed in fine linen, white and clean garments, riding on white horses. Both the Bride and the armies of God wear white. It is difficult to keep white garments clean in a dirty world. They can get soiled so easily. They, therefore, need to be cleansed daily "with the washing of water by the word."

Why has it taken so long for God to put an end to all the misery and suffering of the people of this world? It all centers on God's creative plan and strategy for the church. God has a glorious predestined plan and purpose for His overcoming, glorious church. Could self-centered, end-time churches, like the Laodiceans, be responsible for the delaying of His Coming and the prolonging of suffering in the world?

Jesus' teachings to the church and His prayer to the Father was for that purpose and to that end. "I have given them the glory that you gave me, that they may be one as we are one: I in them and you in me. May they be brought to complete unity to let the world know that you sent me and have loved them even as you have loved me (John 17:22-23 NIV). The church needs to get with it and become submissive to the Holy Spirit, who will help her make herself ready.

"Let us be glad and rejoice and give Him glory, for the marriage of the Lamb has come, and His wife has made herself ready." All the prophetic signs of His Second Coming have been fulfilled and are being fulfilled daily, but the Bride is slow in making herself ready. But soon the Bride and the Spirit will say, "Come." "Even so, come, Lord Jesus." The Bride needs to get herself ready. All heaven is waiting for the consummation of the Age. When the Bride has made herself ready and the glory of her story begins, then judgment will be set in motion to bring the misery of a sin-cursed world to an end.

4. The Shame of Your Nakedness

There was a need for the nakedness of the Laodicean Church to be covered before God. The righteousness of God comes by faith in the atoning death of Christ for our transgressions. It is first revealed as imputed righteousness through the blood of Jesus as a covering for sins. Her nakedness meant that she was trying to stand in her self-righteousness and was not being clothed with God's righteousness.

The temptation of religious pride was for her to establish her righteousness before God through the keeping of church rules. Church rules are needed for orderliness and guidelines within a church in working with one another, but keeping them will not make a church member righteous before God. The shame of her nakedness kept her from being qualified to wear the white garments of God's righteousness. In her neglect she was not applying the principles of Christ's atoning blood sacrifice to her life.

She needed a covering for her nakedness. A covering for her naked-ness goes back to the very beginning with Adam's transgression of God's law. An atoning blood sacrifice is at the very heart of the story of redemp-tion for God's people. It began with the fall of Adam in the Genesis account of creation.

After partaking of the fruit from the forbidden tree, Adam and Eve found themselves naked of God's righteousness. From the beginning God established that there is only one choice, one offering, and one sacrifice acceptable unto Him. That is the supreme substitutionary sacrifice of the Lamb of God "who takes away the sin of the world!" (John 1:29b). At the end of the Church Age, the overcoming, glorious church will be clothed with God's righteousness in Christ Jesus. She will be called "the Lamb's wife."

The first two acts of Adam and Eve's rebellious soul were to clothe themselves of their sinful nakedness and hide from God's divine presence. "Then the eyes of both of them were opened, and they knew that they were naked; and they sewed fig leaves together and made themselves cover-ings…Also for Adam and his wife the LORD God made tunics of skin, and clothed them" (Gen. 3:7, 21).

God rejected the fig leaf covering that Adam and Eve had sewed together. God clothed them with "tunics of skin." The covering of fig leaves represented "the things of men." It was by the works of their own hands. God's covering with the tunics of skin was "of the things of God" (Matt. 16:23). An animal sacrifice was required—likely an innocent lamb—before the sinful nakedness of Adam and Eve could be covered before God. A fallen, proud bridegroom and his bride had to humbly depend upon God for a covering to their sinfulness nakedness.

It was God who provided the sacrifice for Adam and Eve, and it was God who clothed them. Through the animal sacrifice, I believe that God clothed more than their physical body. God clothed their naked, rebellious soul through the blood of the animal sacrifice that He had provided for the forgiveness of sins. "For the [soul] life of the flesh is in the blood" (Lev. 17:11).

When God provided a substitute of an animal sacrifice as a covering for Adam and Eve's sinful state, He was laying the basis for the sacrifice of the Lamb of God who was sacrificed at Calvary for the sins of the world. When anyone makes a personal decision in receiving Christ, it should be based upon what He did through the cross. God provided a way to atone for sinful condition of humanity before His holiness. Christ's blood atone-ment is God's Substitute for the transgressions of all of humanity.

God's church is "His workmanship, created in Christ Jesus for good works" (Eph. 2:10). The basis for the good works of His workmanship is the work of grace that Christ has provided for His church at the cross. There is, therefore, no room for self-glory. God's grace is revealed to the humble at heart.

Instead of boasting in her organizational self-life, that church should have given continual thanksgiving and praise to Him, who satisfied divine justice by dying in her place as her sin substitute. She had left that undone! It was, therefore, necessary for Christ to knock at the door that she may have an open-door fellowship with the Lover of her soul. But it was necessary for "anyone" in that church to hear His voice and open the door to wholehearted affection and devotion with Him.

Fellowship had been broken down between the lukewarm Laodiceans, the Head and other members of the Body of Christ. The covering of the blood of Jesus provides the means where the church may acquire and enjoy fellowship with one another, but she must walk in the light of God's truth. "But if we walk in the light as He is in the light, we have fellowship with one another, and the blood of Jesus Christ his Son cleanses us from all sin." Sins must be brought to the light by confessing them to God through the blood of Jesus. His blood only cleanses in the light. It will not cleanse in the dark.

Confession of sin would have brought anyone in the Laodicean Church out of spiritual darkness—having a wrong relationship with the Lord of the church—in order that he or she could continue to walk in the light as He is in the light. Through the blood of Jesus, confessed sins are forgiven sins.

The fullness of the unity of true Christian fellowship, therefore, does not come until she walks, moves or grows into it. To do this, the Laodicean Church leadership should have confronted the problem of being lukewarm toward Jesus in the life of that church. Of all sins, the sin of spiritual pride is the most difficult to recognize and confess, but the Holy Spirit is faithful and just to reveal to each individual believer in the church that primary sin through the light of God's Word. Spiritual understanding comes according to the light of God's Word as it descends upon life's pathway, and that understanding is needed in these last days. The church needs to bring the truth of His soon Appearing out of the realm of abstract theology into a loving fellowship with the Lord of glory.

5. Anoint Your Eyes with Eye Salve

The man born blind said, "One thing I know: that though I was blind, now I see" (John 9:25). Spiritual eyesight begins at the new birth, but the eyes of that church needed to be anointed with eye salve supplied by the

Holy Spirit in order that she could see with the eyes of faith. The "eye salve" of God's Word will heal those who are visually impaired spiritually. Her eyes had been blinded to entering into more of the fullness of scriptural truth. Only the Spirit of truth can lead and guide the church into all truth. But because of religious pride, He will not lead the spiritually blind. If she could have only seen her lukewarm and halfhearted attitude toward the promised Bridegroom of the church, she could have made the Lover of her soul the great love of her life.

Christianity has no place along the pathway of righteousness for church membership to camp. It is a walk of faith in discipleship as the Holy Spirit leads the church into all truth through the Christ of the Scriptures. In being a true disciple of Christ, therefore, there is no sitting down or standing still. The light and understanding of the Scriptures should have been getting ever brighter each day to the Laodicean Church.

Proverbs 4:18 says, "The path of the just is like the shining sun, that shines ever brighter unto the perfect day." Dawn is the beginning point of light. It is a signal that there is more light to come. Each step of the way, minute by minute, hour after hour, the light of each new day becomes brighter. The light continues to become brighter until the fullness of the noonday sun.

We are living in the end time of church history, and the Holy Spirit is revealing more light upon the Word of God than ever before. Though gross darkness permeates the world around the end-time church, the light of God's Word is becoming brighter and brighter to those Christians who are becoming more and more committed to Him.

Because the church lives in a world of spiritual darkness, the end-time church needs the light necessary to move along the prescribed course that God has laid out for each one of us. In moving forward, the eyes of the church must be fixed upon Him, and faith in His words must become as a lamp to her feet and a light to her path.

Thinking and reasoning that come from our five physical senses are no help for spiritual guidance. "For we walk by faith, not by sight" (2 Cor. 5:7). The world, in its spiritual darkness and emptiness, is facing eternal damnation without Jesus as the Light of the world. Walking in spiritual light, therefore, is a walk of faith. This walk in the light is important because it will reconcile a lukewarm church to God. Understanding revealed truth gives light for fellowship with God and with other fellow believers.

There is a great need for the present-day church to be challenged to love the Lord Jesus with all he heart, mind and soul. Jesus should be "all and in all" in every aspect of church life. As a church, the Laodiceans needed to apply "eye salve" to her spiritual eyesight that she might see the beauty and the glory of the crucified Lamb. The Holy Spirit has come to exalt the Lamb above all others in the midst of His people. He is the Lord of heaven that should be first in all things pertaining to the church.

Eye salve is needed that she may see God's building plan and process through the eyes of faith. God is building the church, His House of Righteousness, with one living stone at a time. The Laodiceans should have seen themselves "as living stones" in being a part of God's great building program. She should have been able to see things and judged them according to the truth of "all Scriptures."

Who can be counted worthy to be identified with such exalted greatness with Him? Persistent preparation is needed for the bride-elect in waiting for her coming Bridegroom. She is waiting with such a great expectation of having an everlasting loving relationship with Him. Jesus said, "Therefore you also be ready, for the Son of Man is coming at an hour you do not expect" (Luke 12:40). The Bridegroom says, "Buy from Me!" Paying the price of self-denial and self-sacrifice of discipleship for His sake is not too high a price for being ready at His coming.

Knowing the true riches of His grace should have been the objective for Christian living in the Laodicean Church. Understanding the true riches of God in Christ Jesus are so important, for His riches are not just for time alone, but "that in the ages to come He might show the exceeding riches of His grace in His kindness toward us in Christ Jesus."

Chapter 8

The Greatest Love
A Need to Repent and Recognize His Love for the Church

"As many as I love, I rebuke and chasten. Therefore
be zealous and repent" (verse 19).

The unique love of the meek and lowly Bridegroom waiting for His over-coming church is revealed in the story about the church of the Laodiceans. The humble Lord over the whole church appealed to that one proud church to repent from her attitude of arrogance and learn to love Him with the same passionate love with which He loved her. She needed to get her eyes off herself and her zeal for temporal greatness in order to become zealous toward the eternal greatness of His self-giving love toward her.

When the focus is on love, a church needs to understand the root and motive of His great love for her is that He "gave Himself for her" (Eph. 5:25). Christ's love for the church and the importance of her eternal worth to Him can be measured by the purchase price that He paid for her. Because of His great love for her, Jesus was holding the Laodicean Church accountable for having a lukewarm attitude toward Him.

Paul brought the love of Christ for the church out of the abstract realm and made a practical and personal application, relating it to the closeness of the love of a husband for his wife in a matrimonial relationship. In Ephesians 5:25-32 Paul exhorts, "Husbands, love your wives, just as Christ also loved the church and gave Himself for her." He goes on to say, "So husbands ought to love their own wives as their own bodies; he who loves his wife loves himself…For we are members of His body, of His flesh and of His bones." Paul describes the matrimonial union of Christ and His church as "a great mystery."

Jesus came to the nation of Israel as her Servant, and the Holy Spirit has been sent to serve the church and her leadership in helping them serve the church organism, which includes the Head. Jesus told His twelve future church leaders, "If anyone desires to be first, he shall be last of all and servant of all" (Mark 9:35). A resurrected Christ told a repentant Peter, "Feed My sheep." Growth of His church organism is most important.

In representing the rule of Jesus over a church organism, church leadership has been called upon to unselfishly meet the need of the whole church Body. God blesses a church in order that she might become a blessing in meeting the need of others. Unlike the rich Laodiceans' self-centered love, the Lord's *agape*, self-giving love, is seeking for church leaders that will passionately love and serve Him as Head over His church organism.

The Laodiceans' bold statement of self-sufficiency revealed how half-hearted they had become toward the Lord. What is important about people being loved wholeheartedly is that they become attached to the person who is doing the loving. Self-love, therefore, cannot be true love. God's self-giving love is a love that serves others. People will seek out and spend money and time on that which they passionately love.

For God's love to be complete, it must be mutually dependent. The love of the world and the God of love are mutually exclusive. They have nothing in common. True love becomes interdependent upon the one being loved. That proud church, therefore, couldn't qualify. "Therefore [the message to the Laodiceans' proud church members could have been] humble yourselves under the mighty hand of God, that He may exalt you in due time, casting all your care upon Him, for He cares for you" (1 Pet. 5:6-7).

The Lord cared deeply for that church, but as a corporeal body of professing Christians, her words of self-sufficiency indicated that she couldn't care less. But there must have been some believers in that church organism who were displeased with that kind of thinking. Those were the ones who would receive the Lord's loving rebuke.

In contrasting the caring rebuke in verse 19 with the humble invitation in verse 20, Jesus was addressing that organism within the proud church organization to repent. Redemption and restoration is a personal and a unique work by the Holy Spirit, who influences and guides believers in a person-to-person relationship to a resurrected Christ.

God So Loved the World / Christ Also Loved the Church

The evangelistic emphasis is John 3:16, which is the story of God's great love for a world that has been condemned in trespasses and sins. The appeal, "Whoever believes in Him should not perish but have everlasting life." The Father has given His Son as a ransom, to cancel the debt of that condemnation in order that the believer might be justified and have everlasting life in Christ Jesus. There is no way to fully picture the reason for God's great love and mercy toward a lost and dying world. God's love for Adam's fallen race is a mystery that's unexplainable, but the world is accountable to God, who has made known His great love to her through the giving of His crucified Son.

No matter how great God's love has been demonstrated toward a perishing world, the Father's love, through His Son, was being demonstrated to an even greater extent toward the lukewarm church of the Laodiceans. The accountability of a lost world is to honor God by receiving His Son who died for their sins. The debt of that church, or any church, was to have a loving commitment to Him "who loved the church and gave Himself for her."

The Father's love caused Him to give His Son for a lost world because of the Son's love for the Father in being willing to give Himself for the church. The church indwells the One who purchased her with His own blood. Having a lukewarm attitude toward Him caused Jesus to feel like vomiting that church out of His Body through the mouth.

The "whoever believes in Him" in John 3:16 is God's appeal to a lost world. The "If anyone hears My voice and opens the door" in Revelation 3:20 is the Lord's appeal to a lukewarm church. God is building a unified church for His own glory, and He is doing it with "one living stone" at a time, fitted neatly in its proper place in relating each to one another in God's building program.

The ransom has been paid for all that believe to be redeemed out of the world. "God so loved the world that He gave…." The verb "loved" is past tense. That love was manifested at Calvary. What Christ has done at the cross for the world has been recorded in the annals of human history. There is salvation in no other name given among men.

To know God's love, the world must come by faith through the cross to know Him in His resurrected saving power and grace. The unbelieving world will be judged for rejecting the one supreme act of God's love at the cross. The Holy Spirit has come to "convict the world of sin, and of righteousness, and of judgment: of sin, because they do not believe (Gk. *eis*) *into* Me" (John 16:8-9).

The "lukewarm" Laodicean Church was being judged for neglecting the ever-present passionate love of Christ for the church. The Father holds the church accountable for Christ's compassionate love for her in what He did for the church through His death on the cross. How is the end-time church responding to Christ fervent love toward her?

The ascended Lord of glory was still making known His great sacrificial love to the self-loving, unrepentant church at Laodicea. If the church of the Laodiceans truly had known Him, she would have glorified the treasures of "the unsearchable riches of Christ" that dwells in earthen vessels rather than glorying in the riches of corruptible earthly treasures that shall perish with the using. Nothing can compare to the value and worth of Christ's love for the church.

The church organism in Christ is the treasure that God has taken out of the world and separated unto Himself. Because of His great love for the church, the Bride of Christ will become the Father's eternal reward to His Son. The faithfulness of the Son to the church merits her great love to Him for His cause.

The church of the Laodiceans at that time had a newborn experience with Jesus, but she had not followed on to learn of Him. It was like He had saved her from drowning in a pool of worldly filth, obscenity and corruption, but she had never fellowshipped with Him long enough to get to know Him in His majestic glory. He had remained a stranger to her. Anyone in the end-time church may learn of Him through the Scriptures as the Holy Spirit reveals Him more and more in the fullness of His great love.

Now Christ was standing outside of that church door knocking. He had called her out of a world of darkness, but she had not developed a continuing, steadfast walk with Him long enough to get to know Him as the Light of the world that penetrates believing hearts and gives complete deliverance from the realm of spiritual darkness.

Christ's self-giving love is the greatest love of all loves. He died for His church in order "that He might present her unto Himself as a glorious church." The Laodicean Church had departed a long way from loving Him as He should have been loved, but He was still pursuing "anyone" in that church who had a desire to learn to love Him in the same magnitude that He loved her.

The challenge of His self-giving love is a challenge of a lifetime; even a thousand lifetimes could not come close to compensate for His great love toward His church. Nevertheless, if the emphasis and focus is kept on the challenge of loving Him in the capacity that He should be loved, there is unquestionably nothing that a church organization can get puffed up about.

Having a Zeal for Jesus

The Lord said to the Laodicean Church, "As many as I love, I rebuke and chasten. Therefore be zealous and repent." The Greek word *zeloo*, translated "zealous" could be translated "full of emotional desire, hot with passionate pursuit" with a desire to walk more closely with Him. The appeal, therefore, is for a strong desire to cultivate the fruit of the Spirit, especially the fruit of love.

The Greek word *zeloo* is also used in 1 Corinthians 14:1 where Paul says, "Pursue love and desire (*zeloo*) spiritual gifts." Here the word *zeloo* could also be translated as "a strong desire, as to burn with desire, or eagerly desire" spiritual gifts. Zeal for both the fruit of the Spirit and the gifts of the Spirit is needed in Christian service.

Being lukewarm meant that the church of the Laodiceans was lacking in having a passionate desire toward fellowship with Jesus. Because of the lack of zeal there was a need for repentance. Repentance should be toward God, and eagerness of faith and love should be the passion of the newborn spirit toward the Lover of her soul.

The Laodiceans had lost their *zeloo* for the Head and Judge of the church. They had become so busy glorifying the works of their own hands, in pursuing riches and wealth, that they had lost the desire to glorify the Father, through the Son, "from whom the whole family in heaven and earth is named." The Laodiceans had lost their enthusiasm to worship the Father in the newborn spirit by the Holy Spirit and in the liberating truth of the ever-unfolding Word of God.

Instead of glorying in temporal riches that perish, her focus should have been on the unsearchable eternal riches of the unchanging Christ. That church needed to rekindle a more thoughtful longing, commitment and devotion to a personal Jesus. People will diligently pursue and give attention to that which they passionately love, whether it is the things of the world or the things of God.

Jesus said, "As many as I love, I rebuke and chasten." In verses 17b and 18, He gave a piercing chastisement. Why was the rebuke so severe? There was so much at stake. Because of Christ's great love for the church, He wants to serve her for her eternal best interests. That church had become lukewarm toward His great love for her. He desired to dine with her with fervency in her worship and love for the truth.

Adam's race has been identified collectively through the fall of one man—Adam, the first man. But the one God-Man, Christ, has sealed off all Adam's evil inheritance through His death as the Last Adam. Now as the Second Man, through His resurrection from the dead, He regenerates, sanctifies and fellowships with His redeemed people on a one-to-one basis. But through each individual's passionate love for Christ Jesus, as a member in the Body of Christ, self-image is absorbed in the oneness and unity of His image in the Spirit of love. The church takes on the identity of the Body of Christ.

Self-glory / God's Glory

Though she did not realize it, the church of the Laodiceans had lost her identity with Him as her loving Lord and Savior. The church is all about Jesus, doing things in His name for His glory, and not doing things "in any other name" for self-glory. Self-glory can neither reveal nor exalt God's glory. If the Laodiceans truly loved Him, she would have relied on the guidance of the Holy Spirit, and the glory of the Lord would have been revealed through her.

The church of the Laodiceans needed to see herself in light of the Scriptures, which was the same way that Christ saw her. Jesus taught that He judges according to that which is written. The Lord does not look on outward appearance of the riches and wealth of a church like the Laodiceans; "the LORD looks at the heart" (1 Sam. 16:7). It is, therefore, important to know the Scriptures, that a church may be able to judge herself in the mirror of God's Word accordingly.

Paul taught that self-discipline, which is necessary to be a winner in an athletic contest, is also necessary to win the prize in the Christian contest. The church wins her Prize with spiritual fitness through self-denial according to the Scriptures. In the realm of all athletic endeavors, physical fitness is necessary to become a winner. Those rewards are about physical endurance and natural talents, which have been received and achieved in the realm of time.

The greatest challenge to members of the Laodicean Church was the challenge in the realm of the Spirit. When spiritual experiences, which promote spiritual growth and development, come by grace through faith, there is no room for self-glory. When a church must, of necessity, confidently and openly depend upon the help of the Holy Spirit for direction and divine guidance, there is no room for self-glory.

Instead of that church engaging in self-praise, she should have been judging herself in the light of the Scriptures. "For if we would judge ourselves, we would not be judged. But when we are judged, we are chastened by the Lord, that we may not be condemned with the world" (1 Cor. 11:31-32). The Lord was chastening the church of the Laodiceans in order that she would not be condemned with the world.

The nation of Israel thought that she was above God's far-reaching judgment in her lofty opinion of herself. As a privileged nation with a covenant relationship with God, she thought that she would not become as broken-off branches. According to Romans 11:17-24, a church should "not boast against the branches. But if you do boast, remember that you [church] do not support the root [Israel], but the root supports you" (v. 18).

The nation of Israel is the root in laying down the ordinances of God, in the writing and preservation of the Scriptures, in the giving of the prophets and apostles, and in giving the Messiah, all of which supports the church. The church of the Laodiceans, therefore, should not have had a know-it-all attitude. She should have been submissive to the Holy Spirit and thankful to Jesus that she had the opportunity to be grafted in where the former branches were broken off (v. 17).

God didn't deal with the nation of Israel according to her being a covenant, privileged people. God dealt with the Israelites for their lack of faith and obedience toward His covenant that He had made with them. "Because of unbelief they were broken off, and you [the church] stand by faith. Do not be haughty, but fear" (v. 20). What should a church fear? Fear what Israel failed to fear. Self-deception! End-time churches have much to overcome, but overcoming the self-life presents the greatest challenge.

Many organizational church systems are taking too much for granted as a privileged church in these last days, but "if God did not spare the natural branches, He may not spare you [the church] either" (v. 21). The spiritual pride and self-conceit that caused the natural branches to be cut off is the same pride and self-conceit that will cause a lukewarm church like the Laodicean Church, as grafted-in branches, to be cut off.

No end-time church system, therefore, should go the same way as the nation of Israel and become presumptuous in her self-confidence and self-complacency. "Therefore consider the goodness and severity of God. For if you were cut out of the olive tree which is wild by nature, and were grafted contrary to nature into a cultivated olive tree, how much more will these, who are natural branches, be grafted into their own olive tree?" (vv. 22-24). Israel is God's olive tree, and with her coming Messiah, she shall be restored to her former glory. The church, therefore, should not be high-minded and take things for granted, as did Israel, but she should be humble and grateful that God has been good and merciful to her as a wild olive tree.

The Love-Hate Relationship

As an example to the church, what did Christ Jesus hate? Hebrews 1:9 tells about the Father speaking to the Son, "You have loved righteousness and hated lawlessness." In other words, Jesus hates the sin of lawlessness. Jesus was led to make a choice to give His life for the lawlessness of sin as an atoning sacrifice. The church, at the present time, is living in an age of violence and lawlessness; so much so that "the love of many will grow cold" (Matt. 24:12). The invitation is to love Him more and more in His relationship to the Body of Christ in these last days of lawlessness.

Continuing to follow Jesus into daily fellowship shows a church's love for Him. But before a church can have a stronger love for Him, she must balance out that love in hating those things that oppose Him. For example, the closer a church draws to Christ, the farther she will be drawn away from the world, because the world is an enemy of God (Jam. 4:4). The Bible says, "Draw near to God and He will draw near to you" (v. 8).

The Holy Spirit has come to reveal His greatness. The appeal in Luke 14:26 teaches what is the cost of becoming His disciple. Jesus said, "If anyone comes to Me and does not hate his father and mother, wife and children, brothers and sisters, yes, and his own life also, he cannot be My disciple." The greatest disciple was the Son, as the Father's humble Disciple. The church at Laodicea needed to understand how the truth of His greatness comes. Any influence that was contrary to the working of the will of God over the life of anyone in that church was to be rejected, even those who had the most influence over them, including the influence of the self-life.

Jesus speaks of denying the self-life, losing the self-life, which is putting off the soulish nature, and here He speaks about hating the self-life. This is all done for Jesus' sake. A church member cannot follow Jesus unless he or she realizes that the self-life can hinder the Christian walk with Jesus. Jesus here speaks about hating the self-life or any other influence that would keep a disciple from persevering in coming after Jesus.

Jesus mentions different close family relationships that could be used as a negative influence on a follower of Christ. Church members, like those at Laodicea, must recognize the old self-life and confront it as the major negative influence against the Christ-life if they expect to receive positive results with God. David's spirit spoke to his soul-life saying, "Bless the LORD, O my soul, and forget not all of His benefits" (Ps. 103:2). David's soul-life, which made the decisions, needed to be reminded to bless the Lord, for it could easily forget the Lord, His ways and His many benefits.

Following Jesus means that you are doing things for Jesus' sake above and beyond doing things for those with the most influence over your life other than Christ, especially the self-life. Life is all about different kinds of relationships: church, family, friends and self. Christ is saying that developing an important, loving relationship with Him should have top priority.

The Laodicean Church certainly had a wrong relationship with Him. She put the goals of her self-life before the purposes of Christ for the church. Moving away from the motive of doing things for the sake of self (self-centeredness) to doing things for the sake of the claims of Christ helps spiritual growth and development of a church.

I have heard people say, "I hate myself!" That is usually for self's sake. But the Bible way is to learn to hate your self-life for Jesus' sake. That's the way to become an overcomer! The self-life can cause a person to do many foolish things, but the secret is learning to depend more and more upon the Lord. Hearing what the Spirit says to the church will show her what is best for Christ's sake. Only He can reveal to a church the fullness of knowing the Christ of the Scriptures with greater devotion and attachment.

Jesus said, "Take My yoke upon you and learn from Me." Accepting His yoke means for a church to put Him in charge over her life as she lives for His sake. That is what gives true meaning to Christianity. It brings every aspect of church life into proper prospective. Doing things for the sake of others is godliness, but it is important how you are motivated, not manipulated, to do it.

The Holy Spirit motivates a church toward doing the things of God for the glory of God. Manipulation involves "the things of men" done for the glory of man. Jesus said that people would either be for Him or against Him. How could that apply to the discipleship message to the church?

The Wrong Kind of Hate

Many false teachers in the realm of Christianity are teaching hate that is not according to the Scriptures. Cult leaders, who take young people away from their parents and a loving family, think that they are doing it for the sake of Christ. But they know nothing about the love of Christ. The self-centered, selfish life of a dictatorial cult leader is in control. They are seeking "their own, not the things which are of Christ Jesus." They replace the self-life of others with their own self-identity. The Holy Spirit is leading Christians to replace their self-life with the self-life of Jesus. A church organism is to lose her self-identity in Christ as the Head of the Body of Christ.

When cult leaders put young people in subjection to their own legalistic teachings, the aspirations and motives behind the influence of the selfishness of their self-life are revealed. Luke 14:26 becomes a favorite scripture for those cult leaders, and they take only the part that refers to hating family relationships, using it to draw disciples after themselves. The collective self-life of the group takes center stage with a legalistic cult leader in control.

By doing so, their legalistic teachings destroy all existing family values and relationships. They bring their young converts into bondage to their dominating ways. If any have experienced the new birth, they do not have the freedom to follow Christ and learn of His great love.

One time a young man visited the church where I was pastoring. He came two or three times over a six-week period. Then one Sunday morning he came with several other young people and an older woman. Before the service was over, with the older woman leading the way, they all left together like a mother hen leading her flock of chickens. The message that was being taught was having your eyes focused on Jesus in your Christian walk. That woman was not about to let her followers get out from under her control. If they would ever fix their eyes on Jesus as the Head of the church, they would soon see the control spirit that she was using over them.

It was obvious that Sunday morning, on a very small scale, that Jesus, as the Head over those young converts, had lost out to a control spirit in the older woman. But the Headship of Jesus is also losing out to the same kind of control spirit in the end-time church on a larger and much more cunning scale.

People might think that it is the will of God in church work to have soulish control over others, but that is not the method of rule that Jesus taught (Matt. 20:25-26). The Holy Spirit leads and guides into all truth. God wants the best for His people by getting the worst out of them through self-denial and being a cross-bearer for Jesus' sake.

The enemy manipulates and intimidates people to hinder them from following the leadership of the Holy Spirit. The Father's appointed leadership is pointing the sheep to the Chief Shepherd by the power of the Holy Spirit, in order that He may exalt Christ in the life of each believer.

Christian service should be motivated by a young person's devotion to the Christ of the Scriptures and not by blind obedience to a cult leader. The carnal self-life of a cult leader will manipulate, or intimidate if necessary, to dominate their disciples. They are deceived in thinking that they have a mandate from the Lord for what they are doing.

Discipleship is associated with being under His discipline as King of God's kingdom. Fellowship is affiliated with His companionship with the church. We cannot be His disciples, having fellowship with Him and with one another, without being under His discipline and rule.

Old Testament Scriptures proclaim that God's kingdom would come to Israel through a Ruler who would be able to shoulder the governmental load. Jesus will fulfill the prophetic announcement, "Of His kingdom there will be no end." Because a church cannot rule her own self adequately, she needs to submit daily to His authority and protective care.

God's kingdom has divine principles that need to be followed. "Blessed are the poor in spirit, for theirs is the kingdom of heaven." Church rules, for the most part, do not cover divine principles for kingdom living that are found in the Beatitudes. The Laodiceans, being lifted up in their self-worth and self-sufficiency as a church, might have had many good church rules, but not one of them was helping anyone in that church to qualify for dining with the King.

Jesus made an appeal to each individual of that church to come under His rulership in order that he or she may have a loving relationship with Him. There is no fellowship between Christ and those who are in rebellion against the church organism, the Body of Christ. We live in a world that knows nothing of His sovereignty.

Judaism represents a religious system that has rejected the rulership of their Messiah. The King of the Jews came to His own people. They rejected their King and had Him crucified by the Romans. As the Jewish Messiah, the great issue and confrontation with Jesus of Nazareth to them would be His rule over them. They did not want to come under His control. Pilate knew that they brought Jesus before Him because of envy.

Jesus is the Son of God and the true Ruler over the Jewish people. But that is not only a commentary against the historical past of the nation of Israel; that is also a commentary against the historical church. There can be no fellowship with the King until His rulership over the people of a church is established.

In dealing with Israel, even in the time of her captivity, God always had His faithful remnant. In His First Coming, Jesus began with a remnant of

Jews as His disciples. Will there only be a small remnant of the church world, compared with her numbers in the millions, truly ready to receive Him at His Appearing?

The Laodicean Church was being confronted with the same issue. It was not an outright rejection of the King as with the chief priests (John 19:15), but eventual rejection can come through the avenue of daily negligence and disregard for the Lover of the church. I don't believe that the church at Laodicea realized it at the time, but to be a true disciple of Christ, a daily, personal fellowship needs to be established with Him. Church leadership must learn to come humbly under His divine discipline and rulership.

Example of True Repentance

In the story of the seven churches of Asia Minor, the Lord called five out of the seven to repent. That ratio might even be higher for the many churches in this end-time era. The story of the prodigal son teaches an exemplary lesson in repentance. When the prodigal came to himself, he began to think differently.

The change in his thinking process led to an inner decision to change the outward direction in the way that he was living. When he came to himself, he said, "I will arise and go to my father, and will say to him, 'Father, I have sinned against heaven and before you, and I am no longer worthy to be called your son. Make me like one of your hired servants.'"

He had not done it yet; he was simply thinking and meditating upon it. Then he acted, "And he arose and came to his father" (Luke 15:17-20a). He went from an arrogant son that said, "give me" my inheritance (v. 12) to the lowly, contrite son that said, "Make me like one of your hired servants" (v. 19). He experienced a change in attitude. That was what the Laodicean Church needed to do.

The change in his thinking process caused him to change the direction that he was going and the way that he was doing things. The evidence that he repented is that he made an inward decision that caused a change in his outward lifestyle. Our heavenly Father, who gives all things to the church in Christ, will change a church member into a mature son or daughter in Christ through an attitude of repentance toward Him.

Members of the Laodicean Church, therefore, needed to repent and make an inward decision that would change their outward actions in true worship and Christian service. The charm of her earthly riches and wealth would have grown strangely dim in the light of His marvelous grace.

When the prodigal son arose and headed toward his father's house, it was confirmation that a change had taken place in his thinking process. That is the definition of repentance. It is an outward action that is evidence of an inner decision. He made a 180-degree turn from the way that he was living.

Jesus, as the way to the Father's house, was standing outside and knocking on the door of the Laodicean Church. Jesus said, "In My Father's house are many mansions." The Father's exalted salvation plan for His church seems impossible to the reason of men, "but with God all things are possible" through the repentance of men. (Matt 19:26). God never overrules self-will in order to achieve or complete His will.

Much emphasis is placed on faith and forgiveness in the end-time church, but without repentance there is no faith for forgiveness. The prodigal son could have talked much about faith while he was living in the pigpen of self-centered thinking and feelings. But he needed to repent in order to have the faith necessary to lead him back into the presence of his loving father's arms of forgiveness.

Jesus' first recorded message was, "Repent, and believe in the gospel" (Mark 1:15). To get out of the pigpen of self-centeredness requires a daily walk with a holy God. God reaches down and picks up contrite souls and brings them unto Himself. Christ Jesus desires to "purify for Himself His own special people, zealous for good works" (Tit. 2:14). That was the invitation Jesus was giving to that lukewarm church.

The prodigal son went from a self-serving attitude to an attitude of servitude in his relationship to his father. He was willing for the father to change him into whatever he wanted to make him. Of course, because of his repentant attitude, the father was not willing to make his forgiven son one of his hired servants. Because of his attitudinal change from a "give me," self-loving son to a "make me," self-giving son, his father gave him more blessings than he could imagine.

Not only did Jesus say, "You did not choose Me, but I chose you," but to those who made their living by fishing He said, "Follow Me and I will make you fishers of men." The Laodicean Church needed to understand that He had not only chosen her, but she also needed to be challenged to experience what He could make her become through a wholehearted, loving fellowship with Him. One might dispute why the Lord would choose a church that He had to rebuke so severely. Why did He choose the twelve and one, named Judas Iscariot, would betray Him? For the purpose that the Scriptures be fulfilled, one of the the twelve would betray Him, but it didn't need to be Judas.

The God that never changes is our heavenly Father, who is in the changing business through His great plan of redemption. That church needed to have a steadfast look in the mirror of God's Word and be changed into the same image of the glory of the Lord "from glory to glory." The changing of her thinking process would come through acting on the message of repentance. "As many as I love, I rebuke and chasten. Therefore be zealous and repent." True love is faithful and tells it like it is. That church needed to repent!

That is God's fundamental requirement for an overcoming church. As exalted members of the Royal Family, the Father's children are developing a spirit of serving one another through an attitude of gratitude. That attitude brings each member of the Body of Christ to honor one another. Each recognizes and appreciates the spiritual gifts and ministerial gifts of the others that makes the Body of Christ complete.

No matter how much God has prospered a church with His material abundance, every church congregation is needy, and God provides for all of our needs according to His riches in glory. But a church's greatest need, in order to please the Father, is to become more like His firstborn Son. That requires a transforming process where a church is changing from the things of the old life to enjoying the new things of God in a more blessed way each day. His blood of the new covenant has provided "a new and living way." The end-time church needs to walk in it.

Because she had boldly declared a proud egocentric statement, the Lord rebuked the Laodiceans. He wished that she were cold or hot. The Lord was condemned for the sins of the dead cold at the cross, which is the same judgment of the world. He would rather reward than rebuke, and it is to the church with the greatest zeal in loving and serving Him that He delights in the giving of all things.

But she was found as a lukewarm church. What is He going to do with her? Because she thought she had no sin, He had to deal with her harshly so that she might see the error of her ways and repent from her sin of indifference and neglect toward His great and tender loving care. A lukewarm church might be defined as a church where the members are serving the Lord at their own comfort and in their own convenience.

The Lord gave a remedy for that church that had become afflicted with a severe "I" problem. She needed to apply God's eye salve ointment (God's liberating truth) in order that she may see the "need" to buy the true riches for abundant living from the Lord God of her salvation. Christ was standing on the outside knocking on the church door with a message for anyone who would repent and open the door to have a mutual passionate, loving fellowship with Him.

Commandment of Love

Love is the fruit of the Spirit; it's not a spiritual gift. Love one another is God's first and great commandment, and not a divine suggestion or a church rule. Spiritual gifts of God and church rules of men might be given to church members, but God's love must be cultivated by the branches that abide in the Vine in order to bring forth much fruit.

Jesus said, "If you love Me, keep My commandments" (John 14:15). Later Jesus told them His commandment: "**This is My commandment**, that you love one another as I have loved you" (15:12). Another way to express that truth would be, "If anyone loves Me, he will keep My word" (14:23).

Loving Jesus, therefore, means being obedient to His words. Keep His words "in the midst of your heart," for they are life to those who find them (Prov. 4:21-22). When the Lord told the church at Ephesus, "You have left your first love," that was the love she once had for the Christ of the church according to the Scriptures. The love of the Ephesian Church for Christ had been replaced by a love for someone or something else from without or within the church in that city.

But the love of the Laodicean Church for Christ had been replaced by her love for riches and wealth. That was revealed by her self-centered attitude as a member of the body of believers. Her lack of love toward other members of the Body of Christ led to an unattached and unsubmissive attitude toward other members in the Body.

Her lack of love toward the Head of the Body resulted in a lack of love for each and every other member of the Body. As members of the Body of Christ, each is to be engaged in doing his part. The Head of the Body is harmonizing each member of His Body in love toward one grand finale. The Holy Spirit is directing the thinking of God's people toward being properly related to the Christ of His Church as the end draws near. The church at Laodicea had a need to accept the challenge of obeying the Greatest Commandment, which is having God's *agape* love.

"Love is the fulfillment of the law [and church rules]" (Rom. 13:10b). Those who are true, born-again Christians will stand before the judgment seat of personified Love for judgment in rewards. The church will be judged according to "the things done in the body whether good or bad." At that time, He need not say, "I know your works." He is the One who knows all things concerning His church.

That church should have asked this question, "How much am I being a channel for God's love?" "The love of God has been poured out in our hearts by the Holy Spirit who was given to us" (Rom. 5:5). Love, as fruit of the Spirit, will do an eternal work for God through humble, submissive souls.

God's nature of *agape* love is the objective in spiritual growth and development in the church. Paul wrote Timothy, "The goal of our instruction is love" (1 Tim. 1:5, NAS). Too many insignificant and wrong instructions given to the end-time church are falling short of that goal in these last days. If God's church does not have love one for another, they have fallen short of the goal that the Father has for Christ's glorious church. Those who belong to the overcoming, glorious church have love for one another.

We need to do whatever is necessary to motivate us to love one another with a sacrificial love. If we are not properly related to one another as members of the Body of Christ, we cannot be properly related to the Head of the Body. If each member is not properly related to the Head and to one another, the Body cannot function sufficiently.

Church rules of a self-sufficient church, like the Laodicean Church, become private property with a "no trespassing" sign. The motive behind that kind of attitude might be to keep the devil out. The rules can become so impenetrable, however, that they leave no room for the Spirit of Truth to exalt Christ Jesus in the midst and to lead them into further truth. As a result, Christ ends up on the outside knocking on the church door.

The Christ of God is personified Truth. Only through the Son can anyone come to the Father of the family of saving truth, who not only is the source of all good things, but who also controls the direction and destination of all things.

God has only one solution for the rebellious soul-life, and it is not social reform or lengthy rehabilitation. It's the death sentence! God's answer, therefore, for the "old man" is execution. But the good news of the gospel is that execution has already taken place in the death of Christ Jesus at the cross. "Knowing this, that our old man was crucified with Christ, that the body of sin might be done away with, that we should no longer be slaves to sin" (Rom. 6:6). It is through His resurrection-life that the church puts on the new man. Christ, as "the firstborn among many brethren," is the beginning of the new creation family.

The end-time church has much to overcome, but "He who overcomes shall inherit all things, and I will be his God and he shall be My son" (Rev. 21:7). That is the predestined goal of the overcoming, glorious church in following Jesus. And the only way to live an overcoming life is dining with Jesus in receiving His wisdom and strength—as hungry hearts, ready to hear the words of righteousness that proceed from His mouth.

Our initial identification with Christ begins at the cross. "I have been crucified with Him" (Gal. 2:20). A church is to be properly related with Him continually until she reaches that inevitable goal of being seated with Him on His throne as Bride to the Bridegroom. That means a church organism needs to cultivate a spirit of humility before the Lord. "Therefore humble yourselves under the mighty hand of God, that He may exalt you in due time" is the universal law for spiritual progress.

Two Main Categories of Love in the Church

There are different levels or kinds of love. The highest form of love is God's *agape* love, which is a self-giving love that meets the need of others. God's love edifies and serves; whereas, the lowest form of love is a self-centered love, which can become so selfish as it grows in strength that it becomes harmful and destructive. That is the kind of love found in a world of lawlessness in these last days.

Meet a person with God's love dwelling within a believing heart and you are edified and enlightened by being around that person. Meet church members of a certain church full of self-centered love and you learn to become cautious and guarded. Self-love was the problem of the church at Laodicea, and it will destroy the spiritual growth and effectiveness of a church.

1. A Love That Edifies

The goal for Christian living is a life that has the mastery of God as love over it. The Laodicean Church might have had a creed about the love of God, but she needed to know God as Love and submit to that love in Christ. "God is love!" The call, therefore, is to become "imitators of God as dear children." That is, "Walk in love, as Christ also has loved us, and given Himself for us." He did it as "an offering and a sacrifice to God for a sweet-smelling aroma." Even the spiritual sense of smell can discern God's love.

Knowledge of the Scriptures that leads to spiritual understanding is very important in the renewing of the mind through spiritual growth and development. But the ultimate objective in Christian service is "to know the love of Christ which passes knowledge; that you may be filled with all the fullness of God" (Eph. 2:19). His love exceeds knowledge. That is the paradox in knowing God's love. Churches recognize that they all have knowledge, but all of them put together do not have all knowledge. "Knowledge puffs up, but love edifies" (1 Cor. 8:1b). God's love abiding within believing hearts has the power to build up and strengthen a church by the Holy Spirit.

"As the Father loved Me, I also have loved you; abide in My love" (John 15:9). A church needs to know what Jesus said in order that she may prove her love to Him by keeping His sayings. If a church is not obedient to the words of Jesus, she is rebelling against the One who spoke the words.

Jesus has commanded the church to love one another, even as He has loved us. One might say, "I cannot love with a self-giving love like His love." That's true; no one can in his or her own strength, but once again the church should not overlook the ability of the Holy Spirit to help her. "The love of God has been poured out in our hearts by the Holy Spirit" (Rom. 5:5). The challenge to any church is to direct the Spirit of love in our hearts toward the Bridegroom who loves the church and gave Himself for her.

2. A Love That Can Destroy

The declaration, "I am rich, have become wealthy, and have need of nothing," reveals a self-serving church. The love of money was a prevailing force within the Laodicean Church. Since no one can serve two masters, God and mammon, that church had become lukewarm in her worship and service to the Christ of His church.

Why was Christ sent to "preach the gospel to the poor?" (Luke 4:18). The basic sin of selfishness and pride is demonstrated in the rich more clearly through the misuse of their wealth and the false security that it provides. That selfishness can run its course from self-indulgence to selfish oppression of the poor. Poor people can be selfish. Because they do not have the temptation of being deceived by the false security of riches, it should be easier for them to repent and humble themselves before God.

In Luke 12:16-21, Jesus tells a parable about a farmer who became wealthy. He pulled down his barns in order to build greater barns to store his crops and goods. He could afford the ease and comforts of this present life, but he failed to prepare himself for the life to come. He had the same problem as the church of Laodicea. He became selfish and self-centered. God said to him, "Fool! This night your soul will be required of you." In providing for temporal treasures, he neglected the eternal needs of his soul. "So is he who lays up treasure for himself, and is not rich toward God."

That rich man was not like a rich man in the Old Testament by the name of Abraham. His heart was not all wrapped up in some temporary earthly building program. Abraham desired a "heavenly country." God, therefore, was not ashamed to be called his God. God has "prepared a [heavenly] city" for all those like him (Heb. 11:16). The objective for a rich church is to not become bogged down with too much emphasis on temporal blessings over eternal rewards, through being faithful to God.

God's kind of love is always reaching out, serving and helping others. The Son of God revealed the Father's love in giving Himself for our sins at Calvary. Though the Father gave His Son for the world that people may have everlasting life, the world does not know about God's kind of love. It can only be learned through knowing Him by experiencing more of His fullness. By nature, fallen mankind is self-loving, lovers of money, and "lovers of pleasure rather than lovers of God." Christ came to save and sanctify the church from that kind of love.

The prophetic statement in 2 Timothy 3:1-4 refers to eighteen moral defects in the end-time church, including the love of self and the love of money, which were the Laodicean Church's problem. Verse 5 refers to the end-time church as "having a form of godliness but denying its power." Godliness is one of the Christian realities that come through a passionate love for Jesus. "A form of godliness" is an appearance of Christian goodness without any true inward reality in having the God-like quality that comes through dining with Jesus.

To have true godliness, the self-life must be denied in order that the Christ-life might have His way in righteous living. Converts to Christianity need to apply the transforming principle of the crucified Christ to their lives so that they might be conformed to the image of the Father's firstborn Son. Christianity is all about the Christ of the Scriptures.

People may be "lovers of themselves" and "lovers of money" and become members of any church organization in the nation, but to go forward and follow Jesus into the fullness of discipleship, self-love and where it leads must be denied and taken to the cross (Matt. 16:24-25). Being a convert to Christ is the doorway where a Christian hears His invitation to follow Him along "the narrow way" in becoming a true disciple of Christ.

Counting the Cost of Discipleship

Jesus said that if anyone had a desire or zeal to come after Him, he must do three things: "Let him deny himself, and take up his cross, and follow Me" (Matt. 16:24). How many in this end-time church generation have zeal to come after Jesus? That was the crux of the problem that the Lord had placed before His church organism at Laodicea.

The first desire and zeal for collective human greatness was through soulish rebellion. In the story of building the tower of Babel, the tower became the product of the works of the flesh through selfish ambition of a united people seeking personal glory. That unholy union brought about an intervention of God in confusing their language, which caused the disobedient work of the tower of Babel to be discontinued.

The church of the Laodiceans had laid the foundation for church building. But the glory of the Lord, as her Beginning, had departed because she had failed to count the cost of finishing it. She had become lukewarm toward Him! Selfish love was preventing her from coming after Him, from having a loving attitude toward continuing to dine with Him.

In Luke 14:26-35, Jesus was at the peak of His popularity. The multitudes that were following Him needed to hear the discipleship message of self-sacrifice. Jesus compared building an invisible church with building a visible tower. Before laying the foundation of that church, she needed to "sit down first and count the cost" necessary to finish it. Jesus was on His way to lay His life down as the sacrificial Lamb of God. He would be laying the foundation of salvation by grace through faith for the church.

Because they had stopped building upon that foundation, the Laodiceans were brought to shame in their lukewarmness before the Lamb of God (1 John 2:28). To be part of God's finished, celebrated building program in eternity, repentant hearts in that church needed to accept His invitation to dine with Him until the end.

In building His church, the Father replaces the desire and zeal for personal greatness with a greater desire and passion to be in a loving fellowship and courtship with His Son. A slothful soul might desire to have the love of God without any accountability toward the God of love. That was the kind of response that the Laodicean Church had toward His great love toward her, and it was not acceptable with the Lover of her soul.

God's kind of love abiding in the lives of believing hearts is the only love that will deliver a church from self-centered love that is the result of excessive egotistical thinking. The Laodicean Church needed to repent from her egocentric thinking. The magnifying power of God's love in Christ is reconciling repentant hearts, as an overcoming church unto Himself, out of an end-time church that has become lukewarm toward Him.

The Laodiceans needed to see the promise of the great provisions that come through dining with Him. Sharing the reward as an overcomer with Him, as revealed in verse 21, will be the answer to her passionate love for Him. He and His church will be as one now and forevermore because who He is and what He means to her.

Chapter 9

The Greatest Relationship
A Need for Fellowship through Hearing His Voice

"Behold, I stand at the door and knock. If anyone hears My voice and opens the door, I will come in to him and dine with him, and he with Me" (verse 20).

The message of Revelation 3:20 has been preached as an invitation to the lost and coldhearted who might see a need to open the door of their hearts in order that they may *enter into the saving knowledge of the Lord Jesus Christ.* But Revelation 3:20 is not primarily an evangelistic message to the lost or coldhearted. It was an invitation given to a church that was lukewarm and religiously content. The invitation of Jesus was to anyone in a lukewarm church that would submit to the Spirit of Truth, that might repent and hear the Voice of Truth. Then that person could open heart's door and dine with Jesus in order to *walk in the saving knowledge of the Lord Jesus Christ.*

The Lord's desire was to reach anyone in that church that would humbly recognize a need for a devoted, loving fellowship with Him. Because of His great love and mercy for the church, Christ was appealing to anyone in that church on an individual and personal basis. He was standing and knocking at the church door trying to get the attention and interest of anyone that might repent and hear His voice.

The membership of that church was not in an appreciative and loving relationship with the Lord over the church. That the Lord Jesus standing outside, knocking on the church door indicated the fact that the Laodicean Church had disregarded His rule. He was trying to get the attention of anyone on the inside of that church to dine with Him.

Neglecting the sovereignty of the Lord over that church led to rejecting the fullness of the message that the Lord had to give to her. Though the Holy Spirit, as the Spirit of Truth, will take the initiative in striving with a lukewarm church, the Son of God, as the Voice of Truth, will only come into the life of an individual through an invitation. If Christ is being ignored, He will not remain in the midst of a church congregation. A church can resist, grieve and quench the Holy Spirit as He strives with her, but for that church to have an affectionate relationship with the Savior of her soul is a goal that she can only achieve with the help of the Holy Spirit.

Hearers must open their hearts' door to Jesus, and dine with Him as the Truth. In loving Him, you love the truth of the Scriptures. A church that is lukewarm to His fervent love needs to repent and dine with Him as she learns to live "by every word that proceeds from the mouth of God" according to the Christ of the Scriptures.

The Laodicean Church members, in all likelihood, had meetings in different homes, which was a practice of the early church. But with her riches and wealth, it is reasonable to assume that the best way for her to exhibit such wealth was to build a magnificent, impressive church building for public church gatherings. Her thinking might have been directed toward the glory of Solomon's Temple as God's dwelling place under the old covenant and not toward the glory of the Person of the Christ of the Scriptures under the new covenant. In His teaching, Jesus referred to His body as the Temple of God.

At the beginning of the Church Age, the church in many cities might not have been financially able to have a privately owned church building of any size for public meetings. If the church at Laodicea had owned a large magnificent church building designated for public worship services, it would have been considered something special. If an impressive church edifice, the material evidence of her riches and wealth, could be seen, that might help explain her self-conceit and boasting. It would also present a visual illustration of Jesus standing outside that closed church door making an appeal to anyone on the inside.

A Person Replaces a Place

If the Laodicean Church were one of the first who wanted to continue the idea of building a Temple of God for the glory of God as Israel did in the Old Testament, she could have been instituting a precedent for that type of thinking in church history.

Under the old covenant God's presence was revealed to Jacob at a place he named "Bethel." Bethel became a divine sanctuary to Jacob where he went for divine help and direction. Later, in the wilderness journey, God's presence was located in the Holy of Holies in the Tabernacle of Moses. Wherever the twelve tribes of Israel camped, the Tabernacle was placed at the center of the encampment. The children of Israel were to have their eyes and hearts focused upon the place where the God of Abraham, Isaac and Jacob dwelled.

After Israel became a nation in their Promised Land, the Temple was built in the city of Jerusalem. Jerusalem has been known since the time of the Tabernacle of David (Acts 15:16) as the place where God dwelt and is to dwell. The Holy of Holies in the Temple at Jerusalem was God's dwelling place. When the Israelites were in captivity, their hearts and minds were focused toward Jerusalem, the city of the great King.

When Daniel was in captivity, there went out a decree from King Darius "against him concerning the law of his God." Daniel "went home and in his upper room, with his windows open toward Jerusalem, he knelt down on his knees three times that day, and prayed and gave thanks before his God, as was his custom since early days" (Dan. 6:10). Daniel worshipped God by facing toward the one place on earth where God dwelt.

Under the new covenant, God's presence is located in the Person of the Lord Jesus Christ and not in any one designated locality. The resurrected Christ has become God's spiritual Temple. Christ dwells in the midst of believers, who are temples of the living God, and the church as an organism is called the Body of Christ.

Different religions have a special place of worship, special forms and words of ceremony. As Mecca is a special place of worship to the Moslems and Jerusalem is a special place of worship for the Jews, many different church denominations have a centralized place of operation and worship. But the Person of Christ, as the living Temple of God, is to be the center of attraction for Christianity. The focus of true Christianity, therefore, does not center on a special place, but it is to center upon a special Person named "Christ Jesus of Nazareth." A wrong focus will cause lukewarmness.

Christ, as the ascended Head of the Temple of God, is seated in the heavenly Holy of Holies at the right hand of the Father. Headquarters, therefore, is where the Head is located, and there is where the hearts and minds of a Christ-centered church are directed. Church headquarters of a denominational church organization is found on earth where the head is seated, but the headquarters of the church organism is found in heaven where the Head is seated.

"If then you were raised with Christ, seek those things which are above, where Christ is, sitting at the right hand of God. Set your mind on things above, not on things on the earth. For you died, and your life is hidden with Christ in God." The resurrected, ascended Christ is the banner under which all Christians should rally, and He hasn't chosen any specific city on earth as His permanent residence during the Church Age.

The woman at the well told Jesus, "Our fathers worshipped on this mountain, and you Jews say that in Jerusalem is the place where one ought to worship." Jesus said to her, "Woman, believe Me, the hour is coming when you will neither on this mountain, nor in Jerusalem, worship the Father" (John 4:20-21).

Jesus was telling the Samaritan woman that there was a time coming that He, as the resurrected Temple of God, would replace the place of worship in Jerusalem. When Christ was crucified, "the sun was darkened, and the veil of the temple was torn in two.""By a new and living way which He consecrated for us through the veil, that is, His flesh." Christ's church is in Christ, and the church can be found in any place where Christ is being honored and reverenced in the midst.

A church's focal point, therefore, should not be on some special place *where she worships*, but her eyes of faith should be fixed upon God's personified Truth *in whom she worships*. "God is Spirit, and those who worship Him must worship in spirit and truth" (v. 23). The Holy Spirit is directing the focus of the church organism, not on the visible things of a church organization but on the invisible Christ of Christianity. Moses "endured as seeing Him who is invisible."

The Jews require a sign. Jesus gave them a sign by saying, "Destroy this temple, and in three days I will raise it up" (John 2:19). That sign ran parallel to the sign of Jonah. Jesus, as the Temple of God, was taken down from the cross and put in a tomb. They thought that they had destroyed that unique Temple, but God raised Him from the grave on the third day. He is now the living Temple of God to His church.

No one can limit the blessings of God, the presence of God or the authority of God to any one city, to any one person, or to any one building on earth. All three dwell in the authority given by the Father to the Person of the resurrected, ascended Christ by the power of the Holy Spirit. Jesus said that He would never leave nor forsake His church. Some of the last words of the resurrected Christ to His church were: "And lo, I am with you always, even to the end of the age." Amen. Now the focus of the church should be on the fact "that God was in Christ reconciling the world unto Himself."

An overemphasis of a church edifice being built at some particular sacred locality might become another religious monument that needs to be dedicated "To The Unknown God" (Acts 17:23). Paul made that point to the superstitious Athenians in his sermon on Mars Hill. Only when Christ is dwelling in the midst of worshippers will an architectural structure pass the test of being a Christian church.

King David realized that building the Temple where God was to dwell had been neglected ever since Israel had the Tabernacle of Moses in the wilderness. God was pleased that King David had concern for His House, but He would not let David build the Temple. It was his son, King Solomon, who would build the Temple.

But God told David that He would build him a house through his seed. It would be a house not made with hands. "He shall build Me a house, and I will establish his throne forever" (1 Chron. 17:12). The prophetic fulfillment of God's House would be Christ, God's Holy Temple. It is in Him where "all things are of God, who has reconciled us to Himself through Jesus Christ" (2 Cor. 5:18). God's dwelling place is in the Holy of Holies of the human redeemed spirit, which is the Christ-life in you, the hope of glory.

A church organization might be represented by a center of operations called "headquarters" at a stationary place on earth. But the concept of the church as the Body of Christ is a maturing spiritual church organism that is growing and developing toward a passionate love relationship with her Head.

Christ's divine church organism is housed, grows and develops across the lines of a multitude of human church organizations. The Bridegroom desires the church for His own purchased possession. The Father is in the process of conforming for His firstborn Son an overcoming church, who is continually being led by the Holy Spirit into mature sonship, with whom He will share the rewards of His Kingdom rule as His Bride.

Importance of Hearing God's Voice

Why is it so difficult to get a lukewarm church to hear what the Spirit is saying to her? The Laodicean Church had become religiously proud and comfortably content. She saw no need to hear the voice of God. Did she think that when she received Jesus, she received all that there was to receive at the beginning? If so, she failed to openly demonstrate it! Jesus said, "He who is not with Me is against Me, and he who does not gather with Me scatters" (Luke 11:23). There was no neutral zone where she could take her stand. The Christ of the church was to be Lord over every aspect of her life.

The Laodiceans were attending church, but they weren't hearing His voice. The members of that lukewarm church organism were paying their tithes to the rich church organization, but they weren't hearing His voice. Most likely, they were reading the Scriptures and observing the sacraments, but they weren't hearing the voice of God.

"If anyone hears My voice and opens the door." The creative or maturing process of spiritual growth and development is based upon dining with Him through hearing His voice. Members cannot open the door of their hearts to Him until they first repent, in order that they might be able to hear Him. The resurrected Christ was still dealing with His own people, who "having ears, (did) not hear" (Mark 8:18). The sheep of His pasture must hear His voice in order to follow Him. A voice of a stranger they will not follow. Following Jesus and eating with Him is the true meaning of Christian worship.

"Blessed are the pure in heart for they shall see God" through the eyes of faith. As they seek after Him, find Him, follow Him, walk with Him, and rejoice in Him, a loving fellowship develops between Him and His disciples. Through worship, prayer and fellowship with Christ Jesus, a personal response to Him makes the Christian life meaningful and important to anyone who desires to hear His voice and follow Him.

At the beginning, God worked with the patriarchs. After three hundred years of walking with God, one day Enoch did not return from his walk; he followed his exercise Partner right out into eternity (Gen. 5:22,24). God also worked with Noah, Abraham, Isaac and Jacob. God worked with His chosen people through Moses, the priests and the prophets.

The era since the death, burial and resurrection of Christ has been the dispensation of grace. God has worked differently with His chosen people in each dispensation, but one thing that has been common with God's people in every dispensation is their ability to hear His voice. "Obey My voice, and I will be your God, and you shall be My people" (Jer. 7:23). One distinctive mark in every dispensation for God's people is hearing His voice in order to obey Him and have fellowship with Him. Jesus said, "My sheep hear My voice, and I know them, and they follow Me" (John 10:27).

If God's people want God's blessings upon their life, they need to walk in the ways that God has commanded them to walk. That comes by rightly dividing the Scriptures. The Holy Spirit, who is the Author of the Scriptures, is the only one who can rightly divide the Scriptures. No one can dine with Jesus unless the Holy Spirit leads him. The church needs to make friends with the Holy Spirit, but the Holy Spirit chooses humble diners for Jesus. For unity and harmony in the end-time church, therefore, it is important for her to be submissive to the leadership of the Holy Spirit so that each church may hear what He is saying to the church as a whole.

"Behold, I stand at the door and knock." The love of Christ takes the initiative. He chose us in order that we might seek after Him. Christ's love for the Laodicean Church kept Him seeking for a fervent, emotional fellowship from anyone in that "lukewarm" or halfhearted church. A lukewarm church might be defined as professing Christians who are trying to serve Christ in their own convenience and leisurely comfort.

In the Gospel narrative, Jesus did not sympathize with the potential disciples who came with excuses why they were not immediately available to follow Him. He told them what was at stake in following Him. They would have to depart from anything that would come between them and a devoted relationship in following Him. There is no other place for Christ but first place in the hearts and lives of His church organism.

No one can follow Jesus with a divided heart. Many times when people have an experience with God, they become very religious and feel like they "have arrived." The summit of the Christian experience for some is reaching the goal of church membership, or the goal of receiving the baptism of the Holy Spirit according to Acts 2:4, or the goal of receiving a ministerial gift or a spiritual gift. But when anyone stops seeking for a closer fellowship with a steadfast heart toward Him, the passion and fresh excitement of that first love for Him begin to diminish.

Jesus did not make an appeal to change the impersonal system of operation of the Laodicean Church organization; instead, He made a personal invitation to the individual within that church organism to come and have a personal fellowship with Him. Deuteronomy 32:9 declares, "For the LORD'S portion is His people."

God can restrict or terminate an independent working system of men by changing the men within the system, as He did in a unique manner at Babel, but He cannot change the independent system itself. Christ came to save and change the hearts and lives of people. The Holy Spirit has come to exalt a personal resurrected Christ in the midst of the church. A passionate love fellowship with Jesus was the solution to the Laodicean Church's problem of self-sufficiency and self-centeredness. Christ can be systematically programmed out of a church system called by His name.

Jesus quoted God's Word to the devil in the wilderness temptation, "It is written, 'Man shall not live by bread alone, but by every word that proceeds from the mouth of God'" (Matt. 4:4).

After the feeding of the five thousand, Jesus said to those following Him, "I am the bread of life. He who comes to Me shall never hunger, and he who believes in Me shall never thirst" (John 6:35). A church should be able to feast daily upon the fresh Bread of Heaven that never gets stale. Because there has been very little spiritual food eaten with the King at His table, many church members in the end-time church are spiritually weak in their walk of faith.

Eating at the King's Table

Not only is Christian fellowship based upon hearing His voice, it is also about breaking daily spiritual bread—"by every word that proceeds from the mouth of God"—in dining with Him and others around His table. An Old Testament example of dining with King Jesus is illustrated by the kindness of King David to Mephibosheth, the son of Jonathan, who was invited to eat at the king's table.

Because of his two lame feet, Mephibosheth, no doubt, needed the help of crutches to walk. My wife and I visited the country home of a life-long friend who was an alcoholic at the time. One spring evening while leaning against a post of his front porch, in an intoxicated condition he said, "The trouble with you Christians is you have to have a crutch to lean upon." Jesus is heaven's Crutch to support the two soulish lame feet of a Christian coming to eat at the King's table.

Four times within seven verses in 2 Samuel 9:6-13, it speaks about Mephibosheth being invited by King David to eat bread at the king's table. Mephibosheth is a type of redeemed humanity in experiencing the restoration of his inheritance and receiving an invitation to eat at the king's table. King Jesus shares a new, eternal inheritance with His church through eating bread at His table.

Perhaps Mephibosheth had heard the story of the friendship between his father, Jonathan, and David before David was crowned king of Israel. Mephibosheth was five years old when his father died. Because of King Saul's sin against God, Mephibosheth and his family had become rejected, an outcast of society living in obscurity.

His nursemaid in fleeing from the enemy accidentally dropped baby Mephibosheth. That accident caused him to become lame in both feet. Life was not treating young Mephibosheth very well and his future looked bleak. But God had a plan for broken Mephibosheth's life. God also has a divine plan and purpose for His church, and He chooses those He wishes to eat with Him at the King's table. Like King David, God will also prepare a table before us in the presence of our enemies (Ps. 23:5).

David wanted in some way to honor his dear deceased friend, Jonathan. So he inquired to see if there was anybody left in the kingdom from the household of King Saul through the seed of Jonathan. Lame Mephibosheth was brought out of the depths of rejection and despair and chosen by the king to eat bread at his table "like one of the king's sons." From the milk of the Word to the Bread of Life is the King's spread.

Mephibosheth went from the bottom to the top of the social ladder in the land by the choice of King David. The lukewarm church of the Laodiceans was at the bottom of the Lord's approval list as a church, but by an invitation from King Jesus "anyone" in that poor church (in His eyes) could accept an invitation to dine with the King.

King David emphasized that lame Mephibosheth was not to be just another dinner guest at the king's table. He was to become a permanent member at the king's table. King David told him, "You shall eat bread at my table continually." The word "continually" was used two different times in the story for emphasis. That implied that he had not been chosen to be a dinner guest only to eat at the king's table on Sunday morning. He had been chosen to eat at the king's table "continually" until he was full.

"If anyone hears My voice and opens the door, I will come in to him and dine with him, and he with Me." Now is the time when "anyone" has an open invitation at anytime to partake of the Bread of Life from the King's table. Lame Mephibosheth is an example of whom King Jesus chooses to eat at His table (1 Cor. 1:26-29). God gives grace to the humble! No flesh shall glory in the presence of the Christ of Christianity. Because the Laodicean Church was full of self-glory, He was no longer in her presence but standing outside knocking on the door.

Mephibosheth, the grandson of King Saul, was an outcast, rejected by his own people, but King Jesus often chooses "anyone" like Himself who has been rejected by His own people to dine with Him. Those in that church, who had no appetite for the King's food, would look down on "anyone" that chose to feast at the King's table. But from a "nobody" to that church, he or she would become a "somebody" to the King by eating bread at His table.

Being born into the royal family was a privilege to King David's children, but they probably did not think of themselves as being privileged. But Mephibosheth's elevation to share a place with royalty at the king's table was a privilege and an honor for him. Perhaps Mephibosheth could praise the Lord with greater gratitude in being able to eat at the king's table. The joy of the Lord would be his strength. The food that he ate in humble adoration and appreciation to the king would digest in a healthy way.

In a spiritual context, some churchgoers think that anything that is said from the pulpit of their church has the Lord's approval. But food that is being served at the King's table must be accepted with repentant hearts. The message to repent was Jesus' first message and also the basic message of the early church. Those with unrepentant hearts may come to the table, but they have no appetite for the King's food. To receive spiritual food of the message of the cross of Christ and to follow His example, people that come to the King's table need to have a contrite heart like Mephibosheth.

Christ is King over God's kingdom of righteousness, and the Laodicean Church had a great need to hunger and thirst after righteousness. Eating at the King's table is what will satisfy a hunger and thirst after God's righteousness. That church needed the help of the Holy Spirit in developing a spiritual appetite to eat at the King's table.

Dining with the King, a church receives spiritual nourishment and strength. His body is the Bread of life and His blood is drink indeed. Jesus said, "It is the Spirit who gives life; the flesh profits nothing. The words that I speak to you are spirit, and they are life." The Holy Spirit enables believers to feed upon Jesus as the Bread of Life.

The Father has given the church His written word, His Living Word, and the spoken word. Each concerns and involves Jesus as spiritual food for hungry hearts. It took fifteen hundred years to write the Bible through dire hardship and much suffering. The resurrected Christ, as God's Living Word, became spiritual food for the church when He gave His life as an atoning sacrifice for the sins of the world. The spoken word comes through the mouth of God's servants, some of whom have spent almost a lifetime serving at the King's table.

Jesus said, "I will come in to him and dine with him, and he with Me." Notice that He first dines with us with what little we have before we dine with Him through His abundant supply. Jesus fed the five thousand and the four thousand (that number could be doubled by adding to the count the women and children) with what few loaves and fishes that the disciples had to give to Him. A church might have little to give, but Jesus can multiply what she has to feed the multitudes with His abounding grace.

Someone who heard Jesus speaking a parable about giving out invitations to eat at a wedding feast said, "Blessed is he who shall eat bread in the kingdom of God" (Luke 14:15b). Not just "anyone" but everyone in the church of the Laodiceans should have been interested in eating Bread at the King's table.

In Luke 14:16-24, Jesus told a parable about a certain nobleman who was giving a great supper and many people were invited. That nobleman is a type of King Jesus. Many should have been interested in such a great supper in which the one giving the invitations showed great delight. But each invitation was met with an excuse; each had something else that needed to be done in preference to accepting the invitation to eat at that evening meal. The end-time church has a big banquet spread from which to dine.

Is the end-time a time for the church to make excuses in regard to eating at the King's table? One of the three excuses was that the person was more interested in the gain of earthly real estate compared to heaven's gain. Another was more interested in testing the strength of his five oxen than the spiritual strength that he could receive through eating at the King's table. The third was more interested in entering into an earthly marital relationship than being honored at the Marriage Supper of the Lamb (vv. 18-20). Those three examples of excuses for not wanting to eat at the King's table illustrate the countless number of excuses that servants of God hear from people who have no appetite for food that is being served at the King's table.

The servant went back to his master with the discouraging news. That angered the master and he extended the invitation to include "the poor and the maimed and the lame and the blind" (v. 21). Even after doing that, the report came back that there was still room for many more.

Now is the time to eat at the King's table, for no one who has a hunger to eat with the King will be refused admittance to dine with Him. But at the Marriage Supper of the Lamb, receiving a seat at that banquet table is by reservation only. Whereas that church had closed her door to Him, anyone, with ears to hear, in that church could open it and dine with Him. But there is coming a time when the door that God has closed cannot be opened. The door that was shut on the five foolish virgins in the parable of the ten virgins and the door to Noah's Ark could not be opened to those who wanted to get in.

Notice the sad ending to the parable of the ten virgins in Matthew 25:1-13, "And while they went to buy, the bridegroom came, and those who were ready went in with him to the wedding; and the door was shut" (v. 10). There is now an "anyone can open the door" policy for lukewarm church members to worship Him. Everyone should take advantage of being able to open the door while there is still time. "For I say to you that none of those men who were invited shall taste my supper" (Luke 14:24).

Jesus Was Not in Her Midst

The Laodicean Church was having church services, but the members were not being led by the Holy Spirit to gather together in the name of Jesus. The One who loved the church and gave Himself for her made this statement, "For where two or three are gathered together in My name, I am there in the midst of them" (Matt. 18:20).

Because of the independent nature of professing Christians, Jesus saw a need to be acclaimed in the midst. He foresaw that a soulish tendency could present itself in the things of men in a religious setting, and a church label would receive more recognition than the acknowledgement of the ultimate purpose of God for His church. The Laodicean Church services should have been centered upon the greater One than us in our midst to show forth His great compassion upon us.

What does it mean to act in Jesus' name? Jesus came in the authority of His Father to do His will that the Father may be glorified. In doing so, the Son lost His self-identity in the Father by speaking the words and doing the things that His Father gave Him to speak and do. By rejecting Jesus, the nation of Israel rejected the Father who sent Him. Anything that is not done for the glory of God is not being done according to the will of God. Where each member of the maturing church organism honors Him as her functional Head, the whole Body functions for the glory of God.

What constitutes or empowers a local church? A Body of believers cannot properly function without recognizing His authority over the church. The Holy Spirit should be honored as His enabling authority in the church to recognize and glorify Christ. Christ is Head of the church organism that gives life to a church organization. A right church is being gathered together by the Holy Spirit for the glory of Jesus according to the will of the Father. A church that glorifies the Son glorifies the Father also.

Assembling together in the name of Jesus gives the glory to Jesus. Through the leading and guidance of the Holy Spirit, that kind of assembly can be accomplished. A gathering that is "being led together by the Holy Spirit into the name of Jesus" becomes a church meeting for Jesus to be present in the midst (Rom. 8:14).

Everything that Jesus did as the Son of Man in the gospel narrative was done by the power of the Holy Spirit for the glory of the Father. When Christ is glorified in the midst of a church, the power and ability of the Holy Spirit is doing it through believing hearts. By virtue of the work of the Spirit of Truth, God's incarnate Truth can be revealed and digested, one morsel at the time. As God's *Logos*, Christ is the totality of God's truth.

Jesus' precise function in the church is the Head of the Body of Christ. The Laodicean Church had lost contact with Jesus as her authority. If Christ does not function over members of a church body as the Head, He does not function at all. That is His predestinated place in the Body. The

Holy Spirit is the Helper in working with the church and preparing her to see the importance of Christ for her very existence and being.

Jesus is not waiting at some designated place called the church sanctuary for church people to arrive. Paul spoke of "a mystery among the Gentiles: which is Christ in you, the hope of glory" (Col. 1:27). After honoring His presence in daily living, Christians bring the indwelling Christ with them as they honor Him in a worship service. The importance of gathering together is to give the Holy Spirit an opportunity to exalt Christ in the midst of His church.

Collective spiritual pride in a church organization can lead professing Christians to have an attitude of disregard, and in some extreme cases, even contempt toward others belonging to another church organization. How can the Father's humble Servant honor haughty humanity? At times, the Lord resisted unenlightened, impetuous, proud, outspoken Peter, but Peter knew how to humble himself before the Lord and repent.

From the beginning, pride has been a barrier separating God from His people. The journey of proud and rebellious Israel to possess the fullness of her inheritance of the Promise Land began 3500 years ago, but I believe the journey is about to end. The journey of God's self-reliant church to possess the fullness of her divine inheritance has also been a long journey. Both Israel and the church have a common enemy, but they also have a common Messiah who is coming soon to give a waiting and watchful remnant the fullness of their inheritance according to the Scriptures. Then Jesus will be the One on center stage of a new order—the Kingdom of God on earth.

The Greatest Invitation

Jesus was giving an invitation to a church, but the greatest invitation is to the world. It is God's invitation to receive eternal life by coming into the saving knowledge of Christ Jesus. But the greatest invitation to a church is the humility of the Lord of heaven toward a lukewarm church. God is a jealous God; that means He has emotions, but the Laodicean Church had lost her excitement and desire to have fellowship with Him. Merciful Jesus was still making an appeal for the affections of that church. Christ was not at the center of the meditations of her heart. She had lost her first love.

Because of the eternal scope of her assigned task, the greatest need for a lukewarm church is to repent and accept Jesus' invitation to come and dine with Him. Because the Laodicean Church was blinded to her greatest need, His personal invitation of fellowship to anyone having a hearing heart for eternal values and rewards was most important. Anyone in that lukewarm setting had the potential of coming to Jesus in fervent, wholehearted fellowship in fulfilling God's ultimate purpose for His overcoming, glorious church.

Salvation's complete story points the church to the coming of the greatest event in the annals of human history. Qualifying for that event comes by invitation only. "If anyone hears My voice and opens the door, I will come in to him." The true Lover of the soul is the only One who can give peace and rest to a troubled soul.

Because the church organism of a Christian institution is all that can qualify to leave this judgment-bound world, she needs to be getting ready to do so. He is only coming for those who have made themselves ready. There is a great need for searching the Scriptures to know more truth. There is an even greater need for prayer in spiritual guidance and understanding. But the greatest need is for a church to humble herself under the mighty hand of God with a wholehearted love and hunger for more of Him in worship and Christian service.

The invitation to dine with Him was to enthrone Him in believing hearts through eating the spiritual food of God's Word. Her halfhearted attitude toward Him was unacceptable. If she would give to Him her whole heart in union and communion with Him, He would share with her what He was sharing with the Father. He would share a throne of glory with anyone who overcomes as He overcame. Great invitations and rewards from heaven do not come without personal sacrifice on the part of doers of God's Word on earth.

To have an ongoing close fellowship with someone, you must become part of the lifestyle of the other. If harmony is not established in a relationship, there can be no lasting fellowship. That is true in the spiritual realm, as it is also true in the natural realm. All church organizations, to better serve the one church organism, must work together in agreement with the Christ of the Scriptures in order to walk in harmony with Him and with one another.

One thing is certain; the Father will choose a Bride for His Son who fervently loves Him and is in total agreement with Him. Knowing Him as the Christ of the Scriptures in His fullness, therefore, is not only the focal point of Christianity, He is also the pivotal point of unity within two different groups of people: the church and the nation of Israel. "Unto him shall the gathering of the people be" (Gen. 49:10, KJV).

Church traditions that resist the purposes of God keep people in spiritual bondage. Church traditions take away from the veracity of the Word of God, and for the most part, they do not change. They become set like concrete, and God will not build upon the solidified sands of the foundation of the things of men.

The rock foundation that God builds upon doesn't change either. The unchanging God is in the changing business. The Father's chief Cornerstone of His building program is the same yesterday, today, and forever (Heb. 13:8). No one can continue to dine in the presence of Jesus very long and remain the same. Church people need to change for the better. Only the Holy Spirit can lead and direct them to dine with Christ Jesus in order for the Father to change them to be more like His firstborn Son.

As a Christian institution, the Laodiceans had failed to be led by the Holy Spirit in fulfilling the purpose of God in Christ Jesus. Self-glory had won out over God's glory. Jesus gave an invitation, therefore, to anyone in that church who might hear His voice and open his heart's door to Him. His great invitation to the people in that church in verse 20 comes between a harsh but loving rebuke that is concluded in verse 19 and the promise of a notable reward for the overcomer in verse 21.

Fellowship with Him from Beginning to End

He was her Beginning or Alpha at the birth and early growth of the church. Loving Him at the beginning of the Christian experience is no sign that church members will love Him more at the end. But the purpose of the Christian journey is having a daily loving fellowship with Him from beginning to end. The objective is to love Him more at the end than at the beginning. "In the place where the tree falls, there it shall lie." The end of this life, as we live it under the sun, is where the tree falls.

An experience with Him as a resurrected, personal Savior is where the love for Him begins. But many church people have a tendency to become so religious in temporal things that their first love for God's eternal Son begins to fade away in the midst of many religious endeavors. Becoming lukewarm toward Him was putting the Laodicean Church in danger of rejecting Him as the Omega or End of her salvation.

The greatest reward that the Bridegroom has to give is sharing His throne with His Bride. That reward is not just exclusively for those who overcome the lukewarm atmosphere of a compromising church system, but it is for all that meet the qualification of loving Him with all their hearts. The Bride will love her Bridegroom more than anything and anyone that is in this world or in a lukewarm church.

Verse 14 introduces Christ Jesus to the Laodiceans as "the Beginning," not as "the Beginning and the End" as He introduced Himself to the seven churches of Asia Minor in the introduction of the book of Revelation (Rev. 1:8). He also introduced Himself in the same manner near the close of the book, "the Alpha and the Omega, the Beginning and the End, the First and the Last" (Rev. 22:13).

He is the Christ of a complete salvation to His church as she fellowships with Him from the beginning to the end. And the thrust of the gospel message is that in knowing Him, we learn to love Him, and fervently loving Him should be the church's objective from beginning to the end.

He was identified to her as her Beginning in His dealings with her at the beginning of the church life, but she was falling short in fellowshipping Him as her End, or Omega. He was calling her unto Himself as her Alpha and Omega, the total Christ representing a complete salvation. She needed to know the importance and meaning of His wholehearted love toward her.

The nation of Israel was guilty of a divided heart toward God many times in her long history under the old covenant. She rejected God in Christ Jesus because she had developed a heart of stone toward Him. The problem in the Laodicean Church had not become that severe, but she had developed a halfhearted attitude toward Jesus. People in the Laodicean Church needed to develop a steadfast heart toward the Son of God.

The promise of an exalted reward to the overcomer in the Laodicean Church belonged to those who overcame a church environment of self-exaltation for self-glory. If anyone has never known Him as Alpha, there can be no knowing Him as Omega. Because of her compromise to a lukewarm position before Him, He was making an invitation to rekindle her first love for Him as her Alpha. What had begun as a rebuke of love turned to a loving invitation for communion and fellowship with anyone who would repent.

Why is it so difficult for the lukewarm to accept an invitation to dine and fellowship with Him in spirit and in truth? Because Israel is a nation that has a covenant with God, she is a privileged nation. Because the church also has a covenant with God, blood-bought believers that form a church become privileged people. But that privileged church thought that she was more spiritual and highly favored toward God than she truly was. She needed to humble herself before the mighty hand of God.

Because of her lack of love for Him, her attention and interest became centered on her own collective self-worth and the material things of this temporal life. One thing is always needful for a congregation like that one. She needed to fall in love with Jesus all over again and obey His words. No one should say, "I love Jesus," and not obey His teachings. Obedience to His words is proof of a church's love for Him. Jesus said, "If you love Me, keep My commandments" (John 14:15).

But Christ is interested in every Christian called by His name. His appeal is: "If anyone hears My voice." He is ready to restore any halfhearted Christian whose eyes have been diverted from Him toward the material things that riches can buy. His own people rejected Him, mocked Him, mistreated Him, and had Him crucified in His First Coming. Now He is coming again, not for a church that has neglected, spurned and shunned His love, but for a people who love Him with all their heart at the time of His Appearing.

Wholeness of heart toward the resurrected, ascended, coming-again Christ Jesus is a heart that is filled with acknowledgment, thankfulness and praise toward His complete redemptive work—the giving of His life's blood as the innocent Lamb of God for guilty humanity. If there were any identification that could be singled out that would best fit His Bride, it would be that she should be called, "the Lamb's wife."

Christ Was Not Her Yokefellow

Jesus gave an invitation to the religious people of Israel that were burdened down with the legalistic teachings of the scribes and Pharisees, "Come to Me, all you who labor and are heavy laden, and I will give you rest. Take My yoke upon you and learn from [of] Me, for I am gentle and lowly in heart, and you will find rest for your souls. For My yoke is easy and My burden is light" (Matt. 11:28-30).

The pride of life with all of its consequences was a heavy yoke for the Laodicean Church to bear. Along with spiritual pride in the realm of a church come legalistic teachings and carnal thinking. He who is "gentle and lowly in heart" offers His yoke of a "meek and contrite spirit." Being yoked to Jesus was for that church to forsake self-will and become yoked to the will of God for her life. True freedom is found in being yoked to Jesus. Sometimes truth appears as a paradox to human thinking, such as "you shall know the truth and the truth will set you free" through being yoked to Jesus.

Jesus did not say that life would be easy; He said that His yoke would be easy. He will be with a church and go with her through every crisis and every trial. In their frustrations and disappointments, church people might dream of a make-believe life of everything going smoothly. The worldly-minded make life out as a joke. Life is no joke; it is a yoke. The yoke of self-denial and being a cross-bearer for Jesus' sake in righteous living is much easier to bear than the yoke of the sins of the world or being burdened down with religious legalistic practices.

Church people may be yoked to a distressful and disagreeable job, financial problems, food addiction, a haughty religious spirit, and a multitude of other controlling, intimidating, manipulative spirits that are not the Spirit of liberty. Many false church systems are under bondage to false doctrines and deceiving religious, legalistic yokes that they know nothing about. Being yoked to a loving Lord Jesus Christ is easy compared to being yoked to lukewarm, legalistic religious practices or the judgment-bound world.

The throne of Christian hearts belongs to Jesus. God can only fill a heart that has been emptied of self-love and love of the world. Only when the laws of God's kingdom have been written on the heart of church members, can they become faithful, righteous servants to the King.

There were some in the Laodicean Church that were carrying an unnecessary yoke that Jesus did not want them to bear. They needed to turn to Jesus for help. He was standing on the outside knocking and speaking to anyone in that church that might hear His voice. Through the trials of His loving relationship with people in that church, He would become more precious to anyone who would repent and open the door.

The end-time church has many reasons for being identified with Christianity, but living the Christian life for the purpose of glorifying Him in fullness of daily fellowship with Him is the supreme reason. The loving fellowship that He provides is the greatest fellowship of all. That fellowship is not just being with Christ in the realm of time, but a fellowship with Him that lasts for eternity. Christian fellowship with Him and His people is a sharing of His interests, objectives, and goals for the church. The more that a church fellowships with Him in the realm of time, the more likely she will fellowship with Him as His Bride in eternity.

That church developed an ecclesiastical system that identified her to the world as Christian. God cannot change an intangible, impersonal, unemotional church system of men, but it is possible for Him to change emotional men within a church organizational system. But man must be in the church system and not the church system in the man. The church organism is to be led by the Holy Spirit into all truth and not led by the rules of a church organizational system into religious bondage.

Knocking on a Closed Door

In the exhortation to receive the good gifts of God, there is a need to persevere in prayer by asking, seeking, and knocking on a closed door. The Lord is emphatic in saying the one that asks shall receive; the one that seeks shall find; and to the one who knocks the door will be opened. A loving, merciful heavenly Father is more than willing to open the door to His children and give good things to the ones who keep on knocking.

But in this story, the One with nail prints in His hands and feet, and a deep scar in His side from a Roman spear, was taking the initiative and knocking on a door that had been closed to Him. That closed door to Jesus was representative of that church's love for her riches and wealth more than her love for Him. That closed door had separated Jesus from the church organism for which He died. It was a door that could only be opened from the inside. The invitation was given to "anyone" in that church who would repent and hear His voice.

There was a need to hear His voice before the door could be opened. The invitation was to those church members, who still had a hunger in their hearts in wanting to know Him more in His fullness. The door to that lukewarm church organism had been closed to Jesus through the influence of a rich, egotistical, self-sufficient church organization.

Rejection and ridicule met Jesus of Nazareth from His own people at His First Coming. It made no difference that He loved His own people fervently. He cried out, "O Jerusalem, Jerusalem, the one who kills the prophets and stones those who are sent to her! How often I wanted to gather your children together, as a hen gathers her chicks under her wings, but you were not willing!" He was willing, but they were not! Because Jerusalem had sown to the wind in unbelief and sinful passions, she would surely reap the whirlwind. Not long after he wept over her, Jerusalem was destroyed in 70 A.D. and her people were scattered to the four winds.

Almost two thousand years ago, Jesus wept over Jerusalem because of her unbelief (Luke 19:41). Today, there is reason to weep over Jerusalem because of her troubles, strife and unrest. "Pray for the peace of Jerusalem: "May they prosper who love you" (Ps. 122:6). But Jerusalem must first find her peace with God before there can be an absence of physical conflict. I believe that the Lord of heaven and earth is getting excited about His soon return to deliver His people by natural descent from their many enemies.

There are many church doors today, like the lukewarm Laodicean Church door, which have been closed to Him. Time is drawing near for the return of the Lord Jesus Christ. For those lukewarm churches that love the things of this world more than they love Him, now is the time for anyone in a *lukewarm* church to respond to His voice of loving kindness and tender care. God's complete salvation in Christ Jesus is available to *anyone* who will come to Him and dine with Him in wholehearted worship.

Israel's spiritual pride and self-righteousness blinded her to the Scriptures that proclaimed the Messiah's First Coming. The nation of Israel had suffered the same spiritual symptoms that were blinding a church like the Laodiceans from being prepared to receive Him at His Second Coming. Jesus was willing to have a wholehearted fellowship with any who would repent from their lukewarm ways, but how many would there be like Jerusalem of old who were not willing? Jesus would tell a church like the Laodiceans what He told the rebellious scribes and Pharisees: "Search the Scriptures" for it is the Scriptures that testify of Jesus in His fullness.

Christ Jesus was rejected by His own people, the nation of Israel, and His own people, the Laodicean Church, were neglecting Him. The problem with the church of the Laodiceans was the same problem that the nation of Israel had. Both took for granted that they had a right relationship with God, which actually, neither no longer had.

The Son was committed to doing the Father's will and that led Him to die the death of the cross. Christ "loved the church and gave Himself for her." The words of a resurrected, ascended Christ in verse 20 reveals that He is seeking the heart and soul of anyone that has been led astray by misplaced emphasis in a lukewarm church. Jesus is saying to anyone who is behind a door of a lukewarm end-time church, which has been closed to Him, to repent and open the door and dine with Him until the end.

Christ has come as the Way to the Father, to show believers the ways of God. Jesus came to live a life before His disciples that was opposite to the ways and thinking of the religious natural mind of that day. Jesus made it quite clear that He was completely dependent upon the Father in everything that He said or did. His life was lived to glorify the Father who sent Him. The life that He lived should be the prime example for the church life. A resurrected Christ said to His frightened disciples in the evening on resurrection day, "As the Father has sent Me, I also send you" (John 20:21).

Chapter 10

The Greatest Reward
A Need to Be Qualified to Receive the Reward

"To him who overcomes I will grant to sit with Me on
My throne, as I also overcame and sat down with My Father
on His throne" (verse 21).

When Jesus taught about rewards of the kingdom in the Bible, it was about kingdom relationships, not about things in heaven. When church members think about rewards today, it is usually the rewards of material things. The things of heaven are emphasized with the gates of pearl, the walls of jasper and the streets of gold. But verse 21 is not talking about streets of gold but a throne that represents a crown of gold.

Verse 21 clearly reveals that rewards are more than tangible things; the most excellent relationship in the universe that an overcoming church can achieve is ruling and reigning with the King of kings and the Lord of lords over a visible kingdom.

At the beginning, the disciples of Jesus were expecting that their Messiah would set up an immediate visible kingdom, as prophesied in the Scriptures. Their hopes were shattered when their Messiah was crucified. But after His resurrection, and before His ascension to the Father, they asked, "Lord, will you at this time restore the kingdom to Israel?" The hope of His soon return to complete the prophetic Scriptures was revived. Many in the early church lived in expectation of the Return of the King to set up His visible kingdom.

Jesus taught about relationship rewards in His kingdom rule. The overcoming church achieves the reward by grace through faith by yielding to Him and loving Him for His wholehearted, self-giving love toward her. Mary was sitting at Jesus' feet and hearing His words, but "Martha was distracted with much serving." Everyone knows that Martha's work was important, including Martha. She wanted Jesus to tell her sister to help her. Jesus told the worried and troubled Martha, "But one thing is needed, and Mary has chosen that good part, which will not be taken away from her" (Luke 10:42). After Mary arose from sitting at Jesus' feet, if she had told Martha that she should be doing the same, Jesus would have told a distracted Mary to keep her heart steadfast toward Him and not compare herself with her sister.

Getting to know Jesus more in His fullness by fellowship with Him in His love takes time and focus. It is not what a church does by self-effort, like the Laodicean Church, but it is what He will make her through dining with Him. The overcoming church is able to say, "By the grace of God I am what I am, and His grace toward me was not in vain."

Many Christians think that rewards are only about heavenly things and having their attention and interest on personal rewards in Christian service would not be appropriate. Jesus taught as much about rewards as He did on any other subject, but the lesson to be learned is not on the love of some reward but on the specific reward of His love.

Since the highest reward is that we might win Him through our love and devotion to Him, longing to be forever with Him cannot be separated from the theme of rewards. Love does not serve to be rewarded, but there is the reward of love. The church belongs to Christ, as personified Love, and He belongs to the church.

Introduction to salvation is coming to the Lord and receiving Him as a personal Savior. The consummation of that salvation is when He comes for an overcoming church. The inspired reward for the overcoming church is winning an eternal relationship with the most exalted Person in the Kingdom of God.

Good relationships give true meaning for living whether in time or for eternity. Verse 21 gives a promise of an exalted reward that belongs to the one who has overcome a church atmosphere of self-exaltation for self-glory. It's not that the atmosphere of a lukewarm church is easy to overcome, but the way out might not be as difficult or complex as being engrossed in damnable heresy or being in bondage and a captive to depraved sinful immorality.

Although God's kingdom has rank and file from the smallest to the greatest, Jesus discouraged that kind of thinking for His church. Jesus prayed to the Father for oneness and harmony in the church, and taught His disciples, "Whoever desires to become great among you, let him be your servant, and whoever desires to be first among you, let him be your slave" (Matt 20:26-27).

The disciples thought that Jesus was going to set up an immediate kingdom. The mother of James and John asked Jesus, "Grant that these two sons of mine may sit, one on Your right hand and the other on the left, in Your kingdom…And when the ten heard it, they were greatly displeased with the two brothers" (vv. 20-24). Perhaps they were thinking the same thing, but the mother of James and John presented the question before they had the opportunity to do so.

That incident gave Jesus an opportunity to teach His disciples how His church should function. Jesus called them together and said, "You know that those who are considered rulers over the Gentiles lord it over them, and their great ones exercise authority over them. "Yet it shall not be so among you, but whoever desires to become great among you shall be your servant. "And whoever of you desires to be first shall be slave of all. "For even the Son of Man did not come to be served, but to serve, and to give His life a ransom for many" (vv. 42-45). When leaders of the many church organizations are all bidding for the goal of a servant's status in serving the one church organism, it becomes much easier to reach the goal of unity and harmony in the Body of Christ.

The church itself, the Bride of Christ, will be the highest in the rank and file in the Kingdom of God. Because she is "the Lamb's wife," she shares with Him in His rule and reign over God's kingdom. Because the church had a past with Him in His pain and suffering, crucifixion and shame for her at the cross, the church will have a future with Him in His rule and glory.

The Reward of a Relationship

The central theme of the story of this book is the relationship between the church of the Laodiceans and her Redeemer. Because of her neglect in building a fervent, loving relationship with the Savior of her soul, her religious works were found wanting. Her halfhearted devotion toward the Lord over the church made Him sick at His stomach. The Head of the Body was ready to vomit her, as a member of the Body, out of His mouth. Because her love for riches was greater than her love for Him, she had no need of help from anyone, and that would include the Head of the church.

That relationship had become one-sided because she had become lukewarm and uncommitted to Him, compared to His wholehearted love toward her. He lives to provide for both the spiritual and physical needs of His church. Because He loved her deeply, He rebuked her severely and harshly for her disobedient attitude. He told her to repent!

The obedient will continue to have a relationship toward an exalted level of reigning and ruling with Christ in His coming kingdom. According to Bible history, only a remnant of that church would receive the reward of the overcomer. But with the help of the Holy Spirit, that story could have a good ending. With His guidance, anyone with a contrite heart in that church could cast all of his cares upon Jesus, for He cared for him.

At the beginning, God created man and woman for a holy matrimonial relationship. The commandment to replenish the earth indicated that there was to be righteous family relationships. The Christian family is the foundation of society and the church. A right church is the foundation of a godly nation. Modern-day society, for the most part, has been unable to see the importance of good working relationships in the home—either that or people are unable to build lasting relationships because of extreme self-centeredness.

There are too many bonds of unholy relationships in these last days. Because of modern-day lifestyles, and the divorce rate being so high, many young people don't even attempt marriage. The human heart has become so rebellious against God that people can't live together in harmony as a family.

Holy relationships are important as a family works together toward mutual goals. The Bible presents the highest goal. The Christian family should all be seeking a devoted relationship toward living a life that is pleasing to Him. Peace and joy are the rewards of righteous relationships. The crux of the Christian life, therefore, should be built upon faithfulness of having a loving relationship to a merciful Lord and Savior.

Being properly related to an all-sufficient Christ, the exalted Head of His church organism, was not a priority to a self-sufficient church like the Laodiceans. The busy lifestyle of many Christians of the end-time Church Age leaves little time for communicating and knowing what makes an interrelated love relationship with Him fruitful and productive.

The Father's Prize for the Overcoming Church

Paul said, "I press toward the goal for the prize of the upward call of God in Christ Jesus" (Phil 3:14). The upward call is the upward drawing of His great love heavenward. Since the reward for the overcomer is not in winning things but in winning Him as the Prize, the eternal reward of a bride relationship with Jesus is the highest of all rewards.

Merciful Jesus wanted a restored relationship with anyone in that church who would hear His voice and open the door to a loving fellowship. His reward is a reward of a personal relationship with those who would overcome as He overcame. He gave His all in the death that He died at the cross for His church. In His resurrected, ascended glory, a living Christ says to His church, "The best that I have to give is Myself in loving you." He is the Father's precious, prize for the overcoming church.

The way to the throne is the way of self-denial and cross-bearing for His sake. To sit with Christ on His throne, the church must overcome as He overcame. Jesus is now sitting at the Father's right hand in His resurrected, ascended glory. He will not share His throne with those who have not been emptied of self-centeredness and selfishness from the throne of their hearts. The Laodicean Church needed to experience a death and burial of self-love before she could experience a resurrection of the love of Christ to sit upon the throne of repentant hearts in that church.

There is lesson to learn in how Jesus earned His reward through living the life of the Overcomer. He came in His Father's name. Because the Father sat upon the throne of His heart, the Son gave the glory to the Father. Now the Father is sharing His throne with His firstborn Son, the beginning of the new creation of God. As a church gathers together to worship in His name, He sits upon the throne of believer's heart. Those who are giving their undivided hearts in loving Him are living an overcoming life by faith. Christ will share His throne with them.

The Lord honored each church member in the Laodicean Church that accepted His invitation and entered into the fullness of His fellowship to the end as a member of the overcoming church. It is never easy being a nonconformist in a worldly crowd or hot for Jesus in a lukewarm church. But the reward of drawing closer to Him for now and eternity is worth it, because winning Him as the Prize is God's Eternal Reward.

Each one in the overcoming church would follow the example of Jesus who "humbled Himself and became obedient to the point of death even the death of the cross." Jesus, therefore, was rewarded His exaltation through His humble obedience to His Father's will. The overcoming church will be rewarded her exaltation with Him through her humble obedience to Him. Christ the King and His Queen have a kingdom to rule over. The Father initiated the overcoming church. He is the One who shall bring her to her appointed destiny. Overcoming pride and rebellion was necessary for the church of the Laodiceans to win the Prize in the person of the Son.

The deceiving power of her riches and wealth drew the attention of the church at Laodicea away from the eternal riches of Christ. Becoming proud of having become prosperous in acquiring earthly things, she neglected her indebtedness in being faithful to the heavenly One. The glitter of her silver and gold had more influence over her than did the God of her salvation. Her riches made her proud at heart. The Lord resisted that haughty attitude.

An angel named Lucifer boasted what he would do through self-exaltation. As a result God said that he "shall be brought down to Sheol, to the depths of the Pit" (Is. 14:13-15). The Bible says, "Whoever exalts himself shall be humbled and he who humbles himself will be exalted." That is an example of a universal, divine principle that is found written in the Scriptures.

As Lucifer is the greatest example of "whoever exalts himself shall be humbled" to the lowest, the Son of God is the greatest example of "whoever humbles himself shall be exalted" to the highest. The Highest One humbled Himself to the lowest position in the universe in His death and burial in order that lowly humanity might be exalted with Him to the highest position in the universe through His resurrection life.

The Laodicean Church owed it all to Jesus. But what was it that held those church members back from giving the fullness of their heart to Jesus? That church had a great debt of love to pay. Because of lukewarm hearts, she was falling far behind in making the payments on her great debt of love that she owed to Him. Jesus is the way to the Father, and she was going the wrong way on a one-way street.

By declaring that she was a "have need of nothing" church, her egotistical words had no value or worth in them. She had become blinded to the worth of her self-centered works. Words and works that qualify for a reward are where God gets the glory. From a halfhearted position toward Jesus, that church needed to develop a steadfast heart toward Him. That church was following the same example of an independent people toward God as did Israel under the old covenant. "For their heart was not steadfast with Him, nor were they faithful in His covenant" (Ps. 78:37).

There is more to the so great salvation in the gospel message than just knowing the place where those who have been justified through the blood of Jesus will spend eternity. Salvation through the redeeming, cleansing, sanctifying blood of Jesus is more than "a heaven to gain" and "a hell to shun" situation. The sooner people face up to that question the easier it will be to come up with the right answers and accept the challenge in regard to winning the Prize in running the Christian marathon race according to His rules.

A Concern to Be Approved to God

The Laodicean Church should not have been so lazy or closed-minded to the study of the Scriptures. The Scriptures would have revealed to her that she had a spiritual need toward God and others. "Be diligent to present yourself approved to God, a worker who does not need to be ashamed, rightly dividing the word of truth" (2 Tim. 2:15).

God's Word, therefore, should be diligently studied with the motive that a disciple might be "approved to God." In following the Christ of the Scriptures into the passion of discipleship, it is necessary to study the unfolding pages of God's Word with the aim of pleasing the One who "loved His church and gave Himself for her."

Being "approved to God" is the highest motive for Christian living. A church is a right church when she has God's approval upon her. No man or woman has been given the authority, according to the Scriptures, to approve people to God. They can be an instrument or a channel of the Holy Spirit to minister to people, to heal and deliver them, and to lead and guide others as the Holy Spirit directs them. Christ judges each church that belongs to Him. "To his own Master he stands or falls" (Rom. 14:4). That is what He was doing to the church of the Laodiceans, and she was not in good standing.

A desire to be approved by men in a church society is a typical, natural desire. The desire may be a good one, but a church must first cultivate a perspective of what it takes to be approved to God? She must first establish a vertical commitment toward God by adjusting her thinking toward Him according to the Scriptures. If God takes the initiative in the life of a church, she must go to the Scriptures to be approved by Him.

So much of the time, a church's thinking and interest may be on nothing more than a horizontal level of the news of the day, which can result in being weighed down with the world and its domestic problems. But a church should never be burdened down with a horizontal focus to the point where current events in the world become a hindrance to her vertical focus for the Soon-Coming event with Him. According to Luke 10:38-42, Martha had a horizontal focus in serving the temporal needs of Jesus and others in her daily chores. Mary had a vertical focus as she "sat at Jesus' feet and heard His word." Both Christian services are important and necessary in the work of the Lord, but the rewards of Martha's work usually can be more readily seen, appreciated and evaluated.

A church does not need to prove anything to God for Him to love her. He has loved her from the beginning. He has proven His love for her by giving Himself for her. Christ was initiating His self-giving love toward the Laodicean Church by the humble invitation that He was giving. He wanted her to learn to love Him with a whole heart until the end because He had loved her wholeheartedly from the beginning.

A church's motivation, therefore, for pleasing God should be based upon the kind of response that she gives toward Christ's self-giving love toward her. How is the end-time church responding to the unchanging love of Christ toward her? The Laodicean Church was too wrapped up in self-love to show Him a wholehearted love.

Great tests of faith are based upon passing the tests and trials in the Christian life. Christ's love for the church was a tested love. Would He give Himself even to the death of the cross for His church? His benevolent concern for lost-dying humanity was the object of His love. But there was also the Father's ultimate purpose for His deserving Son to have a loveable Bride created in His image for the Father's glory.

Jesus passed the test of ultimate self-denial through His prayer to the Father in the Garden of Gethsemane. Jesus took the lost condition of humanity being without hope toward God seriously. The church, therefore, should receive His finished work at the cross and the words that He spoke seriously. The works that she performed as related to obeying the words that He spoke will be her judge.

The Father gave His Son for the sins of the world "that whoever believes in Him" might become a member of the "called-out assembly," separated unto God, as the church. Christ's love was tested and certified by the Father for the benefit of the church. The Father resurrected Him from the dead on the third day for the benefit of the church. So how each individual church identity responds to the fullness of God's grace in Christ Jesus is very important.

What can the church do for His benefit? Can she learn to think about saying and doing things that are for "God who works in you (her) both to will and to do His good pleasure" (Phil. 2:13)? God's love needs a recipient. To be like Jesus, the recipient needs to reciprocate that love in being obedient to God's Word. Genuine love flows outward from Christ through the church and His love deserves a reasonable, faithful response. The Laodicean Church was unenlightened to that scriptural fact concerning her.

Would anyone in the Laodicean Church, called by His name, love the Lord the way He deserves to be loved? As little children are in no position to understand the fullness of parental love for them, that church was in no position to understand the fullness of Christ's love for her. She needed to humble herself before Him in child-like faith.

The facts of Scripture need to be rightly divided and soulish differences need to be set aside. Church traditions and theological systems do not provide the reality needed for souls to walk in the fullness of Christ's love for His church. Loving the praises of men more than the praises of God will also hinder souls from being enlightened to follow Jesus. Being delivered from a self-centered focus by following Jesus is the only way that will lead a church into having a right relationship with Him and with one other.

Spiritual growth and development come through fellowship with Him. There is always a need for a closer walk with Jesus. As He is the functional Head of His Body, the church, then how close can fellowship with the Head be developed with other members in the Body of Christ?

The disciple relationship with Jesus and the church organism is to become so close that individuals lose their self-identity in Him. Paul proclaimed, "It is no longer I who live but Christ lives in me." Christ and the church organism are to become as one mind and one heart in testimony to a judgment-bound world. The church is to do the perfect will of the Lord who commissioned her members to love one another.

He is King over the kingdom of God, but being a member of the Body of Christ, the church has a greater and closer spiritual fellowship with Him and with one another than the relationship between citizens under kingdom rule. Members in the overcoming church are becoming God's foreordained workmanship in Christ Jesus for His eternal glory.

As the overcoming church is being built step by step for God's glory, she is becoming more and more the creative masterpiece that God intends for her to become. Many insignificant doctrinal beliefs are being overemphasized, but the need to be prepared to receive the reward of the overcomer cannot be overemphasized to those who have ears to hear the message.

The Bridegroom's Approval of His Bride

What does it take for the bride-elect to be approved of Jesus? She will not be like the self-centered church of the Laodiceans. The devoted approval of the bride elect by her Bridegroom can be contrasted with His strong disapproval of the lukewarm church of the Laodiceans. Accountability in relation to Christ's unique love for the church might not be a truth that a lukewarm heart wants to hear.

Secular educational institutions promote the theory of evolution as if it were a scientific fact. Believing in the theory of evolution attacks the Genesis account of creation and undermines the beautiful story of the first bridegroom and his bride in the garden of paradise. Believers in the doctrine of evolution, in their blindness of heart, might think that they are released from being accountable to the God of the Bible. Whether the world will admit it or not, it is accountable to God through the death of His Son on the cross.

That lukewarm "need of nothing" church thought that she was no longer accountable to God. But Jesus made it quite clear that she was answerable to His wholehearted love toward her. No church doctrine should try to indirectly take away a believer's accountability toward Christ's great love for the church.

A person that goes by His name as being a Christian is answerable to love Him whole-heartedly. The story of the church at Laodicea pictures Jesus as the loving Lord and Savior who rebuked that church to repent of her unenthusiastic feeling toward Him. Because of His blood covenant sacrifice for her sake, He couldn't endorse the response of her lukewarm devotion toward Him for His sake.

When the focus is upon the ability of God to consummate His ultimate purpose for the church, the focus is upon the sovereignty of God and predestination according to the foreknowledge of God. The Father, with whom "all things are possible," is preparing an overcoming, glorious Bride by the Holy Spirit for His deserving Son.

Whether it is in the world or in the church, when the focus is upon accountability toward God, the emphasis is upon the free-moral agency of humanity toward Him. Each member of that church needed to keep a humble attitude in order to have an ongoing relationship with the Lord. The walk of faith is the way of the Lord where no flesh shall glory in His presence. That walk with Jesus is above and beyond the understanding or ability of any one church, but anyone in the Laodicean Church that heard His voice and opened the door could have a wholehearted loving fellowship with Him.

What God chooses is most important. In emphasizing the sovereignty of God over the life of the church organism, Christ takes the initiative as Head over the church. The church needs to understand how to properly relate the theme of God's sovereignty over her life along with the freedom of choosing whom she will serve. When a church focuses on Christ's approval over her life, she belongs to Him because she was His choice. Christ has purchased the church with His own blood sacrifice.

In material possessions, there are the good, better or best ratings in the approval of consumer goods and other things in the natural realm. The mind must be renewed in order "that you may prove what is the good and acceptable and perfect will of God" in the spiritual realm. That is the inward work of God that abides forever. The church of the Laodiceans needed to experience the renewing process of the mind where each one among them was "not to think of himself more highly than he ought to think" (Rom 12:3).

All good things come from above and prosperity is a blessing from the Lord. But the church at Laodicea became so satisfied and contented with the good blessings from the Lord that the good became an enemy to the best that God had to offer. If she had kept her eyes fixed upon the true riches of God's grace in Christ, the temporal and material things would have taken a back seat to the eternal benefits that He has to give.

In the physical realm of a scale from one to ten, the world classifies the perfect shape and function of a young healthy body as a "ten." To be a "ten" in the shape and function of the soul, the life of that soul needs to humble itself and be under God's control.

Jesus became a "ten," as an inductee in the Hall of Pain, in becoming a success in fulfilling the Father's will as He died on the cross as a substitute for sin, being identified with our sinful nature. Though the world understood the pain, at that time a death on the cross was the death of a law-breaker, a wasted life. But His pain was more than physical. He died in spiritual agony with a broken heart. Christ's death represented the disapproval of God upon our sinful nature in order that we might be approved to God in being identified with the resurrection life of His righteous nature.

The Report Card

Because there is a day when we will be graded for our accountability based upon God's faithfulness; there is a designated time in the future that we could call "report-card day." That's a time that I can well remember during my school days.

Report-card day was always a joyful day for a student who was "a worker who does not need to be ashamed" because he presented a diligent attitude toward the schoolwork and studies that were placed before him (2 Tim. 2:15).

When I taught school, I tried to conduct my math classes according to biblical principles. I let my students know that they were going to be tested regularly on the materials that had been covered in class. They needed to know what to expect from me, and I needed to know what to expect from each one of them. If nothing was being learned, then nothing was being taught.

In the spiritual realm, Bible teachers teach the lesson, but it is the Holy Spirit who gives the tests. The Holy Spirit is faithful to give anyone that is faithful an opportunity to apply the lesson that needs to be learned. Some of the last words that the Master Teacher said to His church leaders were to teach "them to observe all things that I have commanded you" according to the Scriptures.

Friday became the day that I would go to the chalkboard and write "TOF Day." My math students knew that stood for a special day known as "Test on Friday." I developed that technique because I did not want to hear, "Do we have to have a test today?" or "Another test!" The lazy and irresponsible students of the class didn't like it, but I was trying to teach them a lesson in accountability. A lukewarm church will, by her soulish nature, resist the truth of being accountable to God's great love.

The Laodicean Church saw no need for being accountable to God's redeeming grace. They were irresponsible in their commitment to the main theme of His teachings, and that was the message of loving one another. Because of her halfhearted love toward Him compared to His wholehearted love for her, Jesus was on the outside knocking on the church door; thus, making her accountable for His love for her. That "lukewarm" church was being judged for her half hearted attitude toward His loving kindness and tender mercy. She was in danger of being vomited out of the Body of Christ.

Everything was clear-cut. My students knew that Friday would be the day they would be tested on the material we had covered in class during the week. It was their responsibility to be ready. The Lord wants the church to live a life of preparation and expectation where she is ready at all times. "Therefore you also be ready, for the Son of Man is coming at an hour you do not expect" (Luke 12:40).

There came a time when I began writing "DOA" on the chalkboard. Friday and a few special test days had become known as the "day of accountability" for my math students, but for a few unprepared students, "DOA" had become "dead on arrival."

This gave me the opportunity to tell the class. "If I do not hold you accountable for the material that we have covered in class, I cannot be a good teacher. My responsibility is to teach. It is your responsibility to learn what has been taught. Report cards will be out in three more weeks." The church, likewise, will stand before Christ's judgment seat and "each of us will give an account of himself to God" (Rom. 14:12).

To be a good evaluator of the work that the students did in my math classes, I had to keep a record book of the graded work that they did whether it was good or bad. I taught the material, gave the test, judged the performance, recorded their work and gave recognition with the reward of a good report card. In the work of the Lord, the Holy Spirit teaches the lesson that needs to be taught, and the Father takes over from there. He takes care of the testing program in earnest detail by His Spirit through His Word. The Bible makes it clear that God is a God that has a record book. The church is going to appear before the Head of the church in judgment of things done in the body "according to what he has done, whether good or bad" (2 Cor. 5:10).

The students who worked hard and did well in my math classes looked forward to report-card day. At the end of the year, a select few would be awarded and acknowledged at an award assembly. For the overcoming church, I believe the award assembly is related in some way to the wedding celebration known as "the marriage supper of the Lamb."

Paul taught the basis for the exaltation of the Lord Jesus Christ through His acts of humility as recorded in Philippians 2:5-8. A few verses later in that chapter he challenges the church in verse 12, "Therefore, my beloved, as you have always obeyed [the Laodicean Church had not come that far]...work out [in humility] your own [complete, exalted, soul] salvation with fear and trembling." That was not the attitude that members of the church at Laodicea had toward their salvation. Their attitude was one of indifference, having a halfhearted devotion toward Him as God's Salvation.

An attitude of fear and trembling is the most penetrating appeal that can be given to anyone in the church. It is necessary because of a natural human tendency to go our own way and do things independently of God (Is. 53:6). It is not easy to deny the self-life. By nature we want to lean on our own understanding and try to do things for God in our own strength. The report card is the record of progress in receiving an education, and God's report card is the measure of progress in applying scriptural truth to daily living.

In schools of learning according to sense knowledge reasoning, the teaching of the lesson comes before the proficiency test based upon the lesson presented. But if the lesson of humility is to be learned in the Christian walk, learning the lesson follows after the Holy Spirit has given the test.

Philippians 2:12 presents a greater challenge, which covers a greater accountability for the lessons to be learned toward God in order that the church may qualify for an exalted, soul salvation with Christ for the glory of the Father. As Christian parents have a desire for their children to mature into becoming responsible adult citizens in an adult society, the

Father desires His children to mature into the image and likeness of His firstborn Son in the family of God.

Not only does the grace of God teach us to live righteous and godly lives in Titus 2:11-12, but Philippians 2:13 shows how the grace of God works on behalf of the believer: "For it is God who works in you, both to will and to do for His good pleasure." The self-will and good pleasure of the Laodicean Church must die out to God's will and good pleasure for her life. That is being realistic in putting things in proper perspective in order to fulfill the Father's ultimate purpose for His church.

God's good pleasure for the life of that church was for her eternal best interest, but to receive God's best, He must first get the worst out of His people. That goes contrary to the self-seeking and self-serving pleasure of a self-centered church that appeals to the soulish nature of the old self-life.

Paul's Report Card in Christ

The last epistle that Paul wrote was to Timothy. He told Timothy that "the time of my departure is at hand." The time of graduation for Paul was drawing near. Paul had "fought the good fight" of faith. He wrote, "I have finished the race, I have kept the faith." He then boldly declared, "There is laid up for me the crown of righteousness which the Lord, the righteous Judge, will give me on that Day" (2 Tim. 4:7-8a).

Paul had done his homework. He was looking forward to seeing his final report card. Then he added, "And not to me only but also to all who have loved His appearing" (v. 8b). Paul identified himself with a special group of Christians who were also longing for His Appearing. Like Paul, they were also looking forward to the final report card.

Paul's record for living the Christian life would be receiving eternal benefits and rewards for his faithfulness in developing the fruits of Christian character and living a life of faithful Christian service before the Lord. The goal of the crown of righteousness that Paul one day will receive is based upon the day of His Appearing. "And the dead in Christ shall rise first" (1 Thess. 4:16).

Report-card time is drawing nearer for all of us. But, as the day draws closer, each day is not only a day of accountability but also a day of opportunity where we can judge ourselves. "For if we judge ourselves, we would not be judged" (1 Cor. 11:31). The church can judge herself according to God's Word, for the Holy Spirit is testing the church daily to see how she is standing in her wholehearted faithfulness to Christ's commandment of love that is recorded in the gospel message. Paul said in that one commandment of love "is the fulfillment of [the] law" (Rom. 13:10). "The" is put in by the translators. The nature of God's love fulfills all laws or rules that are needed to keep the soul-ish nature in line.

So each church should judge herself to see if she is in compliance to "all Scriptures." The Bible is complete and was "given by inspiration of God...for instruction in righteousness that the man of God may be complete, thoroughly equipped for every good work" (2 Tim. 3:16-17).

If each church judges herself now according to God's written Word without deceiving herself, then she will have a glorious time when God's Living Word judges each one of us at the Judgment Seat of Christ.

The written Word will be the standard for Christ's judgment. "He who rejects Me, and does not receive My words," said Jesus, "has that which judges him—the word that I have spoken will judge him in the last day" (John 12:48). Only a deceitful heart would deny such a convincing and credible message.

The dividing line between justification and condemnation is hearing the Word of God and obeying it. God's Word is justifying the obedient that believe Him in the things that He commands them to do. At the same time, the words that He spoke will condemn those who do not obey them.

If anyone in the Laodicean Church had a hearing heart and was willing to obey Him by walking in the newly created spirit, he could repent and open the door to have fellowship with Jesus. Christ was willing to restore a whole-hearted relationship out from lukewarm circumstances for anyone in that church. The unchanging Christ in an ever-changing world will do the same today as He did yesterday for anyone who sees the need.

God's Ultimate Reward

God's greatest Reward is not found in something special but in someone special. The crown of all rewards, absolutely, is in knowing Christ in His fullness. The marriage of the Lamb will take place when "His wife has made herself ready" (Rev. 19:7). She is making herself ready by being clothed with His righteousness.

Serving Him for the reward of heavenly material gains may be viewed by some as a wrong motive, but serving Christ in order that we may win Him as the Father's Prize for eternity is the most honorable of all motives. Love is the only motive that is acceptable to God for doing anything (1 Cor. 13), and to love Jesus wholeheartedly, having the hope that it is a relationship without end, is the greatest motive for Christian service.

In John 12:1-8, Mary of Bethany broke her very expensive flask of oil, and in loving devotion, she anointed Jesus' feet. Judas Iscariot, who had neither love for Jesus nor the poor, complained that the oil should have been sold and the money given to the poor. That kind of religious talk caused His other disciples to begin to think about the many horizontal needs and they agreed with Judas (Matt. 26:8). But the love of Mary for Jesus caused her to have a vertical focus toward meeting the needs of God.

Jesus said, "Let her alone; she has kept this for the day of My burial. For the poor you have with you always, but Me you do not have always." Was it at that moment of public embarrassment that the devil planted the seed in the heart of Judas Iscariot to betray Jesus? Being properly related to Jesus is the reward. He went away but He is coming back again to those who are ready and waiting for Him. Motivation for doing "good," therefore, should be directly related with a loving personal relationship with the good Shepherd who gave His life for the sheep. Christian service should be based upon being devoted to Him in having the recognition and gratefulness for being chosen to eat with the King at His table.

The Father gave the Gift of His only begotten Son to a lost and dying world in order that the church might believe into Him unto the stature of His fullness. The Father's resurrected first begotten Son receives His Bride unto Himself as His reward. He is her ruling King as she shares His throne with Him to rule and reign with Him.

The Father gave His Son as the gift of eternal life to a lost, dying world, but Christ, the Bridegroom, will become the Father's Reward to the overcoming church by virtue of her steadfast faithfulness to His passionate love for her. The greatest of all rewards that the Father has to give is the reward of His firstborn Son from the dead. According to verse 21, the overcoming church will be identified "with Him" in the fullness of what belongs to Him.

The supreme desire of the Father before time began was that there would be a family of His own kind through a creative act and transforming process to bring forth an overcoming people in His Son. Herein is the Father glorified "to the intent that now the manifold wisdom of God might be made known by the church to the principalities and powers in the heavenly places" (Eph. 3:10).

Out of Adam, God made woman. Out of one, He made two. Then He brought the woman and joined her to Adam in holy matrimony as one. "Therefore shall a man leave his father and his mother, and shall cleave unto his wife; and they shall be one flesh" (Gen. 2:24, KJV). Christ and His glorified church become one for eternity.

There can be no cleaving until first there is a leaving. The Father gave His only begotten Son for the sins of the world. "The only begotten Son, who is in the bosom of the Father" (John 1:18) will also become eternally one spirit, soul and body to His overcoming Bride. He will leave His heavenly Father to be joined to His Bride in eternal heavenly matrimony. The ultimate purpose of the Father for the church will be fulfilled in the Son, as the Body of Christ, and for the Son, as heaven's Bridegroom.

First, there is His spiritual cleaving to the church that begins with oneness in the spirit. "But he who is joined [cleaving] to the Lord is one spirit with Him" (1 Cor. 6:17). Then there is the transforming process from soulish thinking like the world to the renewing of the mind until a maturing Body of Christ functions in oneness having "the mind of Christ" (1 Cor. 2:16). Growth of the church organism is so important!

The resurrected Christ is God's firstborn Son among many brethren. That means there were to be others who would follow Him into the family of God. The marriage of the Lamb of God in holy matrimony to His Bride can also be identified as being between God's firstborn Son and His overcoming church.

The Father is preparing and forming a glorious Bride out of the church that will be worthy of eternal fellowship with His deserving Son. She is being transformed anew day by day into His image. You cannot separate Christ and His church organism. He no longer abides alone like an unburied grain of wheat. He has become the Bread of life, which gives nourishment to all who dine with Him.

Christ is the Gift of His heavenly Father to His overcoming church in the fulfillment of the promise. Christ's death at Calvary provided a way that He and His church might cleave to each other as one from time to eternity. Christ has identified Himself with the church through His resurrection and ascension to the right hand of the Father. The overcoming church belongs to Christ and Christ belongs to the overcoming church. That loving fellowship with Him is not for just time alone but for eternity.

The Father has many precious promises and priceless prizes for His people who believe that Jesus died for their sins. But I believe that the greatest of all awards, which has been predestined from eternity, is the one where the Bridegroom, who led the way by being an overcomer, will be united forever with His glorious church.

Marriage to the Bridegroom will be the reward of the Bride in heaven. Before Christ returns as the church's Reward, she must first receive Him as the Gift of God's Salvation. By receiving Christ into our lives, we are made anew in the spirit by a creative act by the Holy Spirit. The church organism belongs to Him! She is His reward!

.

Chapter 11

The Greatest Helper
A Need to Ask Him for His Help

"He who has an ear, let him hear what *the Spirit says to the churches*" (verse 22).

I t was not until the coming of Jesus as the Son of God that the oneness of the Godhead was brought to light. It was the Son who came to glorify the Father and introduce the Holy Spirit as the Person whom the Father would send in His name. He would take all the things pertaining to Christ and declare them to His church.

It is not within the power or might of God's people to exalt and honor the Christ of the church the way that He should be praised and glorified, without the help of the Holy Spirit. Jesus said that He would "pray the Father, and He will give you another Helper, that He may abide with you forever." He would become the divine Helper to the church.

Without learning to lean on the leading of the Holy Spirit, any church, even those born in the revival fires of the Spirit, would follow the same course as the Laodicean Church. Christ standing on the outside of that church was a certain sign that the work of the Holy Spirit on the inside had been resisted, quenched and grieved. Christ was no longer exalted in the midst of the church congregation. If the Laodicean Church were to experience a restoration out of

217

her lukewarm condition toward Christ, more respect, honor and recognition toward the work of the Holy Spirit would have to be given.

In many areas of the end-time church, the importance of the Person and work of the Holy Spirit is being ignored. The third Person of the Godhead gives the anointing and ability to accomplish through the church what He had accomplished by anointing Jesus of Nazareth with power and might during His ministry on earth. The Holy Spirit should not be the forgotten member of the Godhead. He needs to be recognized and honored for the work that He is doing in the church as the divine Helper to the church. Whatever needs to be done that is of eternal value cannot be done without His help.

The Lord dealt with each of the seven churches of Asia Minor individually. At the end of each judgment, the Lord exhorted all the churches to hear what the Holy Spirit was saying. The Holy Spirit is the Spirit of Truth who leads and guides the church into all truth. One of the greatest mistakes that any Christian or church can make is to see no need for divine guidance. The Holy Spirit is very active in comforting, exhorting and edifying submissive souls in the church. He is present to exalt Jesus in the midst of believers and reveal to the church the things that belong to the Christ of His church. The church belongs to Christ who is Lord over His church.

The Holy Spirit has come as the divine Helper to teach and direct church leadership to be helpers of God's people with a servant attitude. The world considers meekness as a weakness, and a helper or a servant as an inferior status. But the message that Jesus taught—He not only taught it but also lived it—was exactly the opposite to the thinking of the world. Jesus taught how the church should seek greatness. Jesus said, "He who is greatest among you shall be your servant" (Matt. 23:11).

The Son, therefore, was sent as the Servant of the Father, anointed by the Holy Spirit. Jesus, who came to serve His own Jewish people, told His disciples that He had served them as their Helper for a short time, but the Father would send the Holy Spirit to be their divine Helper, in the church, in greater scope and capacity. As the Son and the Holy Spirit were sent in the realm of time as divine Helpers, the Father is building the church with their help. Christ did the work of salvation through His death, burial and resurrection and the Holy Spirit has come to magnify the meaning of that work as the grace of God. But in the oneness of the Godhead, the Son and the Holy Spirit do not feel inferior to the Father. Each has His work to perform for the benefit of the church.

Because Jesus prayed in John 17:22 "that they may be one just as We are one," the thinking of the church should be in line with the work of God in complete dependence upon the unity of the Godhead. The thinking of the church, therefore, is not to be conformed to the independent thinking of the world. Her thinking should be transformed by the renewing of the mind toward the lowly mind of Christ, where a believer shall no longer "think of himself more highly than he ought to think" (Rom. 12:1-3).

Need for the Divine Helper

There are so many things that need to be done for a divided end-time church, and those needs cannot be served without the help of the Holy Spirit. When a church is acknowledging help from the Holy Spirit, she is receiving help from the church's greatest Helper. Because of the soulish, independent nature of Adam's race, a church becomes blinded to her spiritual needs unless the Holy Spirit reveals them to her through the Scriptures. He could not reveal the needs of that church, for she thought she had none.

An unrepentant heart might think that Jesus was too harsh and not justified for severely rebuking a church for being lukewarm toward Him, as He did the proud church of the Laodiceans. But the Holy Spirit can only reveal it to those who have ears to hear. Everyone in the church of the Laodiceans had ears, but only the "anyone" whose hearts were right toward God could hear the Spirit of Truth.

It is not within man to glorify Christ. It takes the work of the Holy Spirit to reveal "the unsearchable riches of Christ." If Christ is glorified, it is the work of the Holy Spirit in the church. "He will glorify Me, for He will take of what is Mine and declare it to you. "All things that the Father has are Mine. Therefore I said that He will take of Mine and declare it to you" (John 16:14-15). Notice that Jesus breaks the rules of grammar when He called the Holy Spirit "He" and not an "it."

Christ, who is *Lord over the church*, was on the outside standing no farther than the church door. He was not standing there idly. He was knocking on the church door that had been closed to Him. He loved that church organism, the Body of Christ, which was now separated from Him by a closed door. The Holy Spirit, who is *Lord in the Church*, was directing as many hearts as were sensitive to Him, and would submit to His instruction and guidance toward hearing the voice of the Lord Jesus Christ. The Holy Spirit strives with humanity to repent; the Son of God invites them to come unto Him.

The church of the Laodiceans had a need for the Holy Spirit to equip and help qualify her to win Christ as the Prize. Jesus shares all things with the ones who have overcome all things; He even shares His throne. A king only shares his throne with his queen. The Bridegroom and His Bride belong to each other. The significance of that holy eternal relationship cannot be overemphasized to the end-time church.

The bond of holy matrimony is a mutual giving and sharing with one another. Jesus, as the Bridegroom, has all things to give to the Bride because the Father has given all things to Him. The only thing that the Bride has to give to Him is her wholehearted, loving commitment, and that was the one thing in which the lukewarm church of the Laodiceans was found lacking.

Words That Come Forth from the Mouth of God

The words that come forth from the mouth of God are anointed words because the breath of God embraces them. The Greek word *pneuma* means both "breath" and "spirit." The breath of God, or the Spirit of God is the One that gives activity and life to the hearing of the *rhema* of God's Word. *Rhema* is a portion of God's *logos*, the totality of God's Word, which is forever settled in heaven and eternity. The Holy Spirit can make a portion of God's Word alive and effective to the hearer at a given time.

"He who has an ear, let him hear" what the Holy Spirit is saying. As the Son of God did not speak His own words during His ministry on earth, but the words that His Father gave Him to speak, the Holy Spirit does not speak His own words, but the words that the Son gives Him to speak. Everyone in that church had ears to hear, but they weren't hearing what was being said. "Faith comes by hearing, and hearing by the Word of God" (Rom. 10:17).

Have you found yourself talking to someone and you know that they are not listening to what you are saying? It's characteristic of a few old-time preachers to put into their sermon every once in a while the phrase, "Are you listening to me?" You have to have a listening heart to hear God's Word.

The hearing of that church was directed toward many temporal things, but it was not being directed toward Jesus. An anointed message—the Holy Spirit is in the message—may be preached to a congregation with good natural hearing, but only those who have a hearing heart will receive faith from the message. That person with a contrite heart is hearing what the Holy Spirit is saying.

One of the great challenges that have been presented to the Holy Spirit in working with the end-time church is getting her ready for Christ's

Appearing. The truth of His soon Appearing needs to be brought out of the realm of theology into an enthusiastic, affectionate union of dining with Him. All other prophecies about His Coming might be soon fulfilled, but there can be no Second Coming until first there is the Rapture.

There can be no Rapture until the Bride of Christ "has made herself ready," and she cannot make herself ready without the help of the Holy Spirit. There are many purposes for assembling the church together in these last days to worship God in spirit and in truth, but getting the Bride ready is the Father's ultimate purpose for the end-time church.

There is exultation in heaven "as the sound of mighty thunderings…Let us be glad and rejoice and give Him glory, for the marriage of the Lamb has come, and His wife has made herself ready" (Rev. 19:6-7). The bride-elect, which is to become the chosen participator on earth in this coming event, should have as much excitement concerning that great event as the excitement of the spectators who are in heaven.

Because the church does not know "the day or the hour" when He is coming—that time can be anytime—the Bride needs to be ready. "He who calls you is faithful, who also will do it" (1 Thess. 5:23-24). Do what? He will consummate His ultimate sanctified purpose for His new creation in Christ after the fall of the old creation in Adam as recorded in the Genesis account.

The Father will have created and formed a new creation in His Son by the work of the Holy Spirit. Since it is the collective work of the Godhead as it was at the beginning, it will also be according to "Our image, according to Our likeness; let them have dominion over" the earth (Gen. 1:26). The "them" of the first creation was Adam and Eve. As that creation was condemned in Adam, the new creation is justified in Christ. Christ's Bride is to be made complete in the image and likeness of the oneness of the Godhead in Christ Jesus.

When the Bible speaks about the Word of God coming out of the mouth of God, it's His anointed words that the church is to live by. In the creation story, Adam received life through the in-breathed breath of God. As the Personified Word is the Son of God, who came to us in the incarnation, the outpouring of the Personified "breath of God," infilling human vessels, came in the Person of the Holy Spirit on the day of Pentecost.

Isaiah speaks about the vast difference between the ways of heaven and the ways of earth and how the earth depends upon the rain and the snow that comes down from heaven and waters the fruit-bearing plants and makes them productive and fruitful. God says, "So shall My word be that goes forth from My mouth; it shall not return to Me void, but it shall accomplish what I please, and it shall prosper in the thing for which I sent it" (Is. 55:8-11). The Word of God, which proceeds forth from the mouth of God, comes with the breath (Spirit) of God, which enables the spoken Word to have power and ability to overcome the world with a mighty triumph over the enemy.

There are many deceiving religious spirits and lustful evil spirits active in the realm of Christianity that call themselves "the church" in these last days. But there is only one Holy Spirit, who is the Spirit of Truth. When He speaks through chosen vessels, He says things that are of eternal value.

One of the primary services of the Holy Spirit is to testify of Christ. "But when the Helper comes, whom I shall send to you from the Father, the Spirit of truth who proceeds from the Father, He will testify of Me (John 15:25). Only the Holy Spirit can testify of and exalt Christ in the midst of His church (Rom. 8:14), but He needs submissive vessels in which to work. Activity of many evil spirits is on the rise in these last days according to the prophetic Scriptures, but there will also be the fulfillment of the one eternal work of the Holy Spirit. The Father's ultimate purpose for His church will be fulfilled.

Because of the interest and care of Jesus for His people, His people are to gather together in His name in order that He may fellowship with them. "In My name" means for His glory, being in obedience to the authority of His words. Only the Holy Spirit can lead God's people together in unity and worship in the name of Jesus.

Jesus' first disciples followed Him up until the early hours on the day of the crucifixion. After His resurrection and ascension and the coming of the Holy Spirit, His disciples followed Him unto death. They followed after Him, laying down their soul-life for His sake, but in the church at Laodicea, the rebellious soul-life was alive and strong.

A church cannot achieve God's approval by something she can do with an independent attitude toward God. God's approval comes by a church being dependent upon the Holy Spirit in everything that she says or does. Christ dying our death makes it possible that a church organism may live a life completely dependent upon God by faith.

The Son of God Is Lord over the Church

Christ's exaltation to the church was achieved through one humble act. As a Lesson in the standard of excellence, He eliminates any grounds for spiritual pride. Accepting the challenge to be more like Jesus will keep a church humble. In Philippians 2:3-8, Paul shows that Christ is God's

Lesson in humility to be learned. The Father sent His humble Son to proud humanity to show the way that God's people should live. Only the Holy Spirit can reveal and give hearing hearts the ability to obey the truth.

Unity in Christianity is found in followers of Christ identifying themselves primarily with the Christ of Christianity and not by a specific church label. Church labels are necessary for mundane business practices in today's modern society. Many years ago the label of a particular church member was indicative of his or her commitment to Christ, but that is not true anymore. Some have become more committed to Christ than most who represent a particular church organizational identity.

The early church had no label except the city where the church was located. Artificial church unity may be found in proudly keeping the identity of a church label and ignoring what the Scriptures require for true unity. Inorganic church unity will be found where there is more love for the organizational church than love for the church organism. One Bible-given label for the church organism is the Body of Christ.

The Laodicean Church had more love for her earthly status of being rich and wealthy than having an ongoing fellowship with heaven's eternal Treasure—Christ Jesus. True unity can be found where each church individually is identified under the authority of the functional Head of the Body of Christ.

As the Son is one with the Father, the Holy Spirit is able to make the church one with Christ in spirit, and in time, united in the restoration of the soul being conformed into His image, and a resurrected body made like unto His glorified body. Then the Father's ultimate purpose for complete redemption will be fulfilled.

Because His Bride has proved herself worthy by submission to His authority through the tests and trials of life, she has become qualified to reign with Him in God's righteous kingdom. The Son of God is Lord over the church, and the church needs to learn to be a helper by being submissive to His authority in all things. The church is to rule as His helper for His cause.

With His Son at His right hand, the Father sits upon the throne of heaven, which represents authority over all things. The challenge of the church is for her to submit to His authority. If all church members are being submissive to the same authority, then church unity is the result. Supreme allegiance and devotion, therefore, to the authority of Christ over His church should be respected and esteemed by individual members of each Christian institution. That emphasis can only be achieved through the faithfulness of the Holy Spirit to glorify Christ through submissive souls within His church.

The Holy Spirit Is Lord in the Church

The Father brought forth His "firstborn among many brethren" (Romans 8:29) in resurrection glory by "the eternal Spirit." God's Firstborn came forth as the elder Brother to the family of God in the realm of time. His bodily resurrection out of the grave by the Holy Spirit has proven the faithfulness of the Father to the church. The Holy Spirit reveals Christ's resurrection as the foundation stone of the Christian faith.

The Holy Spirit directs and guides, giving the church the ability to fellowship with the Father through the Son. Fellowship with Jesus is sharing all things with Him as He shares all things with the Father. That fellowship is based upon a blood covenant with God and it centers in feeding upon God's Word. "That which we have seen and heard we declare to you, that you also may have fellowship with us; and truly our fellowship is with the Father and with His Son Jesus Christ" (1 John 1:3). The end purpose of church unity with the Father and the Son cannot be achieved without the help of the Holy Spirit.

Since the beginning of His ministry in His First Coming, and through His resurrection from the dead, the Holy Spirit reveals that the Father's firstborn Son from the dead is still in charge of His Father's business as He continues to work through His church. The Holy Spirit is the anointing power that makes things happen.

As children in the family of God, the church is to become more and more like the Father's firstborn Son, who is in the image and likeness of the Father. In the growing and developing process as members in the Father's family, the Holy Spirit reveals to each family member his or her gift and calling that is needed in carrying out the Father's business through the Son.

The Holy Spirit, who does the work in building the church in glorifying the Son over all things, has been the most ignored member of the Godhead throughout church history. The overall picture of His work is a complete church that functions for the glory of the Father through the Son in self-denial and cross-bearing for Jesus sake.

The Father is building the church by the Holy Spirit through the Son as He works as the one true Mediator between God and men (1 Tim. 2:5). The Son gives the church the words to say and the Holy Spirit gives her the ability to say them. A church can do nothing to help in the work of Christ unless she submits to the Holy Spirit as her divine Helper. The Holy Spirit is the Helper in the church, as the church is maturing to be a helper to the Son in carrying out the Father's business. In obeying the Son, the church is helping the elder Brother to do and to complete the Father's business.

As the Kingdom of God is a kingdom where righteousness reigns, the Father's family is a close-knit new-creation relationship where righteousness dwells. In the Father's family, there is a spiritual DNA family likeness between the nature of the Father's Firstborn in resurrection glory and all other family members. The Father's family is born through the planting of the eternal incorruptible seed of God's Word.

Being a loving, attentive, faithful member of the Father's family is more important to the Father than some individual outstanding performance that one may do as a family member. But "being what the church should be" to the Father will lead the church in "doing what she should do" in her faithfulness to Him who has separated her from this present evil age for His own glory. The Holy Spirit provides the birth, the growth and the ability needed to become faithful, maturing members in the family of God.

Three Sermons with Two Words from the Godhead

You could say that the gospel story records three sermons for the church from the Godhead: one by the Father, one by the Son, and one by the Holy Spirit. Each sermon contains a message of only two words. The person of Christ is the central theme of each sermon. Obviously that was not the case of the sermons that were being preached from the pulpit in the Laodicean Church.

The Father told Peter, James and John, "Hear Him," in His endorsement of the Son. The Son said to the tax collector, Matthew, "Follow Me," in calling one of His twelve disciples. Jesus said that when the Holy Spirit comes, He will "glorify Me."

The resurrected Christ is the key and central Person in the Father's great building plan of salvation being worked out in the realm of time by the Holy Spirit. The three sermons with two words from the Godhead, therefore, center on the Christ of the church. Why should the thought-life of the church of the Laodiceans be church-centered and not more Christ-centered? If her thinking had been Christ-centered, the Body of Christ would have been honored. You can't promote the Body without exalting its Head.

The three accounts are as follows: When Peter, James and John went with Jesus to the Mount of Transfiguration, "A cloud came and overshadowed them; and a voice came out of the cloud, saying, 'This is My beloved Son. *Hear Him*!' Suddenly, when they had looked around, they saw no one anymore, but only Jesus with themselves." Hebrews 1:2 says that the Father has in these last days spoken to us by His Son. As the Logos, Jesus is the last message of God to humanity. The prophets of God had much to say about God and His people, but when God wanted to say everything that needs to be said, He summed it all up in a two-word message "Hear Him!" He sent His Son as the personification of His Word. There are many misrepresentations of the Christ of the Scriptures in the realm of Christianity. But as the last Word, Jesus is the One who gives the church a true picture of the Father. He is the full and final revelation of God. If people reject that revelation, they can't expect to hear from God in some other way (John 14:6). After the introduction of Jesus of Nazareth as His Son, the Father had a two-word message for the church: *"Hear Him!"* Days earlier at Caesarea Philippi, the Father had revealed His Son as the Messiah to Peter and the other disciples; now on the Mount of Transfiguration, the Father shows His endorsement of His Son to Peter, James and John.

Every word that Jesus said, as recorded in the gospel story, is very important and a church needs to take heed that she does not neglect the message. In this dispensation of the Holy Spirit, it is necessary that we pay careful attention to what He speaks. If the message spoken through angels was dependable, the transgressors and disobedient were justly punished, how shall we escape if we neglect so great a salvation. "Watch therefore, and pray always that you may be counted worthy to escape all these things that will come to pass, and to stand before the Son of Man." The "lukewarm" church of the Laodiceans needed to take the words that Christ spoke more seriously.

When Jesus passed by Matthew, the tax collector, He preached to him a message that contained only two words: *"Follow Me"* (Matt. 9:9). Matthew arose and followed Jesus, faithful to the end. That is a definition of true Christian discipleship. Christianity is not just another religion with a code of ethics as church rules, nor is it about belonging to the right church organizational system. It is a new-creation race of people uniting God and man in Christ. As the old creation was identified with the fall of the first man, Adam, the new creation is identified with the new life of the second Man, Christ Jesus. This new creation of God comes from Emmanuel, "God with us." It is the God-man race.

When Jesus chose the fishermen and the tax collector to be His disciples with the message, "Follow Me," they had no idea how great a challenge His calling to them would become. Discipleship is following the Christ of the Scriptures to the end of the Christian journey as His disciples hear what He has to say pertaining to His church. Jesus said, "My sheep hear My voice, and I know them, and they follow Me" (John 10:27). A steadfast heart is needed to hear the voice of Jesus until the end. There is no looking back toward the things of the world. Jesus said, "Remember Lot's wife." Lot's wife was not a type of the Bride of Christ.

The command to follow Christ Jesus sums up the true meaning of Christian discipleship. There is no standing still in God's building program. The Holy Spirit is continually directing the church's building program towards its predestined fulfillment.

When Jesus called His disciples He told them, "Follow Me and I will make you fishers of men." It's not important what you were at the time He called you, but what He is making you to become as you continue to follow Him. No one can follow Jesus for very long and remain the same. Abraham had his faults in not fully obeying God and he made his mistakes in not fully believing God, but in his ongoing walk with God, Abraham became the only man who "was called the friend of God" (Jam. 2:23). David sinned against God and had to reap what he sowed, but in his enduring walk with God, David became a man after God's own heart.

There is no spiritual maturity in an end-time church unless there is a steady spiritual growth and development in Christ. The Lord always presents a challenge to go forward to the next spiritual level. If church members are not properly related to Christ, it matters not the orthodoxy of their church doctrine. If right church doctrine is not obeyed and acted upon it is dead doctrine to that church member. Insignificant church doctrines are being overemphasized too much of the time, compared to the emphasis on having the opportunity to enter into His caring fellowship through dining with Him.

A Christian disciple has been called to please the Lord through self-denial and cross-bearing in following Him to the end. With a puffed up attitude, that poor, rich church could not be drawn toward Him. A church, like the Laodiceans, in her lukewarm relationship with the Lord does not stand still. She will accept His invitation to come and dine and become more and more passionately in love with Him, or her divided heart will cause a cooling down trend in her relationship toward Him.

We are now living in the Holy Spirit dispensation as He is preparing the overcoming church for the soon coming of her exalted Bridegroom. Sermons need not be long when the Holy Spirit has anointed them. In announcing the coming of the Holy Spirit to the church, Jesus summarized the purpose and goal of the Holy Spirit's work in two words. Jesus said that the Holy Spirit would "**glorify Me.**" The Holy Spirit is in the glorifying business and it is not about a particular church, a gifted servant of the Lord, or even Himself. It is not within the power or ability of a soul or a church to glorify Christ. She needs to submit to the Holy Spirit to help her do so.

Without the help of the Holy Spirit, a church cannot be successful and prevail in glorifying Christ. Self-glory will replace God's glory like it did in the church of the Laodiceans, and that is one example of falling "short of the glory of God" (Rom. 3:23). Not only does the Holy Spirit direct the thinking and use the tongue of each church member to say it; He also inspires and directs the church to be doers of God's Word for the glory of God in Christ.

In the beginning Elohim said, "Let Us make man in Our image, according to Our likeness" (Gen. 1:26), as He created Adam and his bride to have dominion over the earth. Now there is a new beginning in Christ Jesus where all things have become new, and each member of the Godhead has His role and place in bringing forth a new creation in Christ Jesus where "all things are of God."

Jesus made reference to that fact to His disciples when He said, "All authority has been given to Me in heaven and on earth. Go therefore and make disciples of all the nations, baptizing them in the name of the Father and of the Son and of the Holy Spirit." The church is to glorify the Father through obeying His Son by submitting to the power of the Holy Spirit operating in and through a believer's life.

The Laodicean Church was living at the beginning of the Holy Spirit dispensation. Living the overcoming Christian life is all about dining with Jesus. At the heart of the gospel message is the work of the Holy Spirit as the promotional Agent for Jesus. The exaltation of the Son is not only the objective, but also the scope of the gospel message.

Be Filled with the Spirit

The end-time church needs the help of the Holy Spirit to redeem the time to do the greatest good for the glory of God. The end-time church needs to know that it is the will of God for her to "not be drunk with wine, in which is dissipation," but to "be filled with the Spirit" (Eph. 5:18). The negative command is not to be drunk with wine. The positive command is to "be filled with the Spirit." As the eternal Spirit directs church members in everyday affairs, He provides a feature of quality to the limits of time.

When a scripture in the New Testament refers to believers being filled with the Holy Spirit, it is always related to some kind of speaking. Being intoxicated with wine is compared to being filled with the new wine of the Holy Spirit. Intoxicated people are usually very talkative with empty words, but a spirit-filled person's tongue might become an instrument of the Holy Spirit for a two-fold edification—the edification of the person doing the speaking and the edification of the church being exhorted and comforted.

"Speaking to one another in psalms and hymns and spiritual songs, singing and making melody in your heart to the Lord giving thanks always for all things" (v. 19). *Speaking* God's Word, *singing* and *giving thanks* to Him are three different functions of the tongue inspired by the Holy Spirit that edify the church. One of the evidences of being filled with the Holy Spirit is giving thanks. The Bible says, "In everything give thanks for this is the will of God concerning you. Do not quench the Spirit" (1 Thess. 5:18-19). It is the will of God, therefore, to stay thankful and be filled with the Spirit.

As believers meditate upon God's Word, the Holy Spirit purifies the soul. "My heart was hot within me; while I was musing, the fire burned. Then I spoke with my tongue," says the psalmist (39:3). When the *rhema* of God's Word becomes alive by God's Spirit, it is the burning fire of divine illumination to the newborn spirit.

Speaking the words of the Lord with anointed singing and giving thanks are an outcome of being filled with the Holy Spirit. Being filled with the Holy Spirit, therefore, uses the tongue aright in giving the expression of thanksgiving with an overflow of joy. David was excited about the Lord when he said, "My cup runs over." When the Holy Spirit uses the tongue, it is aright and it is one way in redeeming the time out of the hands of the devil in prayer.

The Prayer Helper

The church prays to the Father through the authority that He has given to the Son as the "one Mediator between God and men," but the Holy Spirit teaches us what to say in the ministry of prayer. Because insufficiencies and needs of the world and the church are so great and far-reaching, a church does not know what to pray for as she ought to pray. The Holy Spirit is an effective prayer helper to intercessors who pray with an unknown tongue about things that they know nothing about.

Evidently, the church at Laodicea did not understand the importance of the ministry of prayer and saw no need to enter into it on the behalf of fulfilling the purposes of God in meeting the need of others. The greatest Helper is most effective through the prayer ministry of the church, but He needs willing channels that will humble themselves before God in worship and in prayer.

In Luke 11:5-13, Jesus teaches the importance of perseverance in prayer. He tells a parable about two friends. One friend goes to his friend's house at midnight and makes a request for food to help another friend who is on a journey. Jesus taught that the request was granted on the basis of his persistence on behalf of his friend and not on the basis of their personal friendship. Many intercessory prayers of the church are answered on the basis of steadfastness and perseverance more than on the basis of their status as a child of God in the family of God.

Jesus goes on to teach that the persistence of prayer in asking, seeking and knocking to a loving heavenly Father will be rewarded. The key, in reference to an intercessory prayer ministry, is the gift of the Holy Spirit. Persistent prayer is important and the Holy Spirit must be the Helper and Teacher in that important realm of prayer.

"If you then, being evil, know how to give good gifts to your children, how much more will your heavenly Father give the Holy Spirit to those who ask Him!" (Luke 11:13). Jesus was pointing out to His disciples, as children of the family of God, that the Holy Spirit would be given to them as their future Teacher in prayer. Anyone who can begin a prayer with "Our Father in heaven" is qualified to ask his heavenly Father for the gift of the Holy Spirit to be his prayer Helper. The Holy Spirit is teaching the end-time church how to become more effective in the prayer ministry.

Receiving the gift of the Holy Spirit in verse 13 was Jesus' answer to the question that was asked Him in Luke 11:1. "Lord, teach us to pray, as John also taught his disciples." The Holy Spirit was to become the prayer Helper of the church. Jesus said that when the Holy Spirit comes, "He will teach you all things" (John 14:26).

Of the all things that needed to be taught to the Laodicean Church, there was a need for an effective prayer ministry. Prayer covers a broad theme in the ministry of the church, and it is very important that it is taught properly. The prayers of John the Baptist and his disciples were of the old order. Prayer in the new order would be on a much higher spiritual level.

The Holy Spirit will motivate and lead a church to pray, and that includes teaching her how to pray. The Laodiceans needed an active prayer ministry within the church. She needed to learn to pray as she leaned on the Holy Spirit as her prayer Helper. The Holy Spirit would have led and guided that church *into all truth*, especially concerning the importance of an active prayer ministry.

"He who has an ear, let him hear what the Spirit says to the churches" in these last days. The Holy Spirit is preparing a bride-elect for her Bridegroom through wholehearted worship and prayer of the end-time church. The Holy Spirit is the one who prepares the heart of the bride-elect to seek for the approval of her Bridegroom. The Laodicean Church was blinded to the Bridegroom's disapproval and rejection of her attitude of self-sufficiency.

According to the prophetic message in Joel 2:28, the Holy Spirit would come "in the last days" (Acts 2:17) and He would teach Christ's disciples how to pray in becoming effective witnesses in the work of God (Luke 24:25). The end-time church needs to make friends with the Holy Spirit and become more submissive to His divine guidance.

The church of the Laodiceans had a great need to make friends with the Holy Spirit and receive His help in a multitude of ways. If she would become submissive to Him, the Holy Spirit was capable of leading her into all truth. The Laodiceans might have had a doctrine or teaching concerning the baptism of the Holy Spirit, but I'm sure that Paul could have told that church as he did to the tongue-speaking Corinthian Church, "I thank my God I speak with tongues more than you all" (1 Cor. 14:18). That indicates to me that Paul had an active ministry as a prayer intercessor.

Exaltation of the Son

The Holy Spirit was sent by the Father to glorify the Son. If the help of the Holy Spirit were not available, asking self-loving religious people to have a wholehearted love for God would be too much to ask. The Holy Spirit was working in the Laodicean Church initiating the reconciliation of a lukewarm people with God by working with the contrite in heart. Loveable Jesus, on the other hand, was rebuking and chastening that lukewarm church organism with love to be zealous and repent. Jesus was inviting anyone who could hear His voice to open the door unto Him, to dine together in union and communion with Him.

When the Son of God came in the realm of time as the Messiah of the Jews, He was anointed by the Holy Spirit to do works of mercy. He first came as the great Helper primarily to His own people, the nation of Israel. "How God [the Father] anointed Jesus of Nazareth [the Son] with the Holy Spirit and with power, who went about doing good and healing all who were oppressed by the devil, for God was with Him" (Acts 10:38). Though "He came to His own," Jesus was always willing to help anyone who came to Him with a need.

Since the day of Pentecost, the Holy Spirit has come into the realm of time to be the Helper to the church. Jesus is now seated at the right hand of the Father as the exalted King over all things, which begins in and through His believing people, the church. The Father has exalted His Son through resurrection from the dead and ascension to His right hand. The Holy Spirit, as Lord in the church, is exalting the Son of God in the hearts and minds of His people that they may come to Christ Jesus, as Lord over the church, and dine with Him until the end.

When Jesus came as a Servant to His own people, He represented the love of the Father who sent Him. Jesus was always ready to meet the need of those who sought Him out in faith. He knows what is in the hearts of those who are filled with unbelief. Jesus came first to His own needy people, "the lost sheep of the house of Israel," but when a Gentile came to Him in faith with a need, merciful Jesus met that need.

Jesus, however, was able to help very Jewish religious leaders. When people step over into the office of religious duties and affairs, it is important that they see a need to remain meek and submissive before Jesus as the Head of the church organism.

Jesus is the *Logos* of God and there is always a need for church people to come and feed upon Him, as the Word of God, more and more in His fullness. To those who have a desire to walk in the truth, the Holy Spirit will reveal to the needy additional truth. A church is to walk in the truth until she fulfills the fullness of the Father's ultimate purpose for the church. The predominant need for everyone in the lukewarm church of the Laodiceans was contained in Jesus' invitation to open the door and dine with Him.

Christianity, without receiving the help and direction of the Spirit of Truth, gives rise to doctrinal error with unemotional formality and ritualistic worship. Forms and ceremonies take the place of wholehearted Christian worship. That allows an unenthusiastic attitude toward the Christ of the church to creep into congregational worship and Christian service. Only the Holy Spirit has the ability to take worship and Christian service up to the next level in Christ.

The Father's humble Servant over the church still meets the need of the needy. He is drawn close to those who look to Him to meet a need, and though she didn't think so, the Laodicean Church was truly a needy church. The Head of the church, therefore, was unable to rule over that "need of nothing" church who had little faith toward Him and less love for Him. He was ready to meet the need of communion and fellowship to anyone in that church, who would open his heart's door and begin to love Him fervently.

The Laodicean Church thought that the riches of material gain would bring true satisfaction, but it doesn't. She would eventually realize that temporal things could not satisfy the eternal longing of a hungry soul. The end-time church gives testimony to that fact. But the Holy Spirit could speak the things of Christ to the humble in that church that would bring reality and true satisfaction to each needy soul.

The Holy Spirit has come to meet the need of humanity by exalting the Christ of His church. The sinner has need of a Savior. The sick has need of the Great Physician. The church organism, as the Body of Christ, has need of a functional Head. Even the Lord Jesus Christ has a need! Because He had a need for devoted fellowship with that church organism, the lowly, lovable, loving Lord of glory was rebuking a lofty, lukewarm church to repent of an unenthusiastic temperament toward Him. The issue to the end-time church is not the fact that church people identify themselves as being Christians. The question is, are they committed Christians?

The same Holy Spirit that anointed Jesus of Nazareth with power has come in His name to be the divine Helper to the church to encourage and comfort those who bring their prayer requests to the Father. As the Lord Jesus Christ was sent, as a Helper, primarily to be a help to the nation of Israel, as He glorified the Father. The Holy Spirit has been sent as a Helper to help the church, as He anoints her, to glorify the Son. The greatest witness to a lost, dying world is a maturing, united church organism, which is called the Body of Christ, which is overcoming a judgment-bound world.

What Is the Holy Spirit's Business Finale?

The Holy Spirit's last assignment and business is getting the end-time church ready for her coming Bridegroom. The Holy Spirit has come to do a work in time for many eternal purposes, but His ultimate purpose is getting the Bride ready for her Bridegroom. As Christ came to fulfill Scriptures concerning Himself in relationship to His Bride, the Bride is fulfilling Scriptures concerning herself in relationship to her Bridegroom.

The Holy Spirit provides the ability and power necessary to help the Bride make herself ready. He is dependable and capable in doing what needs to be done. The end-time church should not be like the Laodicean Church, but she should see a need to submit to the Holy Spirit for His help in making herself ready for her coming Bridegroom.

A church organization like the church at Laodicea won't qualify, but the Holy Spirit is preparing her meek, submissive members for the coming of her exalted Bridegroom. That momentous event, which is coming soon to planet earth, is God's complete plan of salvation for His church. The end-time church should not underestimate the scope of God's great salvation plan and be found responding to it in a lukewarm manner.

The churches in America should not be lulled to sleep in the comfort and convenience of the material prosperity of this present age. The message to an end-time lukewarm church, therefore, is to "awake, you who sleep, arise from the dead, and Christ will give you light. See then that you walk circumspectly, not as fools but as wise, redeeming the time, because the days are evil" (Eph. 5:14-16).

If the days were evil at the dawn of church history, what do the Scriptures foretell in comparison to the last days of the Church Age? The end-time church should not be like the church of the Laodiceans. She should have a daily affectionate and attentive communion with the Lover of her soul in order that she "may have confidence and not be ashamed before Him at His coming" (1 John 2:28). The Holy Spirit exalts Jesus in the midst of the church that belongs to Him. He purchased her with His own precious blood.

The world needs to repent in order to come *into the saving knowledge of the Lord Jesus Christ.* The church of the Laodiceans needed to repent in order to *walk in the saving knowledge of the Lord Jesus Christ.* Only the Holy Spirit can motivate and direct submissive hearts to see a need to dine with Jesus as the Bread of Life.

The day is coming soon when the Holy Spirit will have completed His final and most difficult and important assignment, and the Father and the Son say, "Amen!" The bride-elect is waiting in anticipation for that soon-coming event saying, "Even so come, Lord Jesus!" Whether a Christian bride has made the best catch possible or not, every expectant member of the Bride of Christ has the hope of knowing the Best is yet to come!

Chapter 12

God's Ultimate Purpose for His Church

A Need to Fulfill God's Ultimate End for the Church

"And we know that all things work together for good *to those who love God*, to those who are *the called according to His purpose.* For whom He foreknew, He also predestined to be conformed to the image of His Son, that He might be the firstborn among many brethren (Romans 8:28-29).

God has many great promises. The greatest promise is to anyone who will persevere in dining with a resurrected Christ in loving, committed fellowship will be conformed to the image of His firstborn Son. The church that overcomes an unbelieving world will share the reward of the overcomer with Him. Because of her lukewarm feeling toward the Lover of her soul, the church of the Laodiceans had lost the desire to follow the call of God toward fulfilling the Father's ultimate purpose for His church. The Father's ultimate purpose for His church family is to move toward spiritual maturity by being conformed to the image of His firstborn Son. As the Firstborn, His resurrection represents the cornerstone for new-creation living. Understanding the Father's purpose for His church puts everything else concerning the church in proper perspective.

Before members of that church could go forward in pursuit of spiritual growth and development in Christ, the wholehearted love that they had lost for Christ must first be restored. A loving communion with Him is one essential element that provides progress toward spiritual maturity. The purpose of God for "anyone" in that lukewarm church, who would accept His invitation for a restored wholehearted fellowship with Him, would be to find true satisfaction *in Him.*

"And we know that all things work together for good *to those who love God."* The Holy Spirit will help submissive hearts learn to love Jesus as He loved the Father. The love of Jesus was a self-giving love, fulfilling the Father's great plan of salvation for the church. The Church of the Laodiceans was a long way from having the kind of love and obedience toward Jesus that He had toward the Father.

As a church, the Laodiceans had a self-centered love rather than a sacrificial love toward the Father's ultimate purpose for His church. She had a love for wealth and the material things that riches could buy rather than a love for the Word of God that opens the door to the treasure house of the unsearchable riches of Christ. No end-time church organization should develop an attitude of self-sufficiency like the Laodicean Church. God's will should take precedence over self-will in Christian service, and God's glory be exhibited rather than self-glory. It is God's will for the end-time church to be united. Since there is one Head over the church organism, that is the church that will be unified.

The basis for her exalted, eternal good would be to love God with her whole heart. Jesus has made it known that those who love Him will keep His sayings. To love Him is to obey Him. Lost souls need to receive the evangelistic message in order to be saved, but the gospel of good news was written to the church for her admonition and understanding. Church members, like those of the Laodicean Church, need to confidently acknowledge the fullness of the purpose of the gospel message to the church.

In new-creation living, the Christian home and the local church family need to recognize that they are an important part of a larger church family known as the family of God. Members of the family of God in each church organization need to learn the importance of spiritual growth and development toward the image of the Father's Son, "the firstborn among many brethren." As members of the church organism are identified with a particular church organization, it also becomes important that church members are taught the importance of growth in spiritual maturity in royal family living.

According to His Purpose

In speaking of "the called according to God's purpose," notice that the word "purpose" is singular. Romans 8:28 has always been an inspiration to me during the time of tests and trials. But until recently I never realized where faith in that scriptural fact was leading. It is the basis that is needed to understand the direction and destination of the tests and trials of the Christian life. Through God's foreknowledge, the overcoming church has been "predestined to be conformed to the image of His Son, that He might be the firstborn among many brethren."

The Father's ultimate purpose for members of His family is the building of an overcoming church. As the Firstborn of the family of God has fulfilled and will continue to fulfill all Scriptures concerning Himself, Romans 8:29 is a scriptural fact that the bride-elect, as members of the Father's family, is fulfilling for herself.

Abraham, as a type of the Father, sent his servant, as a type of the Holy Spirit, saying, "Go to my country and to my family, and take a wife [type of the Bride] for my son Isaac [type of the Bridegroom]" (Gen 24:4). Notice the bride for Isaac was taken out of the family of Abraham from the city of Nahor in Mesapotamia. The Bride for Christ will be taken from the Father's family from those who are ready and waiting. It is, therefore, important to study Genesis 24 in order to see what it was about Rebecca that qualified her to be chosen as the bride of Isaac. Also in contrast, as Adam's bride was taken as a rib out of his body, the Bride of Christ will be taken out of His Body (the church) as that member closest to His heart.

It is the ultimate purpose of the Father that in spiritual growth and development of royal family living He will have family members maturing to be conformed to the image of His firstborn Son. As God made a mature bride comparable to Adam at the beginning of the Genesis creation, He is making a Bride in the likeness of His Son who is the Beginning of a new creation where "all things are of God." From the beginning to the end of salvation's story, the grace of God teaches the church that she cannot save herself.

What does it mean to be "the called according to His purpose?" God has an ultimate purpose! Jesus fulfilled the Father's purpose for His life in His First Coming. He did not come in His own name or speak His own words. He came to say and do everything according to the will and glory of the Father. The ultimate self-giving purpose that the Son accomplished for the Father's sake was that "He humbled Himself and became obedient to the point of death, even the death of the cross" (Phil. 2:8). As the fall of Adam was through one act of transgression, through Christ's one final act of obedience at the cross, the Father has exalted the Last Adam, as the Second Man, above all and over all in new-creation living.

Because of her selfish, self-centered agenda and self-appointed goal, the church of the Laodiceans was traveling an independent course away from God. Her self-appointed purpose for self-glory was not God's ultimate purpose for His glory. There was no yielding to God's authority for completing His plan and purpose. The scope of her understanding and purpose for God's complete salvation plan was far below the Father's exalted purpose in Christ for the church.

The Laodicean Church, as an organization, was not interested in knowing God's ultimate purpose or how to experience its fulfillment. She had her own shallow, self-willed plan of salvation, and she thought that she had already achieved it. After twenty years of dedicated Christian service, Paul said in Philippians 3:10, "That I may know Him, and the power of His resurrection and the fellowship of His sufferings, being conformed to His death."

As a solitary, immortal, incorruptible Seed, Christ first had to suffer and die before He could experience the power of resurrection life. As a member of the Body of Christ, Paul had to first know Him in the power of His resurrected life in order to know Him in "the fellowship of His sufferings, being conformed to His death." The end purpose for Paul knowing the fullness of Christ in the Christian experience was that he, "by any means, may attain to the resurrection from the dead" (v. 11) like unto His glorious resurrection. Paul had become a member of the Father's family through faith in the firstborn Son, but he was zealous to be made complete in being conformed to the image of the firstborn Son.

The more of the power and sufferings that Paul experienced together with a resurrected Christ in the Christian journey, the more he was entering into knowing the fullness of the Christ of the Scriptures. Paul, therefore, was seeking to know the Christ of the Scriptures more in His fullness in daily experiences. The more of Christ's fullness that Paul experienced, the more he entered into the fullness of God's complete salvation plan for his life. Paul had zeal to dine daily with Him.

Salvation was not found in belonging to or keeping the rules of the Laodicean organizational church system. Salvation comes by faith in a crucified, resurrected, ascended Lord of glory, who desired to take complete control over every aspect of the church life of the Laodiceans for their own eternal good and best interest. The fullness of God's salvation comes by having an ongoing relationship with a resurrected Christ.

Were the Laodicean Church minds being "corrupted from the simplicity that is in Christ," which was causing her to ignore His grandeur? There was a need for that church to seek God in knowing Jesus, as her Salvation, in more of His fullness. Knowing complete salvation cannot be separated from experiencing more of the fullness of the Christ of her salvation. The

Lord had not forsaken that church. He was still interested in "anyone" that would hear His voice and open his or her heart's door to His loving care.

Any member of that church organism who accepted Christ's invitation and continued with Him until the end would be granted the reward of an overcomer. That meant the Bride would be sharing with the Bridegroom the same crown as an overcomer. If the reward, as recorded in Revelation 3:21 was not in the Bible, no one could have visualized it or believed it. Even though that scripture is recorded, it still takes the Holy Spirit to reveal its magnitude and its importance in the Father's total salvation plan.

The church is so important to the great Architect of the universe that He has made her a predestined participant in His great plan of complete salvation in Christ Jesus. Just as Jesus was "the Lamb slain from the foundation of the world" (Rev. 13:8), the church, as "the Lamb's wife," also was chosen in the Lamb from the foundation of the world.

God's Foreknowledge of the Church

In the foreknowledge of God, He has laid down His awesome, amazing plan of salvation from beginning to end. The Laodicean Church had a good beginning in new-creation living but she needed, as a church, to endure to the end. Christ's kingdom of righteousness is without end, but there shall be an end to the Church Age.

The Father doesn't need to change the script as the story unfolds. He doesn't make any mistakes. Nothing happens by accident on your journey to God's ultimate purpose for your life. Our heavenly Father is never taken by surprise. You belong to God as a new creation in Christ Jesus. The God that indwells eternity and works in time is from everlasting to everlasting, and He knows all things from everlasting to everlasting.

He is the Father-God of love, who loves and faithfully watches over each and every member of His family. The Laodicean Church should have believed that God was able and willing to fulfill His ultimate divine purpose in every detail for her life. But that unbelief in God's ability to bring into being a complete work in Christ is also found in many sectors of the end-time church.

That church organization should have accepted God's foreordained plan for His overcoming church organism; then she would have had no problem with self-sufficiency or self-importance. She needed to trust the God of the Scriptures and not lean to her own understanding. Whatever is according to the Scriptures doesn't need to be fully understood, but believed without doubting. What is impossible for man is possible with

God. He is perfect in His authority and ability as the divine Creator of the church to design His salvation's plan to its predestined fulfillment. All Scriptures will be fulfilled!

The Father has had a foreordained plan for the church through His Son from the beginning, and that plan is based upon people having faith in that plan for their life. A loving heavenly Father motivates believers to become submissive to His predestined ultimate purpose for their life in Christ Jesus. You are chosen of God!

At the beginning of revelation knowledge, it is the purpose of the Father *to reveal* His Son as "the Messiah" and *to uphold* what His Son has to say. "Hear Him!" Now the emphasis is placed upon the Father's ultimate purpose *to reward* His Son with members of the family being conformed to His own image for mature fellowship.

In the foreknowledge of God, Jesus as the Lamb of God would live, die and be resurrected as the firstborn from the dead. He would ascend to heaven and come back to earth as the anointed King over God's righteous kingdom. Any people, therefore, that are related in a blood covenant relationship to God are predestined. That would include both the nation of Israel, under an old covenant, and the church, under a new covenant. Each has a different inheritance, but both are predestined according to God's foreknowledge.

Because there is no way our finite minds can fully understand it, a heart full of faith and love toward Him is needed to believe in the Father's exalted, complete salvation plan for the believer's life. In Galatians 5:6, Paul speaks about a faith that works through love. Romans 8:28-29 reveals a love for God that works through faith in trusting that the ultimate purpose for God's church family is being consummated for our life.

Understanding Complete Salvation

To better understand complete salvation beginning with the light given in Ephesians 2:8-10, there are three terms that we need to understand: God's grace, His foreknowledge, and His predestined plan. These three theological terms need to be properly understood in their relationship to one another.

The experience of salvation begins with faith in the truth of Jesus' death, burial and resurrection. Since salvation is based upon what Jesus did for the church, each individual must receive it by grace through faith. Since all have sinned, salvation begins with people coming out of the world to Jesus as repentant sinners. To recognize the truth about one's lost condition without God requires a humble act of repentance before God.

The first step of the long Christian pilgrimage in living the overcoming life is learning the daily lesson of humbling oneself before God and His Word in order to be led by the Holy Spirit into all truth. The reason so many false religions and cults make such a penetrating impact on Adam's fallen race is that anyone can join them without ever taking that first step of humbling the self-life in repentance before God.

Complete salvation covers a wide scope, but through the entire journey, there is no place to stop and build a monument of works (like Babel) where the flesh can glory. When a church organization wants to stop and glory in something in the Christian journey, she can glory in what the grace of God has made her through Christ's sacrificial death at Calvary.

The Laodicean Church had no insight that she had a delinquent debt of love toward the Lord Jesus Christ that needed to be paid with supreme interest in loving Him with all her heart. When God's amazing grace is not highly esteemed, His extravagant love ceases to operate effectively in a church organization.

Paul said, "By the grace of God, I am what I am." Boasting in the grace of God humbles a believer at the foot of the cross where Paul said, "But God forbid that I should boast except in the cross of our Lord Jesus Christ, by whom the world has been crucified to me, and I to the world" (Gal. 6:14). That church was glorying in her wealthy status, but she should have known that there is always a need for the operation of the grace of God in her collective church life.

Complete salvation includes a diverse, all-inclusive experience that covers being justified, redeemed, sanctified and delivered from all kinds of spiritual deceptions and physical bondage. Working out God's exalted salvation, therefore, was an obligation that they should have taken God seriously with a wholehearted love toward the Savior.

Those who think they are predestined for heaven need to know that salvation is not a residential dwelling place in time. But the Father predestined the church "to be conformed to the image of His Son." It is a journey, an ongoing process of events, which covers the tests and trials of life that produce the fruit of Christian character.

Spiritual growth and development goes from bearing fruit to bearing more fruit until a disciple bears much fruit as a branch abiding in the true Vine. Bearing "much fruit" is very important and glorifies the Owner of the vineyard (John 15:1-8). The Father can truly be glorified through the fulfillment of His ultimate divine purpose for the church in Christ. The Son glorified the Father in becoming our sin Substitute. The Father will glorify the Son by giving to Him a sanctified people, a Bride made in the image and likeness of the Godhead, as it was in the Genesis account of creation. With God all things are possible through faith in His Word.

Predestination covers the Father's collective purpose that will be consummated in Christ Jesus. Since the predestined Jesus of Nazareth has a twofold relationship with God's people—one as Lord over the church and the other as the future Messiah of the nation of Israel—the church and the nation of Israel are both predestined people. The complete story of the church at Laodicea relates the potential fulfilling of God's plan for His obedient people as the church organism becomes properly related to its Head.

Because no one knows that they have made God's ultimate purpose until the Judge comes and imparts His judgment on the matter, no one can glory in the predestined course that God has laid out for them. But they can be grateful to God in knowing that He is in charge over their life. But they won't know that they've made exalted, complete salvation in Christ until the first resurrection of the dead is completed in Christ.

Complete salvation would have to cover that the "whole spirit, soul and body be preserved blameless at the coming our Lord Jesus Christ" (1 Thess. 5:23). The born-again experience is a spiritual experience where God becomes alive in spirit to a believer. "He who is joined to the Lord is one spirit with Him" (1 Cor. 6:17). It does not say one soul with Him.

If there is to be spiritual growth and development in the newborn spirit, the old independent soul-life against God (Is. 53:6) must be denied or put off in order to walk with God. Salvation is not complete, however, until the faithful shall experience a resurrected body that is formed like unto His glorious resurrected body.

If God's great plan of qualifying for complete salvation were revealed to a church like the Laodiceans, there would be no way that she could stop at a self-appointed place in the Christian journey and declare, "I have need of nothing." If the understanding of salvation is only on the level of a heaven to gain and a devil's hell to shun, then the viewpoint of salvation for a "need of nothing" church might quickly be concluded.

A theology can come out of a narrow concept of salvation where a church receives nothing more than the key to heaven's pearly gates, and she can forget about everything else concerning God's great plan of salvation. If a church goes no further than thinking she has been granted the key to the pearly gates of heaven, she might be tempted as a church organization to selfishly close her church door to all other members in the Body of

Christ. But with that kind of narrow spiritual insight, she is also closing the door to the loving presence of the Head of the Body Himself.

All born-again, evangelical Christians would have to agree that a church like the Laodicean Church was not a church organization that would qualify for the Rapture. Only the church that qualifies for the Rapture at His coming can be labeled "the right church," and the end-time church will have to wait until the Rapture takes place in order to find out which church members are waiting and ready.

The Father's Promised Bride for His Son

The Father has purposed in His heart from the beginning to bring into being a glorious, overcoming Bride that is worthy of His Son. That exalted salvation could not possibly be the plan of man. That plan is beyond human reasoning, therefore, the plan could not be for the purpose and glory of man. God has predestined the church in Christ as an overcoming church organism for His purpose and His glory. That plan calls for a lowly, submissive church to yield herself to her Maker in order to permit Him to create her completely anew for a coming, exalted, deserving Bridegroom.

Jesus said, "For the Father judges no one, but has committed all judgment to the Son" (John 5:22). But when the mother of Zebedee's sons asked Him, "Grant that these two sons of mine may sit, one on Your right hand and the other on the left, in Your kingdom." Jesus answered her by saying, "To sit on My right hand and on My left is not Mine to give, but it is for those for whom it is prepared by My Father" (Matt. 20:20-23).

Who would be found worthy to sit on the right hand or the left hand of the King? That would mean that there is a very close relationship with Christ in His kingdom rule that the Father has reserved to judge. The Father desires to specifically reward the faithfulness of His Son with a special people that only He could declare worthy for such an exalted honor. That is the Father's choice for His deserving Son, not a judgment.

The Father is so interested in each individual in the church that He has his or her life story planned out in every detail beforehand. That is exciting! As the perfect example for the church, God's only begotten Son was the only One who could and would fulfill the script concerning Himself in every detail for His life as it is written. The script was written for Him beforehand in the Old Testament Scriptures. As yet, He hasn't fulfilled all Scriptures concerning Himself. There are also many prophetic scriptures in the New Testament yet to be fulfilled concerning Christ and His church.

God has predestined believer's life in such detail that He brings specific people into your life, working through them, to direct you along your appointed pathway. Sometimes it may be people to try you and test you. We may not pass all the tests; Peter didn't. But, like Peter, we need to repent and stay humble before God. No end-time church organization needs to go the way of the Laodicean Church, which was an independent course unattached from Christ that was not directed by the Holy Spirit.

As an example of being a committed Christian, Paul had a prescribed course set out for his life. The end-time church also has a prescribed detailed course set out for her life. The end-time church has the same challenge with different kinds of trials and tests to overcome as did Paul in his day.

We all have different gifts and callings of God. The end-time church thinks of Paul as a great apostle, but during his ministry, there were many in the church at Corinth, and perhaps in other churches, that didn't think very highly of Paul. When you have church division, like that in Corinth, a party spirit would cause lukewarm church people not to accept a Christian committed to the degree of the apostle Paul.

It is, therefore, important that we direct our thinking toward God being in complete control over our lives. Though we may not understand it, the people that He uses to help direct us or even to test us are a part of God's divine plan for our life in Christ. The God who controls the heavenly bodies that speed through the sky with precise timing is the same God who directs each member of His church for His glory on the basis of their faith and obedience to His Word.

What does God teach through the tests and trials of life? According to the Genesis account of creation, God is a God of detail, excellence, accountability, purpose, oneness, diversity and completeness. If that was true of the Genesis account of creation with Adam, it is also true of the Gospel account of the new creation in Christ Jesus. The eternal new-creation process in Christ is still in progress in the realm of time.

You can be "confident of this very thing, that He who has begun a good work in you will complete it until the day of Jesus Christ." Not only does a church need to know, but she also needs to believe in God's ability and wisdom to complete the work that He has begun in her. God can complete His work in a church in the face of every contradictory circumstance that the enemy might bring against her.

Working Together for Good

When God's people come to the place where they believe that God has predestined their lives in every detail, they have the peace of mind that all things are working together for their eternal best interests, "to those who love God, to those who are called according to His purpose."

As God's plan for each life is revealed in Romans 8:28, it directs us toward its goal and ultimate purpose which is contained in Romans 8:29. God is love, and we need to trust and be committed to that love. That "need of nothing" church organization was not going to commit herself to anyone, even the Lord Himself.

When a church puts God's love in charge over her life, her eternal best interests are being served and worked out. As she continues to put her trust in Him, He shows Himself trustworthy. Considering that God has one ultimate predestined purpose for the church, there can only be one ultimate good that she, as a corporeal spiritual organism, should be experiencing daily.

What is the one ultimate purpose of God's will and good pleasure that is working in each believer in Christ? It is to be conformed to the image of the Father's firstborn Son. To be properly related to Him, as a member in the Body of Christ developing a more mature relationship with Him as the Head, should be the supreme aim for Christian living. God's purpose for the church is first for His divine favor; then, it works out for her eternal good.

To believe that all things work together for good takes more faith and trust at some times than it does at other times. When things are working for the good of the soul-life, the soul might be troubled with testing and trials. Things working for our eternal good might not be working for our temporal good. The exalted good of God may be brought out from the depths of the devil's evil through God's workmanship in Christ Jesus. The highest good for an offspring of God is being predestined to rule and reign with the eternal Son of God.

One of the greatest hindrances to overcoming faith, which is necessary to promote spiritual growth and development in the Body of Christ, is the soulish "things of men" that resist the spiritual "things of God." The soulish things of men in the arena of religion are committed to many things, but because of a wrong focus and misplaced emphasis, none of them provide for spiritual growth and development for "the new man" in Christ.

Because it is a Bible fact, the church organism may try to develop rules to promote church unity. Church unity, however, cannot become a reality until there is spiritual growth and development in the rule of love in the direction of the many different church organizations.

Through spiritual growth and development, the Father's new-creation family is "predestined to be conformed to the image of His Son, that He might be the firstborn [firstfruits of resurrection glory] among many brethren." The one ultimate purpose of God's new-creation life in Christ is to experience complete reconciliation of the church and the restoration of all things (this includes Israel) for the Father's glory. The new life is the maturing Christ-life, and it is the outcome and product of truth. His incorruptible seed abides forever!

Man's Free Will / Sovereignty of God

There is a division in the end-time church among sincere born-again believers not being able to rightly divide all Scriptures that refer to both the sovereignty of God over the church and the free moral agency of people in the church. Jesus chose His twelve disciples and they chose to follow Him, but Jesus said of Judas Iscariot, "One of you is a devil" (John 6:70).

All authority originates in the Father and progresses through the Son by His Spirit. The Father knows all things from everlasting to everlasting. The Son knew only that which the Father revealed to Him. For example, He did not know the exact time of His Second Coming. Also, it would be His Father's choice to decide which disciple would sit on His left and which on His right when He sets up His Messianic kingdom.

One proof of the Father's sovereignty is that the Bridegroom will have a glorious overcoming Bride. The sovereignty of God will be glorified in the ages to come through a new creation of redeemed people that had the freedom to choose, who chose to love God fervently and serve Him with all their heart.

One example of free moral agency is an end-time church that, for the most part, is a divided church. A divided church organism can choose to act upon the Scriptures and dine in loving fellowship with Him. This would dissolve disunity in the church and lead toward church unity through spiritual growth and development.

God knows in advance how you will react, and how people that you meet will react in any given situation. That makes the people that God has placed before you in your Christian walk more meaningful to life's overall picture. Out of eternity into time, our heavenly Father has charted out the life of each family member in Christ. Faith in the faithfulness of God to His Word will bring it to fulfillment in the life of each believer of "the household of faith."

Because the Laodiceans did not recognize the need to give God thanks for directing their lives in all things, that church was not walking according to God's will. By nature, people have a tendency to focus too much on the negative. They must remember God's way of doing things is to bring good out of evil, joy out of sorrow, and victory out of apparent defeat for His divine purpose and glory. If you believe that certain people have been put along your designated pathway by God, you can "in everything give thanks, for this is the will of God in Christ Jesus for you" (1 Thess. 5:18).

In coming into the saving knowledge of the Lord Jesus Christ, it is important that we start the journey with our eyes fixed on the Author of our faith. But as we progress in the Christian race, in order that we might complete it successfully, it is also important to have our focus upon the exalted Christ at the right hand of the Father, not only as the Author, but also as the Finisher of our faith (Heb. 12:2).

You have been chosen to be a member of God's precious family, pre-destined to be conformed to the image of His firstborn Son. When God's exalted, soul salvation is presented from the Scriptures in such a dimension and magnitude for His own will and good pleasure, it will present an awe-some challenge to the end-time church. The challenge is to "work out [in humility] your own [exalted soul] salvation with fear and trembling; for it is God [His grace] who works in you both to will and to do for His good pleasure."

Christ, the Trailblazer, was the humble soul who merited exaltation for His church by pouring out His righteous soul unto the death of the cross (Phil 2:5-11). The overcoming church must also work out, by God's grace *working within*, her salvation in Christ. Because you don't know that you've made it until you've made it, no one can glory in complete, exalted salvation, which should not be perceived thoughtlessly.

The Christ-life shall become more precious and meaningful to believ-ers each day as they obey His words of instruction from the Scriptures. The more that we get to know Him the more that we learn to love Him. Loving Him means keeping His sayings (John 14:15). We get to know Him in a greater way by acting on His words through blessings and tests of life in daily service unto Him.

God's new-creation life in Christ Jesus can only be brought to matu-rity through experiencing the fellowship of His sufferings, which were brought into the world through the fall. Our perfect Savior "learned obedi-ence by the things which He suffered" (Heb. 5:8b). Christ's sufferings are also being experienced on the behalf of the Body of Christ. The testing and trials of the overcoming church work a greater ministry for His sake as she continues to reach out to Him. That is the means by which she "may be per-fect and complete, lacking nothing" (James 1:4b).

Christ gave His life for Adam's fallen race, who are dead in trespasses and sins (Eph. 2:1). He exalts the people who are called by His name, who will humble themselves before Him, in this end-time Church Age. Those who become submissive to the authority of His words, Christ will make them overcomers with Him.

God's Predestined Course Laid Out

In relating her to an architectural masterpiece, the church has been saved by grace through faith for good works (Eph. 2:8-10). That mystery of the church was hidden in God through His new creation in Christ Jesus. In revealing His manifold wisdom, the Father's accomplished eternal purpose for His church family will be laid open to the principalities and powers in heavenly places (Eph. 3:10-11).

Spiritual growth and development, through the renewing process of the mind, brings the church into a more comprehensive scope in understanding scriptural truth. In the growing process, there are certain scriptures that are neglected or ignored because of the lack of understanding or application. Acting on scriptures that refer to denying the self-life and being a cross-bearer are important to God's overall program of complete redemption, but those scriptures, during a time of wealth and prosperity, are often neglected or disregarded in the teaching of the gospel message.

The church at Laodicea needed to acknowledge, not necessarily fully understand, the daily experiences that would point her toward God's pre-destined course and goal for His overcoming church found in Paul's epistle to the Romans. The overcomers in that church needed to believe more in God's love, and that all things were working together for her good as she had been called according to the Father's one ultimate purpose.

The Father's specific predestined end is for the church to be conformed to the image of His firstborn Son among many brethren. That should have been the objective for the lukewarm church at Laodicea. The means to reach that objective, however, was not by keeping the facts of church rules but by being submissive to the leading of the Holy Spirit as He continues to guide into all truth.

"In Him also we have obtained an inheritance, being predestined according to the purpose of Him who works all things according to the counsel of His will" (Eph. 1:11). God's predestinated course for the lives of His people is according to His divine purpose, which is also according to both His own will and good pleasure.

The Laodicean Church needed to accept by faith the sovereignty of God's love over every area of her life and choose to reciprocate that love with enthusiastic zeal. Believing that she had been predestined by God to be conformed to the image of His Son meant that she had the liberty to recognize and walk in the new things of God while putting off the old things of men. In the freedom of choice, "anyone" could make the decision to follow the Christ of the Scriptures all the way to fulfillment of His ultimate purpose for each life.

Christ met the church people of the Laodiceans just where they were. He was willing to bring "anyone" in that church into fellowship with Him on the basis of His Word. To know Him more in His fullness is an upward calling. Paul pressed "toward the goal for the prize of the upward call of God in Christ Jesus" in order that he might "know Him" (Phil. 3:14, 10a) in the fullness of the Christian experience.

The spiritual journey for that church began when the Lord first chose her. From that point onward, it became an upward journey that continued until the believers reached the predestined goal of spiritual maturity in Christ Jesus. That goal can only be brought about by the transforming power of the Holy Spirit, who is not only called the Spirit of Truth but also the Spirit of liberty in Christ. The spirit of bondage is found in the world and the things of the world. Because that church was no longer looking in the mirror of God's Word for a closer fellowship with Jesus, the Holy Spirit could not transform her more into His image from glory to glory.

The mirror of God's Word would reveal the inconsistency and differences between how that church stood and what the Word of God had declared her to be in Christ Jesus. Many things in the realm of the soul-life of those church members needed to be addressed and corrected. Those corrections were necessary for anyone in that church to continue toward the predestined goal of putting on the fullness of Christ, who came in the image and likeness of the invisible God.

But "the things of men" were winning out over "the things of God" in the Laodicean Church. Spiritual bondage within that church hindered the Spirit of liberty and grace from exalting the Christ of the Scriptures in her midst. Those church members needed God's grace to enter into His gates with thanksgiving and go through His courts with praises where they could come into the Holy of Holies to dine with Him in the fellowship of His presence.

Anyone that heard His voice would follow on to see His glory in the mirror of His Word. Then thanks to Him could be given for the liberty of having fellowship with Him. Spiritual liberty was needed for those who chose to be transformed into the Lord's image "from glory to glory" by the power of the Holy Spirit as they developed a steadfast look toward the glory of the Lord in the mirror of His Word through fellowship with Him.

God's Foreordained Workmanship

The church glorifies the Father by choosing to continue to abide in the true Vine until she brings forth "much fruit" (John 15:8). Ephesians 2:10 says that God's foreordained workmanship is a creative work of art, a handiwork of God. God's foreordained plan for His overcoming church is revealed in the story of the creation of man and woman in the Garden of Eden. It was conceived in the heart of God before the foundation of the earth.

The Genesis account of creation begins with a story about a wedding of a man and a mature woman who were created in the image and likeness of God. The Church Age ends with the story about a wedding of the exalted Second Man and the overcoming church that has been transformed into the mature image of God's firstborn Son.

It is the will of God that the church would lawfully, by the grace of God, obtain a future exalted position with Christ through a present humble position before Christ that leads to faith and obedience to His words. Unlike the thinking and ways of the Laodiceans, the Bride of Christ's forthcoming position with her exalted Bridegroom comes by the way of humility, through self-denial and cross-bearing for His sake.

The fallen angel, Lucifer, tried to illegally grasp that exalted position through rebellion against God. He wanted to live independently of his Creator by exalting himself above God's Throne. As a result, he became the father of all evil. God said to him, "Yet you shall be brought down to Sheol, to the lowest depths of the Pit" (Is. 14:15).

From the beginning, in His foreknowledge, God knew that the angel Lucifer would want a higher created position than the one that had been granted him. He would rebel against his Creator by wanting to make himself equal with God. But God, however, had predestined an exalted position for "a special people." He would send His Son who would humble Himself and become the Father's suffering Servant in purchasing a church for the Father through His sacrificial death. The Father would be glorified through the Son in fulfilling His ultimate purpose for the church, and in turn, the Father would reward the Son.

God's redeemed race will be identified with God's eternal "Lamb slain from the foundation of the world" (Rev. 13:8b). As members in the Body of Christ have lost their identity in the Head, the Bride of Christ will lose her identity in the Lamb. She will be identified in eternity as "the Lamb's wife" (21:9).

Because of what Christ has done for the church at the cross, and what He means to the church, her predestined course centers on God's Son as the slain Lamb of God. The title of "the Lamb," in relationship to Christ or His church, is used twenty-eight times in the book of Revelation. Since the predestined overcoming church shall be known in eternity as "the Lamb's wife," God has had a purpose for the church in her relationship with the crucified Lamb "from the foundation of the world."

The glory of the Father's story, therefore, is found in His church becoming a glorious workmanship as His creative, foreordained masterpiece. Predestination is based upon the foreknowledge of God. He knows beforehand those who will walk in trustworthiness and righteousness according to His Word. Those are the attributes that are needed to be a part of "His [glorious] workmanship, created in Christ Jesus for good works, which God prepared beforehand that we should walk in them" (Eph. 2:10b). Since God's plan for His church was prepared beforehand, the church is to receive that new and living way as she walks in it by faith.

To follow in the particular plan and course that God has chosen and laid out for His church, she must resist all the opposing, deceiving and controlling forces and evil spirits that would come against her. She also must be submissive to the Holy Spirit who leads and guides into all truth. No work will ever be accomplished or completed in Christ Jesus without the help of the Holy Spirit.

Predestinated Messiah / His Predestinated People

Whether it is a nation or the church, anyone related in any way to God's predestined Messiah is a predestined people. The story of the Bible, which centers in Christ and His predestined people, covers two covenants—both the old and new covenant. The chosen people of God, as Israel and the church, are so classified under the two covenants of God. The unchanging God is a covenant-keeping God. The same God that will keep His covenant promises to the nation of Israel will also keep the promises of a better covenant to the church.

Because Christ is the promised long-awaited Messiah of the Jews, the nation of Israel has been a predestined indestructible nation for 3500 years. It was necessary for God to set aside a nation to cradle the Savior of the world.

Because the predestined Lamb of God loved the church and gave Himself for her, the overcoming church is also a predestined people. According to the God of the Bible, human history pivots around the predestined Messiah. Since the overcoming church has been identified in Him according to the Scriptures, everything pivots around that one indestructible church organism in Him. He gives true meaning for living and dying.

Outside of Christ, there is no predestined glory for anyone. The chosen nation of Israel was set apart by God to bring forth her Messiah. In order for the nation of Israel to receive her full inheritance of the Promised Land, she will eventually have to humble herself and claim her true Messiah as the One whom she had pierced (Zech. 12:10).

How does a person become part of God's foreordained church? It begins by grace through faith in the crucified Lamb. The cross was not only the pivotal point for the world to receive life through His death, but it is also the foundation stone of God's building plan for His church. Without the new covenant based upon Christ's death and resurrection, there would be no further need for the existence of Adam's fallen race.

The eyes of the church, therefore, should be focused on Jesus as she presses "toward the goal for the prize of the upward call" (Phil. 3:14a) in following the Lamb all the way to the end of the spiritual journey that God has set before His overcoming church.

Why is the overcoming church predestined to be conformed to the image of the Father's firstborn Son? Christ's death on her behalf at Calvary was planned before the foundation of the earth "in bringing many [mature] sons to glory." The more the church becomes aware of Christ's resurrection power and the fellowship of His suffering in daily living, the more that God's predestined purpose for her life becomes a living reality.

Because of Christ's relationship to the nation of Israel through His physical birth, Israel has a predestined physical inheritance with her Messiah. From the manger in the little town of Bethlehem through His hometown of Nazareth, God's chosen Child of Israel grew to maturity. From His death on Golgotha's hill through the empty tomb, He has ascended to "the right hand of the throne of God." God's chosen crucified King of Israel is coming with His church to rule over the nations from the throne of David in Jerusalem. Only the Prince of Peace can bring peace to the troubled city of Jerusalem.

Christ is also having a chosen overcoming church prepared for Him by the Holy Spirit. She is being molded and groomed to be a proper ruling queen with Him. Born-again believers, therefore, are to grow and develop to maturity into an exalted spiritual inheritance with Christ. The chosen people who belong to His maturing church organism, "the glorious church," have a divine destiny to fulfill.

Predestination is God's planned, exalted and glorified purpose for the people of God who have become committed to Christ. The Bridegroom will receive the overcoming church as His Bride, and she will rule and reign with her King, "the Lamb of God." The nation of Israel, at a given moment in time, will receive the Christ of Christianity as her King. He will rule over the Israelites and their Promised Land from the throne of David for a thousand years as "the Lion of the Tribe of Judah."

Predestinated Nation / His Predestinated Church

Israel is God's predestined nation with a divine destiny, which will be played out in the course of human history. Christ loves His own people according to the flesh. Even though He is now their rejected Messiah, the Bible declares that one-day He will be acknowledged as the King of the Jews. The Spirit of Christ spoke through the prophet Zechariah (1 Pet. 1:10-11): "They will look on Me whom they have pierced; they will mourn for Him as one mourns for his only son, and grieve for Him as one grieves for a firstborn" (Zech. 12:10). It makes no difference whether we understand it or not, but it is important that we believe it, because it is predestined to come to pass.

One of the greatest miracles that I have observed in the twentieth century has been the rebirth of the nation of Israel in one day—May 14, 1948. And along with that miracle, the Six-Day War took place in June 1967, where Israel gained possession of the Old City of Jerusalem for the first time since 70 A.D. After being in exile for almost nineteen hundred years without a land to call her own, she had kept her God-given identity, being set apart by God as distinct, unique ethnic group, and she has once again returned to her God-given land according to the Scriptures.

Many Jews feel they are no different than any other people. But they are! God made them different! The church is separated unto God as a different people. It is not easy being identified with the true God in a godless world with so much hatred and envy.

Since 1948, the tiny sovereign nation of Israel has been the central theme of the political world more than any other single nation on the planet. One day she shall be the central theme of the whole world in a different light. The King of kings and the Lord of lords shall rule the whole earth on His throne from the city of Jerusalem.

The world has seen and is seeing and hearing with the natural senses the struggle of Israel against her enemies in possessing the fullness of her Promised Land. In contrast, there is the struggle of the overcoming church against her unseen spiritual enemies in possessing the fullness of her spiritual inheritance in the good fight of faith. A comparison can be made between the one Promised Land of Israel for the soon coming King of the Jews with the one ultimate promise of the church for her matrimonial union with her soon coming Bridegroom.

Since the things which are not seen are eternal, the spiritual battle and the reward for endurance in spiritual warfare is on a higher plane. As the (no named) woman was taken out of Adam in a paradise on earth, the (no named) church will be taken out of Christ in the paradise of heaven. The church in eternity will be without a name, but not without an identity. Her identification label in the kingdom of God will be "the Lamb's wife."

Christ is the active Head of His church, the Body of Christ. Even though Christ loved the church so much that He gave Himself for her, in many areas of the end-time church He has become the neglected and ignored Christ of the Scriptures. What is the reason that God's nation or God's church isn't doing very well in possessing the inheritance that God has promised each of them? The King of Israel or the Head of the church is not being given the preeminence that He deserves. Christ is the rejected King of the nation of Israel, and for the most part, the neglected Head of the end-time church.

The Scriptures declare that Christ is going to have an overcoming church that is also called "a glorious church." The Holy Spirit is preparing her and will have the glorious church ready to present in the realm of time to the Coming Lord. Christ is eager to receive His church unto Himself. The Bridegroom shall present His Bride unto Himself in the realm of eternity.

Ephesians 5:27 is a New Testament prophetic declaration about Christ's glorious church that will come to pass whether I understand it or not, or whether I believe it or not. Though I do not understand how or when it will be done, I believe it will come to pass. As I now believe that I'm a member of the serving Body of Christ, He is my blessed Hope and my desire is to one day become a member of the reigning Bride of Christ.

Predestination, therefore, covers two realms: the temporal and the eternal, the seen and the unseen, the physical and the spiritual, the natural and the supernatural. Both realms are centered in two titles of Jesus, who is both the Son of Man in time and the Son of God of eternity. He is now and forever the God-Man of eternity that is reconciling the church with God. He is both the King of the Jews and the Head of His church. He is the Supreme One, who is to be at the center of all things at all times pertaining to His church, and one day He will also be at the center of things pertaining to His nation of Israel.

Christ was born of the Virgin Mary in the town of Bethlehem as the Son of God. Christ, who purchased His chosen, overcoming, glorious church with His own precious, innocent blood at Calvary, was from "the Seed of the woman." The portrayal of His humanity, as the Son of Man over the nation of Israel, was as a member from the line of the royal "Seed of David." The portrayal of His divinity, as the Son of God through His resurrection and His indwelling presence in His new-creation people, is called "the Church."

All of the Old Testament prophecies concerning the relationship of the nation of Israel to her Messiah will be fulfilled. "Unto us a child is born, unto us a Son is given and the government will be upon His shoulder…of the increase of His government and peace there will be no end" (Is. 9:6a-7a). Isaiah was saying "unto us" meaning that the promised Child was to be born to the Jews as their King. Isaiah said that He was given "unto us" as the Son of God to rule and reign over us, the nation of Israel. That has not taken place yet, but it is God's prophetic word and it will come to pass. "He came to His own" and He was rejected, but "He loved them to the end" (John 13:1).

Abraham, as the father of many nations, has been given a covenant promise with God through the promised child Isaac, a special section of chosen real estate called "the Promised Land." God, as the Father "from whom the whole family in heaven and earth is named" (Eph. 3:15), has given the church a covenant promise with Him through the promised child Jesus, a special exalted position with Him in the family of God. Both promises to Israel and the church are predestined; thus both will be fulfilled.

According to his natural seed, God promised Abraham that "multiplying I will multiply your descendants…as the sand, which is on the seashore" (Gen. 22:17b). The *sand of the seashore* illustrates a people of the seed of Abraham who have been given an inheritance of a Promised Land upon earth.

After almost four millenniums of Jewish history, the complete fulfillment of that old covenant promise has yet to be achieved. Also after almost two millenniums of church history, the fullness of the new covenant promise of a visible glorious church has yet to be fulfilled. We are living at a pivotal time in Bible prophecy with the nearness of the Coming of Christ, "whom heaven must receive until the times of restoration of all things" are fulfilled (Acts 3:21a). As the church is being restored to her promised inheritance, Israel will also be restored to her promised inheritance.

According to his spiritual seed, God promised Abraham an inheritance through Christ Jesus, "the heavenly Man" (1 Cor. 15:48). "And multiplying I will multiply your descendants as the stars of the heaven" (Gen. 22:17a). The glory of the *stars of heaven* portrays an inheritance with Christ in His ascended glory. The resurrection of the dead is like the different glories in the celestial. "There is one glory of the sun, another glory of the moon, and another glory of the stars; for one star differs from another star in glory."

With the glorious church, predestination centers on a blameless, sanctified, chosen united people whom Christ will present unto Himself. These redeemed ones are the chosen, special people of God who will rule and reign with Him for God's glory.

There are, therefore, two categories of the children of Abraham. His natural lineage, through the promised seed of Isaac, shall be his descendants numbered corresponding with the grains of sand on the seashore. His spiritual lineage, through the promised seed of Christ, shall be His descendants numbered corresponding with the stars in the heavens.

Israel is to be viewed as the minute hand on God's prophetic time clock for the church in these last days. God's nation will one day obtain her Promised Land through an old covenant promise that God made with Abraham (Gen. 15:18-21). God's overcoming church will win her Bridegroom through a new covenant promise made through the cross.

God has already foreordained His good works for the church to be carried out for His glory (Eph. 2:10). That noble Sacrifice was made "through the eternal Spirit" at a given time in human history, and He shall present His glorious church unto Himself out of time in the realm of eternity.

Promised Land / Promised Bride

The nation of Israel's focus, therefore, should be on possessing the fullness of a specific Promised Land based upon the prophetic promise of God as revealed in the Old Testament Scriptures. Possessing the fullness of her inheritance based upon God's blood covenant of circumcision with Abraham centers in receiving her Messiah.

It is unprecedented, as we enter into a new millennium, that the small nation of Israel has such a high profile in the political arena of the nations of the world, where nations stand either for her or against her. Once again, there is a close parallel and contrast in the spiritual arena of the Christ of His church, where Jesus said that if you are not for me, you are against me.

In the political arena, it looks like an impossible task for Israel to claim her vast inheritance as promised by God to Abraham through Isaac. In the realm of the church, it looks like an impossible task for God's people to qualify for the high standards and moral principles proposed for the glorious church as promised in Ephesians 5:27.

The result of the church's focus as the glorious, overcoming church, on the other hand, is winning the Prize of a special, promised Bridegroom, which is also based upon the truth contained in the prophetic Scriptures. That predestined promise may be delayed but it will be fulfilled. But that promise is dependent upon the church's love, faith and hope in the ultimate purpose and promise of the gospel message that makes a believer part of God's prophetic fulfillment for the overcoming church.

Since becoming a nation in 1948, Israel has been fighting her enemies all around her for her very life and existence as a sovereign nation. The political and religious enemies against the nation of Israel do not want her to achieve her predestined inheritance as a nation. But the vast Promised Land belongs to Israel, which was given to her by the God of Abraham, Isaac, and Jacob (Gen. 15:11-15). "The earth is the LORD'S and the fullness thereof" (Ps. 24:1), and the Almighty can give it to whomever He wishes.

The same is true of the "glorious church not having spot or wrinkle or any such thing, but that she should be holy and without blemish" (Eph. 5:27). The enemy is also doing all that he can to prevent the church from coming into her predestined inheritance as a glorious, overcoming church. In relation to His healing ministry, Jesus laid down a divine principle for receiving anything from God—"According to your faith let it be to you" (Matt. 9:29). The end-time church needs to apply that faith principle in accordance with her predestined fulfillment in Christ in order to claim it by faith and live in the hope of His soon Appearing.

God does His work through the universal faith principal. "Without faith it is impossible to please God." "For whatever is not from faith is sin" (Rom. 14:23). As faith in His divine purpose for His church unites and gathers, unbelief in that purpose separates and scatters. Jesus said, "He who is not with Me is against Me, and he who does not gather with Me scatters abroad" (Matt. 12:30).

As the Father's firstborn Son from the dead is completely identified with the Father in all things, the church is being challenged to be completely identified with her Head, the Son of God, in all things. The thinking of the Body of Christ is continually being brought into subjection and harmony with the mind of Christ, the Head of the Body (Phil. 2:5). The end-time church has much to overcome!

Jesus is coming again to His nation of Israel, but first He must rapture the church in order that she may share in His Second Coming. As the Promised Land is God's promise to His chosen nation, the unique and mysterious relationship of Christ and His Bride is God's promise to the chosen church.

Since the King of God's kingdom is related to the predestinated nation of Israel as King of the Jews, He is also related to the church as the predestined Bridegroom for His overcoming church. Then His Bride will also have a relationship to Israel as her predestined Queen. But Jesus is the King of kings and the Lord of lords over the whole earth. His rule and reign is forever and ever!

"The Lamb slain from the foundation of the world" will receive unto Himself an overcoming church that has been predestined before the foundation of the world. She will be known throughout eternity "as the Lamb's wife." Before Jesus comes again to the nation of Israel, there will first be the Rapture of the Church and the Marriage Supper of the Lamb because "His wife has made herself ready" (Rev. 19:7).

The Father is the Master Architect of the building plan. The Holy Spirit is directing the building of the church, and Christ Jesus is ruler over that building program. The destiny of the Bride of Christ in eternity is a set goal for her waiting Bridegroom. The work has begun and shall be fulfilled by the Holy Spirit in the realm of time.

Abraham's seed has a covenant promise with God through the Seed of David to reign over the Promised Land. Abraham's Seed has a covenant promise with God through the Seed of the woman for a special people called the glorious church. That covenant promise has been sealed with His own blood as the Lamb of God, and will be completed in eternity with a wedding to a chosen united people who shall "collectively" be called the Lamb's wife.

To be made complete, the nation of Israel is waiting to receive her Coming Messiah. To be made complete, the overcoming church is waiting to receive her Coming Bridegroom. The nation of Israel does not know it yet, but she and the church are waiting for the same Person.

According to our soulish reasoning and finite understanding, preparing such a special people for such a momentous climatic event appears impossible. But God has predestined it from the foundation of the world for His glory and "with God nothing shall be impossible" (Luke 1:37; Matt. 19:26). It is not important for the church to know *how* it is going to be done, or when it is going to be done in "that day and hour." But what is important, God has an ultimate purpose for His church, and it is going to be done. Jesus admonished the church to be ready and waiting for Him at His Appearing.

That special church's membership role contains all the saints of God who have been predestined to dwell harmoniously with one another as one glorious church with the Lord Jesus Christ as the Head. Some things may be hard to take and difficult to understand in the realm of time, but for God's predestined ones, He is in control of every situation and circumstance. He has an exalted destination for His precious saints in Christ Jesus like none other in the universe.

The overcoming church, which was initiated by the Father in the Son, overcomes the world and "shall inherit all things" with Christ (Rev. 21:7). She will inherit all things with Him because she has, through Him by the grace of God, overcome all things in Him.

The work of God's grace teaches a church that it is a continual work of submissiveness to the truth of dealing with her own independent soulish nature. The finished task becomes an awesome and diligent work. The overcoming church, as the Body of Christ, therefore, will meet the ultimate purpose of God through a humble attitude of fear and trembling, "not to think of himself more highly than he ought to think, but to think soberly" (Rom. 12:3).

Anyone in the lukewarm atmosphere of the church organism of the Laodicean Church who repented could hear His voice and open his heart's door to Jesus. As long as professing Christians are dining with Jesus, they have the opportunity to go all the way with Him as overcomers. There would be those in the church of the Laodiceans who would go from being lukewarm toward Him to becoming an overcomer with Him. Those who become members of the overcoming church organism become dear to the heart of the Father and the Son in fulfilling His ultimate purpose for the church.

Book Summary

A Need for a Church Organization to Serve the Church Organism

Jesus taught the gospel message by making comparisons. He taught many of those comparisons through parables, going from the known in the physical realm to the unknown in the spiritual realm, going from the temporal to the eternal. The church of the Laodiceans had a good beginning, but "the end of a thing is better than its beginning" (Eccl. 7:8). The score at the end of the game of life is the score that actually counts.

No member of the end-time church organism aspires to be found guilty in going the way of the Laodicean Church as compared with the way of the Bride of Christ. Whereas the church of the Laodiceans reached her own self-appointed objective, the Holy Spirit is preparing the bride-elect to reach her God-appointed objective.

The Laodiceans had a wrong attitude in the eyes of the Lord. God doesn't measure a church as being right or wrong according to human standards but according to the Scriptures. The root problem of being lukewarm toward Him was her love for the world and things of the world being more fervent than her love toward Him.

The Bride of Christ in eternity will come out of the church organism, which is the Body of Christ in the realm of time. As the bride of Adam was formed from a rib taken out of his body in the Garden of Eden, Christ will present His Bride unto Himself in heaven's paradise. The right church, therefore, is the one growing and developing church organism contained in different church organizations that are providing for her spiritual nourishment and development through dining with Jesus.

A comparison between the Laodicean Church's indifference and luke-warm emotional attitude toward the Head of the church organism can be contrasted to the fervent emotional pursuit of the bride-elect toward her Bridegroom. That shows the broad range of the wrong and right emotional spectrum of the church toward the Savior of her soul. The bride-elect is interested in fulfilling the Father's ultimate purpose for the church as she works at perfecting her devoted relationship with her coming Bridegroom.

What standard of measurement do we want to use for evaluating whether a church is right or wrong? The importance of evangelizing the lost, getting people redeemed and ready for heaven, is one standard that might be used. Teaching the discipleship message, preparing a church to watch and be ready as she eagerly waits for her Coming Lord, is another standard of measurement that might be used.

Romans 12:2 says, "Do not be conformed to this world, but be transformed by the renewing of your mind, that you may prove what is that good and acceptable and perfect will of God." Using these three standards of measurement for a right church, therefore, necessitates evangelizing the lost. But going no further than entering into the saving knowledge of Christ might be classified as being a thirtyfold church in bearing fruit from the Vine while fulfilling the good will of God. But others may go further and function in the Body of Christ as a sixtyfold church in bearing more fruit from the same true Vine. That is where hearers are obedient to the words of the Lord warning the church to be ready and waiting at the time of His Appearing, which would be the acceptable or well-pleasing will of God.

Yet the perfect will of God is fulfilling the ultimate purpose of the Father. That is the hundredfold church, which shall bear much fruit. Jesus said, "By this My Father is glorified" (John 15:8). The overcoming church shall become the Father's deserving matrimonial workmanship for His worthy Son. The Bride is passionately in love with her compassionate Bridegroom. It is by His grace through her faith, which works by love, that she wins His eternal favor.

The lukewarm Laodicean Church did not have the close devoted fellowship with the Lord Jesus Christ to qualify her for having overcoming faith. As a church, she believed in God, but she did not take God seriously and believe God. Compassionate Jesus challenged members of that church to repent and develop a zeal and passionate love toward His wholehearted love toward her. They could identify themselves as being Christians, but they were Christians that had not committed themselves to Him.

A wholehearted love is the foundation that makes a church ready to dine together with Him, experiencing spiritual nourishment and development.

That kind of relationship with the Lord is the kind of fellowship that would qualify a committed people for His Appearing, and to become the overcoming church sharing His throne.

Because of His magnificent greatness and importance to the Body of Christ, a grateful and indebted end-time church will give more time to pleasing Him by hearing His voice and speaking His words. Emphasizing the importance of spiritual unity in the Body of Christ is what pleases the Head of the Body.

A Church Organization / The Church Organism

When people ask the question, "To what church do you belong?" they are thinking in terms of belonging to one of thousands of different church organizations. Because there is only one Body of Christ, all true born-again Christians belong to the same church organism. One born-again believer, therefore, can answer that question by saying to another born-again believer, "I belong to the same church as you do."

As I entered a taxicab recently, I noticed hanging down from the rearview mirror a display card with the words, "I love Jesus." I told the driver that I liked his display card about Jesus. Then I said to him, "We belong to the same church!" He was startled and didn't know how to answer me.

Because of the thinking of most church members, people can only belong to the church that they attend. There may be people who attend the same church organization as I do; yet, they many not know Him well enough to love Him. But all of us who belong to the same church organism should continue to love Him more than we did the day before.

There are a countless number of church organizations but there is only one church organism. Though the organism is contained in the organization, a church organization is not greater than the church organism. The organizational leadership should not lord it over the organism. The Lord values the free will of the redeemed in His church organism, and so should each church organization.

Before the Lord sent His disciples forth as the first church leaders, He told them, "He who is greatest among you shall be your servant" (Matt. 23:11). Greatness of organizational church leaders, in the eyes of the Lord, is found in how they best serve the church organism. It was quite evident that the organism in the Laodicean Church did not primarily belong to the church organization. That church organism was accountable to the Head who was making the appeal, giving the rebuke, and offering the invitation.

The Father sent His Son as a Servant to serve the nation of Israel. The Son prayed to the Father to send the Holy Spirit to serve the church. The

Holy Spirit motivates unity in the Body of Christ and gives each member the ability to be committed to the Head of the Body. Without realizing it, the leadership in that proud, self-sufficient church organization was ignoring the humble, all-sufficient Christ who was the Head over His church organism. By closing the church door to members of the Body of Christ, the Laodicean Church had also closed the church door to the Head of the Body. The Head cannot be separated from His church organism; Christ and His church are one.

Christ was dealing with the Laodicean Church both as a church organization and a church organism. He had harsh words to say against the attitude of a rich, self-sufficient church organizational system, which housed the church organism that belonged to Him. Jesus had not forsaken the church at Laodicea, but He was resisting the arrogance of a rich, self-contained church organizational system.

The end-time church might learn from the mistakes of the Laodicean Church. Through misplaced emphasis as a church organization, she guided and directed—by ignoring the work of the Holy Spirit—the church organism to become lukewarm toward the Head of the Body of Christ. At the same time, that organism needed to be made aware of the thoughtful, positive approach of Christ Jesus who was reprimanding her.

That church organism had been given birth in a growing, prosperous church organization, but she had become lukewarm toward Jesus. The Lord, who had justified her by forgiving her sins, was now the same Lord who was condemning her for her halfhearted commitment toward His great love. Merciful Jesus had not forsaken the church of the Laodiceans. He was reprimanding her and challenging her to repent from her halfhearted love toward Him as compared to His wholehearted love toward her.

The *zoe* life of Christ was in the church organism that made up that church organization. But it was the church organism that was accountable to Christ's wholehearted love for her. Being identified with a church organization, which loved the riches and wealth of this world more than she loved God, caused that church organism to have a divided heart between the rich church organization and the riches of Christ. The organism lives for Christ and must go out to meet Him.

The organism in that organization was still in the Body of Christ. The Head hadn't yet vomited those body members out of His mouth. To develop and experience soul prosperity, the church organism must live a life of dependency upon the One who gives life, but that church organization independently boasted in her riches and wealth.

The Lord, therefore, disqualified her from being a right church. The solution to the problem of self-sufficiency as a church organism was to repent of the heart attitude of being lukewarm toward Him. A church organization can independently function without God's help, but a church organism has experienced spiritual birth and lives on the spiritual food and nourishment that comes from the life-giver and life-sustainer Himself.

A church organism, housed in a church organization, needs to depend upon the rest of the Body of Christ to function. Ephesians 4:16 says "from [the Head] the whole body, joined and knit together by what every joint supplies, according to the effective working by which every part does its share, causes growth of the body for the edifying of itself in love." The organism of that church might have been assigned as connecting joints that supplied and shared in loving service and edification to other parts of the Body of Christ.

Church-Centered Focus / Christ-Centered Focus

A church-centered focus had developed in the Laodicean Church. That focus took away the Christ-centered focus needed for the church organism to have spiritual growth and development by having a loving attached fellowship with the Head. There has been too much church-centered focus in the end-time church with emphasis upon belonging to a certain church organization where the Christ-centered focus of belonging to the one church organism becomes completely ignored. Being self-centered is a weakness of a church organization; being Christ-centered is the strength of its church organism.

If church people have the wrong focus in God's ultimate purpose for His church, the Holy Spirit is hindered in uniting all born-again believers together as one developing and maturing Body of Christ. The ultimate, mature goal for the Body of Christ is for each functioning member to be directed with "the mind of Christ." Then the Head directs each maturing member of the Body to edifying one another in love.

There is the need for a church organization to develop a Christ-centered focus for its church members, but many born-again Christians have never been taught the importance of the church organism, the Body of Christ. The Laodicean Church possibly didn't even know that the church organism even existed. It is important to encounter and understand that the character of a growing and developing church organism is alive and well.

The mature Body of Christ is the church that the Head is eager to receive unto Himself at His Appearing. Evidence of the maturing church organism is that the Body of Christ is becoming more like the Father's firstborn Son. Will the Bride of Christ come out of the Body of Christ in heaven's paradise from a rib that is closest to His heart?

The Laodicean Church organization should have seen herself as a needy church in a servant's role helping and supporting the spiritual nourishment of the church organism. But because of her pride and self-centeredness as a church organization, she had become a hindrance to the church organism rather than a helper.

If the one Christ-centered church organism, which is housed in each church organization of the end-time church, were honored, then the church organism in all other churches would also be honored. But there is a tendency for a church organization, like the Laodicean Church, to become only church-centered in her thinking. That places the importance of a church organization and her head over the importance of the church organism and the Head of the Body. That was what caused that church organism to become lukewarm toward Christ. The chief Shepherd told a repentant Peter, "Feed My sheep!"

The attitude of self-importance of that church organization had promoted selfishness within the church membership toward the Body of Christ. The leadership might not have been the total cause for the development of the party spirit, but they did not discourage it. The apostle Paul warned the Corinthian Church of the danger of the party spirit.

As an apostle and servant to the church, Paul promoted the Christ-centered focus for the church organism. He said, "For all things are yours: whether Paul or Apollos or Cephas, or the world or life or death, or things present or things to come—all are yours. And you are Christ's, and Christ is God's" (1 Cor. 3:21-23).

The reason the Lord was addressing the church organism to open the door was to receive overcoming faith through spiritual nourishment from Him by dining with Him. Because of a heart full of love for Him had been taken away from Him as her functional Head, that lukewarm church organism couldn't experience any spiritual growth and development.

Is church growth in membership and attendance of a church organization more important to the church leadership than spiritual growth and development that will bring unity to the church organism? There is joy in true growth of a church organization, but John, the elder wrote, "I have no greater joy than to hear that my children walk in truth." That greater joy was in reference to the spiritual growth of the church organism.

If emphasis is placed on the growth of an organization at the expense of the development of the church organism, a church-centered focus becomes more important than a Christ-centered focus to that church organization. What is important is that the Head of the church organism is coming soon for those who are watching and ready.

Because of self-centeredness, a church organization develops a preference to turn the eyes and hearts of the people from the importance of the Christ-centered church organism to the importance of being identified with a specific label of a church organization. Too much emphasis upon the importance of the many different church organizations and their labels come at the expense of the importance of the one church organism.

Many denominations go to the Bible for the right label as a church organization, but many have chosen a particular label from the Bible for their church denomination that pertains to the church as an organism. In the early church, the Bible label for a church organization was the name of the city where it was located. The apostle Paul, however, gave the one significant biblical label for the church organism—the Body of Christ.

The Importance of the Church Organism

The church organism cannot grow and develop without the help of a church organization, but a church organization with its administrative structure and programs can function quite well in a world of darkness without the presence of the living church organism. Many end-time, main-line church denominations might be "having church" without one born-again believer in its congregation. That would be an example of the function of a church organizational system without the presence of the church organism. Jesus isn't involved with a dead church with no living organism.

Some church denominations of this end-time era have become independently self-sufficient, like the Laodiceans, and have developed an attitude that causes division in the church organism, the Body of Christ. If there is to be greater improvement in church unity, there needs to be more emphasis upon the importance of the one church organism that operates by recognition and submission to the one functional Head.

In many denominational and theological systems of the end-time church, servants of the Lord are not measured by their ministerial or spiritual gifts in the Body of Christ. Neither are they measured by the fruit of the new-creation spirit that the Holy Spirit is cultivating in their life as maturing servants to the church. The bottom line is—are they committed to wearing the invisible right denominational church label? An outward vocal commitment to a church organization (to be heard of men) gives no assurance that one is being faithful to the Head as a member of the Body of Christ.

Church members might glory in their church label without any help from the church leadership. It is the responsibility of the more mature church leadership, however, who wants to please God rather than men, to place the emphasis where it belongs. The emphasis belongs in the growing unity of the church organism where all true believers are identified by the same church label. That label is the Body of Christ! And there is the Father's ultimate purpose for the church in eternity, the label of the Bride of Christ.

The glory of the Laodicean Church, as an organization, took away from the glory of the church as a maturing organism. The Head of the Body of Christ was longing for a loving fellowship to be reestablished within that lukewarm, indifferent church organism.

The dual function of the Laodicean Church was that she was a body of believers that formed a church organization called the church of the Laodiceans. As a church organization, that church had a system of operation. The Laodicean Church's system of operation was on a small scale compared with the immense major church denominations as we know them today. But within a church organization, there is an underlying theological system, a system of church rules and practices, an office of church administration, etc.

Since that church's organizational leadership was not honoring Him as her functional Head, Jesus did not use protocol in addressing that lukewarm church organism to repent. He was on the outside making a direct appeal to the church organism on the inside to repent from her lukewarm status before Him.

Christ honors His church organizations, but the leadership of that organization hadn't honored Him nor did they welcome or exalt His presence in the church services. Because of neglect in giving Him the proper recognition, He did not honor the leadership of that church organization because He was no longer a part of it.

Jesus introduced Himself as "the Faithful and True Witness" to that church organism, in which He is the most vital part. He was giving an invitation to anyone in that church organism to open the door that had been closed to Him, come unto Him and become a functional part of the Body of Christ by dining with Him on spiritual food.

An organizational system of operation is the impersonal and unemotional entity of a church. As a church organization, she could break up and be dissolved, like the work at Babel, but as an impersonal, unemotional church organization, she could not repent from having a lukewarm relationship with the Head of the church. Jesus was dealing with His church organism that had been hindered in her expression of emotions toward Him by the operation of an egotistical organization. The duty and work of an impersonal church organization is to promote the importance and greatness of its personal spiritual church organism toward the functional Head. The greatest enemy in serving Christ is the self-life, and the solution to the problem is to lose self to the Christ-Life and live for His sake.

We can conclude, therefore, that the church at Laodicea, as a church organization, had become a wrong church in the eyes of the Lord. As a church organization, she did not recognize herself in a servant's role to Christ, as the Body of Christ, where she was responsible to the Head of the Body. The worship service of that lukewarm church, therefore, had become less and less Christ-centered until the Head of the church was ostracized to the outside of His church. But Jesus does not lose His wholehearted love for His church organism. He wanted that lukewarm church organism to be restored as devoted functional members in the Body of Christ by dining upon the Bread of Life.

As His Second Coming draws near, the end-time church for the most part, is making the same mistake as did the nation of Israel under the old covenant in her long history before the First Coming of her Messiah. Being the chosen people of God under a new covenant in Christ, the church becomes a privileged people to God in Christ. Experiencing the blessings of God, being not aware that all are based upon the grace of God, will make church people spiritually proud. The Holy Spirit will not lead and guide a proud church "into all truth." The universal law, which God's people must recognize in building His church, is that God resists the proud but gives grace to the humble.

Through carnal competitive pride in the church world, disunity arises between the glory of a church organization and the glory of the Body of Christ. The Holy Spirit was sent to edify, comfort and exhort the church organism for glory of the Head, whereas men glorify a lukewarm church organization for the glory of men.

The rich Laodicean Church organization had emphasized her self-worth and self-importance at the expense of not teaching the church organism where the eternal true riches of God could be found. Man may glory in the increase of growth and size of a church organization, but the Father is glorified in the fullness of growth and development in spiritual maturity of the church organism. The ultimate purpose of the Vine is to produce much mature fruit that contains reproductive seeds, which when planted and watered, will eventually produce the mature image of His firstborn Son, the true Vine.

When the Head of the church organism gets the glory, therefore, it comes at the expense of a church organization receiving the glory. "He must increase, but I must decrease." That statement made by John the Baptist could apply collectively to the increasing worth of the church organism in the eyes of the Lord, with the decreasing worth of a church organization, like the church of the Laodicean Church, in her own eyes.

Growth and Development of the Church Organism

Everyone, as a member of the church organism in the Laodicean Church organization, could accept the invitation that the Lord had given. They could become eligible for the crowning reward of the overcomer. Jesus said that anyone could hear His voice and open the door and dine with Him, "To him who overcomes I will grant to sit with Me on My throne, as I also overcame and sat down with My Father on His throne."

By saying, "as I also overcame," Jesus was contrasting overcoming the proud, lukewarm church system of the Laodiceans with His confrontation with the proud religious system of Judaism of the nation of Israel. Jesus and His overcoming church would inherit from the Father the same kind of a reward.

People that think religiously without the renewing of the mind do not have their hearts in tune with the leading of the Holy Spirit in the Christian walk. Because of their lukewarm relationship with the Christ of Christianity, the Laodicean Church had leveled off on a religious plateau in her Christian walk. If she failed to trust in the Holy Spirit, who leads into all truth, to lead her forward to the next level, that church would never get to a higher spiritual level.

Leadership in the right church organization, on the other hand, listens to what the Holy Spirit is saying. The Holy Spirit is getting the Bride of Christ ready by glorifying Christ in the midst of organized Christianity. Jesus said that when the Holy Spirit came, He would "glorify Me." The Holy Spirit is in the glorifying business, but it is not about a right church organization, a gifted member in the Body of Christ, or even the Holy Spirit Himself. They all may be honored, but it is the Head of the Body who is to be glorified, and He no longer abides alone; He and His church organism are one.

The complete church organism, which is identified by the Head, is what the Holy Spirit has come to glorify. You can't glorify the church organism by putting down its particular church organizational identity. But it is important to know which of the two that needs to receive the distinction for the purpose of church unity.

The Laodicean Church might have been experiencing evangelistic growth as a church organization—that is essential—but that was not the underlying issue that was confronting that church. The important scriptural factor that was needed was for Jesus to be in the midst of that church's operation and advancement for the benefit of spiritual nourishment and growth of the church organism.

Christ is one with His church organism. That is why the unity of the Body of Christ is firmly established upon the rock of His faithfulness and under His Headship. Glorying of that lukewarm church organization came at the expense of the glory of that divine church organism. As a result, there could be no spiritual maturing in the church organism that was being housed in that church organization. Christ was a faithful witness to that proud, self-sufficient church organization. It was necessary for Him to chastise and rebuke that lukewarm church organism with His loving kindness and tender mercy.

The right church organization denies the glory of her collective self-life and picks up her cross for the sake of His church organism. As His helper, she is more interested in the glory of the Lord than self-glory. Overcomers, as leaders in a church organization, will fulfill God's ultimate purpose as members of His church organism.

The right end-time church is longing for His Appearing as "those who eagerly wait for Him He will appear a second time, apart from sin, for salvation." That means that she will not be found in a lukewarm, unenthusiastic predicament before Him like the church of the Laodiceans. Christ loved the church (each born-again believer in that church organization) and gave Himself for her.

There is a misplaced emphasis, in many areas of the Body of Christ of the end-time church, on temporal, material things that hinder in having a steadfast heart toward Him. Spiritual growth and development of the church organism is necessary to promote unity in the Body of Christ. As the Body of Christ matures in having the senses exercised to rightly discern spiritual things, leadership in the end-time church will see the importance of church unity, and that pleases the Lord.

Which Church Is Wrong?
Order Form

Postal orders: 20341 N. 109th Ave.
Sun City, AZ 85373-9751

Telephone orders: 623-566-3860

E-mail orders: dlpopesr@juno.com

Please send *Which Church Is Wrong?* to:

Name: _____

Address: _____

City: _____   State: _____

Zip: _____

Telephone: (_____) _____

Book Price: $15.00

Shipping: $3.00 for the first book and $1.00 for each additional book to cover
shipping and handling within US, Canada, and Mexico.
International orders add $6.00 for the first book and $2.00 for each
additional book.

Or order from:
ACW Press
85334 Lorane Hwy
Eugene, OR 97405

(800) 931-BOOK

or contact your local bookstore